POINT AND FIGURE CHARTING

WILEY FINANCE EDITIONS

OPTION MARKET MAKING by Alan J. Baird

MONEY MANAGEMENT STRATEGIES FOR FUTURES TRADERS by
Nauzer J. Balsara

GENETIC ALGORITHMS AND INVESTMENT STRATEGIES by
Richard Bauer

FIXED-INCOME SYNTHETIC ASSETS by Perry Beaumont

THE NEW TECHNICAL TRADER by Tushar Chande and Stanley S. Kroll

POINT AND FIGURE CHARTING by Thomas Dorsey

THE NEW TECHNOLOGY OF FINANCIAL MANAGEMENT by
Dimitris N. Chorafas

TREASURY OPERATIONS AND THE FOREIGN EXCHANGE CHALLENGE
by Dimitris N. Chorafas

TRADING ON THE EDGE by Guido J. Deboeck

TRADING FOR A LIVING by Dr. Alexander Elder

STUDY GUIDE FOR TRADING FOR A LIVING by Dr. Alexander Elder

THE DAY TRADER'S MANUAL by William F. Eng

MANAGED FUTURES IN THE INSTITUTIONAL PORTFOLIO by
Charles B. Epstein

DYNAMIC ASSET ALLOCATION by David A. Hammer

ANALYZING AND FORECASTING FUTURES PRICES by
Anthony F. Herbst

GLOBAL ASSET ALLOCATION by Jess Lederman and Robert A. Klein

UNDERSTANDING SWAPS by Jack Marshall

INTERMARKET TECHNICAL ANALYSIS by John J. Murphy

FORECASTING FINANCIAL AND ECONOMIC CYCLES by
Michael P. Niemira

INVESTING IN INTANGIBLE ASSETS by Russell L. Parr

FRACTAL MARKET ANALYSIS by Edgar E. Peters

CHAOS AND ORDER IN THE CAPITAL MARKETS by Edgar E. Peters

FORECASTING FINANCIAL MARKETS by Tony Plummer

INSIDE THE FINANCIAL FUTURES MARKETS, 3RD EDITION by
Mark J. Powers and Mark G. Castelino

RELATIVE DIVIDEND YIELD by Anthony E. Spare

TRADER VIC II: ANALYTIC PRINCIPLES OF PROFESSIONAL
SPECULATION by Victor Sperandeo

THE MATHEMATICS OF MONEY MANAGEMENT by Ralph Vince

PORTFOLIO MANAGEMENT FORMULAS by Ralph Vince

THE NEW MONEY MANAGEMENT: A FRAMEWORK FOR ASSET
ALLOCATION by Ralph Vince

TRADING APPLICATIONS OF JAPANESE CANDLESTICK CHARTING by
Gary Wagner and Brad Matheny

SELLING SHORT by Joseph A. Walker

THE FOREIGN EXCHANGE AND MONEY MARKETS GUIDE by
Julian Walmsley

TRADING CHAOS: APPLYING EXPERT TECHNIQUES TO MAXIMIZE
YOUR PROFITS by Bill Williams

FIXED-INCOME ARBITRAGE by M. Anthony Wong

TRADING AND INVESTING IN BOND OPTIONS by M. Anthony Wong

CORPORATE FINANCIAL RISK MANAGEMENT by Dianne B. Wunnicke,
David R. Wilson, Brooke Wunnicke

A COMPLETE GUIDE TO CONVERTIBLE SECURITIES WORLDWIDE by
Laura A. Zublake

POINT AND FIGURE CHARTING

The Essential Application for Forecasting and Tracking Market Prices

Thomas J. Dorsey

John Wiley & Sons, Inc.

New York • Chichester • Brisbane • Toronto • Singapore

Copyright © 1995 by Marketplace Books, Inc.
Published by John Wiley & Sons, Inc.

Library of Congress Cataloging-in-Publication Data:

Dorsey, Thomas J.
    Point and figure charting : essential applications for forecasting
and tracking market prices / Thomas J. Dorsey.
        p.   cm. — (Wiley finance editions)
    ISBN 0-471-11961-X (Cloth)
    1. Stocks—Prices— Charts, diagrams, etc.   2. Speculation.
3. Stock price forecasting.   I. Title.   II. Series.
HG4638.D67   1995
332.63'222—dc20   95-3091

Printed in the United States of America
10 9

FOREWORD

I first met Tom Dorsey in 1985 at a conference in St. Petersburg, Florida. Tom was employed as the options strategist for Wheat First Securities and I had just started in a new position as senior vice president for the Philadelphia Stock Exchange. I was invited to this conference to give a presentation to Tom and other individuals representing regional brokerage firms around the country on what was "new" at the Philadelphia Stock Exchange. Since that time, Tom and I have become good friends. We have a great deal in common, we both love the music of the 1950s and 1960s, motorcycles, and share a passion for the business that we're in.

When Tom first asked me to write the Foreword for this book which is everything you want to know about point and figure analysis, I was flattered but also I was concerned because I knew very little of the art of point and figure analysis except that it has existed in one form or another over the last one hundred years. Today, it is a skill known by very few people in our business. Tom Dorsey is one of them. He dusted off this art form some years ago and has become an expert in reading the chart patterns that the Xs and Os of the point and figure charting create. With that information, Tom Dorsey predicts the future. The outstanding feature of this art is that it permits tracking the history of a particular stock each and every day. Furthermore, based on this pricing history, any given chart-formed patterns enable Tom Dorsey to predict the future price of a particular stock. Those of us that know little about this aspect of technical analysis might refer to Tom as a psychic or a witch doctor but after you think about it, it makes perfect sense. Stocks, like people, civilizations, and weather, form patterns.

While I would not put Tom Dorsey on the scale of Nostradamus, what Tom does is not much different! Think about it. How was Nostradamus able to accurately predict future events such as natural disasters, population explosions, and religious wars? He did it by studying the history of many areas of civilization as well as geological patterns. By doing so, he became an expert on foreseeing future events because, just like most other aspects of life, a pattern was formed and those who have the insight to read those patterns, have the ability to look into the future. I am certain that becoming a psychic is not quite that simple, however, this book will give you an idea on how the art-form of point and figure analysis almost becomes a precise science.

Tom Dorsey publishes what we call *The Philadelphia Report*. On a weekly basis, he takes each and every one of the stocks on which we trade options, devises strategy recommendations on those issues for the benefit of thousands of brokers who have signed up to receive this report. Tom's track record over the life of this report, is nothing less than impressive. Many brokers utilize this report as if it were religion. I know that if you are interested in and enjoy following the financial markets, you will be fascinated reading the pages before you. Most importantly, through this reading you will gain some knowledge of a unique personality . . . Tom Dorsey.

JOSEPH S. RIZZELLO
Executive Vice President
Philadelphia Stock Exchange

ACKNOWLEDGMENTS

Where can I begin with acknowledgments? There are so many people who were directly or indirectly involved in this book. Had it not been for my wonderful wife Cindy, I would never have believed it could be done. She has always seen in me something I could never see. Her endless support kept me going throughout this project. I would like to recognize my children Thomas, Mitchell, and Samantha for understanding why their father spent all his spare time on the book and not with them. They are the greatest. I sincerely thank Tammy DeRosier, one of my ace analysts, for her effort in putting all the chart work together. The charts were all done by hand. It was her devotion to detail that resulted in the finished manuscript. There is much more to writing a book than meets the eye as I discovered in short order. I would also like to thank Joshua Parker and Dennis Johnson for taking the time to give the book a good proofreading. The comments and changes you recommended have really helped the book flow much better.

None of this would have ever happened if Jim Crocker had not given me a chance to be a stockbroker at Merrill Lynch back in the mid-1970s. I knew the investment business was my life's work the first day I applied for the job. My special thanks to A. B. Jones for setting me straight after my first whirlwind year of production trading options by saying, "Tom, ain't but one way to make money in the stock market. Slowly." He was right, dead right. I would also like to acknowledge Dan Thompson. I went to college with Dan, and it was he who told me Merrill was hiring and encouraged me to submit an application. If it hadn't been for that urging, I might not be in this business today.

I owe a debt of gratitude to Marshall Wishnack, President of Wheat First Securities, for having enough faith in my abilities to allow me to develop and manage Wheat's Options Strategy. When I worked for Marshall, he was the Director of Research at Wheat. He is also one of the most accomplished technicians on Wall Street who favors the Point and Figure method. When I started the Options Strategy Department, I was smart enough to know my stock-picking abilities at that time were limited. To fill that side of the equation, I hired Steve Kane. Had I not hired Steve Kane to assist me in my department, I don't know what stock analysis methods I would be using now. Steve was the person who brought the Point and Figure method to my department, and it is through him I had my awakening. Steve taught me the methods of Point and Figure Technical Analysis that changed my life. It is interesting how an idea or some small piece of information can so profoundly affect a person's future. Since that day, I have tried to pass this message on to other professionals on Wall Street. If my business life can go through such a major, positive change, the same thing can happen to anyone else who will take the time to learn this method. I feel a profound responsibility to teach this method to others needing guidance in their investment endeavors. In my mind, the true test of success is having a positive, long-lasting effect on someone's life. I try to accomplish this by teaching this method to other professionals who manage people's money.

My sincere thanks to Steve Mitchell, Managing Director and Head of Options Strategy at Alex Brown. He had faith in my firm early on and was one of the first companies to take our research systemwide. I also want to thank John Felber. He is a Partner and Director of Options Strategy and Correspondent Research. He too had faith in us. Their unending support will never be forgotten. John Platt at Raymond James, Lyn Lane at Rauscher Pierce, Tom Hart at PaineWebber, Eileen Phelan at Morgan Keegan, Mike Bickford at Kidder Peabody, Dalton Givens at Interstate Securities, Bill Brown at Bear Stearns, Bill Kissell at J.P. Morgan, Don MacLeish at Northern Capital Management, Dick Tougas at Connecticut National Bank, and Bob Morris at Lord Abbett Funds also supported us. In the early days of developing our company, this support gave us confidence that we just might stay in business.

I would like to thank Ken Spence, the former Director of Technical Analysis at Salomon Brothers, for his belief in our work. When he signed on as a client, it spoke volumes about our viability on Wall Street. We knew then we were here to stay. His comments to me over the years have always given me strength in my conviction that we were unique and on the right track. Ken is now a partner in a major hedge fund, Ethos Capital Management. He is still a valued client and, in our opinion, is one of the Wall Street greats.

My big buddy Jim Yates, where do I begin to thank you? I knew I wanted to start my own company by the time I was 40, but taking the first step was tough. Jim and I spent many veal scallopine lunches in Vienna, Virginia, discussing my venture. Jim convinced me to quit my upper management, good-paying job, with a big bonus and security, for a dream. It seemed like a good tradeoff to me. Actually, aside from marrying Cindy, it was the best decision in my life.

Watson, my partner, gave up the opportunity to become Director of Option Strategy at Wheat to join me in my dream. Your unwavering loyalty to me and the company have played a major role in getting Dorsey, Wright & Associates where we are today. We have only yet begun. Sue and Tammy, you have paid your dues in this company. My thanks to both of you for your hard work and loyalty for all these years. We've been through tough times together. You two were the backbone of the firm early on. Watson and I couldn't have made it without you. Hang in there, we only have 40 more years left. My thanks to you Jay for all your hard work. You have been the perfect addition to our team.

I want to give thanks to my mentor, Mike Burke. He has been in my corner the whole way. Mike is one of the greatest analysts on Wall Street and tops in the Point and Figure method. I can't begin to say how much I have learned from him. Mike is one of the most positive people I have ever met. He has been there to answer my every question for 10 years. He unselfishly taught me much of what I know about technical analysis. We've been down the road together over the past decade. I would also like to thank Lee Grey, the founder of Chartcraft/Investors Intelligence, and his son Rick for their friendship over these years. They are the greatest. The whole crew at Chartcraft/Investors Intelligence is a tribute to the investment business. It's no wonder they have been in business for over 40 years; they just keep getting better.

Lastly, my thanks to my wonderful mother and father for having faith in my abilities all my life and for always being there for me no matter what. My dad provided the greatest inspiration a son could have. I'll never forget watching him graduate from Florida State University at age 47. He was an eighth-grade dropout who joined the Army in World War II as a Private and retired from the Army 30 years later as a Lieutenant Colonel. During his career he saw three wars. My dad spent 10 years in night school getting his degree. He showed me where there was a will there was a way. I attribute my success in the university and my strong work ethic to you, Dad. You showed me the way.

THOMAS J. DORSEY

CONTENTS

1. Introduction to Point and Figure Charting 1

Point and Figure Charting: A Lost Art 1
The History of Point and Figure Technical Analysis 2
Why You Should Use Point and Figure Charts 3
In the Beginning 4

2. Point and Figure Fundamentals 7

Charting U.S. Surgical 15
Trend Lines 18

3. Chart Patterns 27
Recording the Battle between Supply and Demand

Statistical Probabilities of Chart Patterns 30

4. Constructing and Managing the Trade 65

The Bullish Catapult Formation 67
The Bearish Catapult Formation 69
Managing Your Stop in a Short Sale 69
Managing the Trade 71
When to Sell 73
Taking a Profit—What to Do When Things Go Right 73
Some Helpful Guidelines in Managing a Trade 77

5. Using Relative Strength Calculations 79

Relative Strength—The Chartcraft Method 79
Moody and Parker's Relative Strength Study 86
Relative Strength as a Short-Term Indicator 88

6. The New York Stock Exchange Bullish Percent 91
The Most Important Market Indicator

Introducing the NYSE Bullish Percent Index 91
NYSE Bullish Percent Risk Levels 98
Significant Facts about the Bullish Percent 103

 7. **Other Market Indicators**   **109**

     Other Technical Indicators   109
     Trend Charts of Market Indexes   126
     Bond Market Indicators   135

 8. **Sector Analysis**   **141**

     Sector Analysis with Bullish Percent Indexes   141
     A Review of the Six Risk Levels   145
     The Majority of Risk in a Stock—The Sector and
        the Market   147

 9. **Trading Options Using Point and Figure**   **197**

     Call Definitions   198
     Put Definitions   200
     Put Versatility   200
     Selling Puts—The Underwriter   202
     Puts as Insurance Policies   204
     Rule of Thumb for Deltas   206

10. **Trading Commodities Using Point and Figure**   **211**

11. **Putting It All Together**   **217**

     Step 1. Evaluate the NYSE Index—Who's Got
        the Ball?   218
     Step 2. Evaluate the Two Short-Term Indicators—
        Who's Got the Ball Short Term?   219
     Step 3. Select a Sector—A Crucial Decision   222
     Step 4. Select a Group of Fundamentally Sound Stocks
        from the Chosen Sector   224
     Step 5. Evaluate and Inventory the Chart Patterns for
        Your Group of Stocks   224
     Step 6. Select Your Entry Point and Set Your Stops   229
     Step 7. Know What to Do When Things Go Right   230
     Conclusion   231

     Index   **233**

1

INTRODUCTION TO POINT AND FIGURE CHARTING

POINT AND FIGURE CHARTING: A LOST ART

The Point and Figure method is not new by any stretch of the imagination. It is, however, a lost art. I say lost art simply because most investment professionals and individual investors have lost sight of the basics of just what causes the prices of securities to fluctuate. In today's rapidly evolving technologies, the irrefutable law of supply and demand has been all but forgotten. New methods of security analysis continue to crop up capturing the ever-expanding curiosity of the investment public. It seems everyone is searching for the Holy Grail, a computer program that will throw off the winning trades each day. A long time ago when I was a stockbroker at a major firm on Wall Street, I learned there is no Holy Grail. The key to success in this business, and any business for that matter, is confidence. According to my dictionary, confidence means "firm belief or trust; self-reliance; boldness; assurance." Relative to success in the securities business, the key term in the definition is self-reliance, and it is the one trait most investors and stockbrokers lack. Investors today are increasingly averse to making their own decisions, which is why the mutual fund business has grown to record levels. The irony is that 75 percent or more of professional money managers never outperform the broad stock market averages. Nevertheless, most investors look at the stock market as an enigma. It confounds them that the market does not react in what would seem to be a logical pattern. Increased earnings expectations should result in price appreciation of the underlying stock, right? Not necessarily. In many cases, the exact opposite takes place.

1

THE HISTORY OF POINT AND FIGURE TECHNICAL ANALYSIS

The first person to record stock price movement was Charles Dow in the late 1800s. At the turn of the twentieth century, some astute investors came to notice many of Dow's chart patterns had a tendency to repeat themselves. Back then, there was no Securities and Exchange Commission; there were few rules and regulations. Stock pools dominated the action and outsiders were very late to the party. It was basically a closed shop of insiders.

The Point and Figure method of charting was developed as a logical, organized way of recording supply and demand. These charts provide the investor with a road map that clearly depicts that battle between supply and demand.

Everyone is familiar with using maps to plan trips. When we drive from Virginia to New York, we start the trip on I-95 North. If we don't pay attention to our navigating and inadvertently get on I-95 South, we are likely to hit Key West, Florida. The way to prepare for a journey to New York from Virginia is to familiarize yourself with the map, check the air in your car's tires, begin with a full tank of gas, bring coffee, and make sure the children have some books and toys. In other words, plan your trip. Most investors never plan their investment trip. By learning the Point and Figure method of analyzing supply and demand, investors will be able to plan that trip. Nothing guarantees success, but the probability of success is much higher when all the possible odds are stacked in the investors' favor. Somewhere along the road, you might be forced to take a detour, but that's OK as long as you stick to your original plan. This book will outline the best plan for financial success when you are investing in securities.

When it is all said and done, if there are more buyers in a particular security than there are sellers willing to sell, the price will rise. On the other hand, if there are more sellers in a particular security than there are buyers willing to buy, then the price will decline. If buying and selling are equal, the price will remain the same. This is the irrefutable law of supply and demand. The same reasons that cause price fluctuations in produce such as potatoes, corn, and asparagus cause price fluctuations in securities.

Two methods of analysis are used in security evaluation. One method is fundamental analysis. This is the method of analysis most investors are familiar with. It deals with the quality of the company's earnings, product acceptance, and management. Fundamental analysis answers the question *what* security to buy. The other basic method is technical analysis. The technical method answers the question *when* to buy that security. Timing the commitment is the crucial step.

Fundamental information on companies can be obtained from numerous sources. Many good, inexpensive publications are available that deal strictly with fundamental analysis. Most brokerage firms provide their customers with fundamental recommendations. The technical side of the equation is much more difficult to find as there are few in the securities business who are doing quality technical analysis that the average investor can understand. This book is designed to teach readers how to maintain and interpret Point and Figure charts that can guide their investing.

WHY YOU SHOULD USE POINT AND FIGURE CHARTS

The investment industry is overloaded with different methodologies on evaluating security price movement. There are methods that use bar charts, ancient Japanese candlestick charts, Gann angles, Elliot waves, and many more. The only method I have found to be straightforward and easy to understand is the Point and Figure method.

The charts are made up of X's and O's. Recording the movement of a security using this method is very much like recording a tennis match. A tennis match can last 12 sets. Each player can win a certain number of sets, but it is in the final count that one wins the match. In the Point and Figure method, we are only interested in the culmination of the match, not the winner of the underlying sets. The patterns this method produces are very easy to recognize—so simple that I have taught this method to grade schoolers in Virginia. I have always maintained that simple is best.

The concept underlying the method must be valid. Supply and demand is as valid and simple as it gets. I am not saying other methods aren't valid, it's just that most people can easily understand supply and demand because it is a part of everyday life. Why not make it a part of your everyday investing?

The greatest market indicator yet invented was developed by Chartcraft in 1955. It is called the New York Stock Exchange Bullish Percent Index. We have used it for many years with great success. In that time, we have refined it as the markets change, but the basic philosophy is still intact. I have devoted Chapter 6 of this book to a discussion of this indicator. Our sector rotation method, which is explained in Chapter 8, is a derivative of the Bullish Percent Index and was also developed by Chartcraft. Once you learn these basic principles, your investor confidence will increase tremendously. You will soon find yourself acting rather than reacting to different market conditions. This method changed my life, and I strongly believe it can do the same for anyone who will take the time to read this book and implement the investing principals contained therein.

IN THE BEGINNING

It took me years of operating in a fog in the brokerage business before I came across the Point and Figure method. I started my career at a large brokerage firm located in Richmond, Virginia, in late 1974. In training new employees, the firm focused primarily on sales. As trainees, we were drilled in the philosophy that the firm would provide the ideas and our responsibility was to sell them. The first four months at the firm was devoted to study. Every potential broker must pass the Series 7 examination to become registered with the New York Stock Exchange. The course was extensive—covering everything from exchange rules and regulations to complicated option strategies. Once we had passed the exam and completed five weeks of sales training, we were ready to be unleashed on the public.

As in any other profession, experience counts a lot, and we were severely lacking in that area. The market had just gone through what seemed to be a depression, losing about 70 percent of its value. Prospecting for new accounts was a difficult task at best, but those of us who survived spent the next four years building a book of business and learning by trial and error. Each morning, we had mounds of new recommendations from New York to sift through, all fundamental. We were not allowed to recommend any stocks our firm did not have a favorable opinion on; the rule was no thinking on our own, it could cause a lawsuit. Our job was to sell the research, not question it.

Over the years we had some tremendous successes and some tremendous failures, definitely not a confidence builder. Much of my spare time was spent searching for some newsletter writer who would be infallible, kind of like searching for the Holy Grail. This search only proved that the newsletter writers were better at selling than they were at picking stocks. The ship was basically rudderless, but we forged ahead. Now, almost 20 years later, nothing much has changed in the way business is done. There are some new bells and whistles and fad investments, but the backbone of the industry continues to be equities or equity derivative products. During my tenure at this firm, I specialized in option strategies. Options were relatively new, having been first listed for trading in April 1973. I spent much of my spare time studying this investment tool, and in 1978 I was offered the opportunity to develop and manage an options strategy department at a large regional brokerage firm home-based in the same town. It was an irresistible challenge, so I embarked on this new adventure.

Overnight, my clientele changed from individual investors to professional stockbrokers. I was now responsible for developing a department that would provide options strategy ideas to a sales force of 500 brokers. It was at this moment that I had to be totally honest with myself. Just how much did I really know about the stock market? I knew that, when all was said and done, my success at selecting the right stocks to underlie our options strategies would ultimately determine the success or failure of my department. The answer to that question was startling.

After four years of working as a successful stockbroker, I had very little knowledge of how to go about selecting stocks on my own, much less evaluating sectors and the market itself. I was used to doing what the firm directed. The one thing I did know was relying on the firm's research was likely to be hit or miss, just as it had been at the previous firm. It was clear to me that developing a successful options strategy department meant I would have to find someone who was adept at stock selection.

During my search, one name continued to crop up as an adept stock picker: Steve Kane, a broker in our Charlotte branch. I contacted Steve and explained my new adventure to him and offered him a position in my department. He decided to join me. My grand plan was that Steve would provide the stock, sector, and market direction, and I would provide the option strategies to dovetail his work.

As any craftsman would, Steve brought along his tools, which consisted of a chart book full of X's and O's on hundreds of stocks and a Point and Figure technical analysis book written by the late A. W. Cohen. (This book is no longer in print.) Each week Steve would fastidiously update these charts of X's and O's and use them to make his stock selections. Over the first year, Steve did very well. Stocks he selected to rise generally did. Stocks he felt would decline generally did. His calls on the market and sectors were also very good. The team was working well, and best of all, we were self-contained. We were a technical analysis and options strategy department rolled into one. We weren't always right, but we were more right than wrong and most important we had a plan of attack.

Just as things were looking good, a specialist firm on the New York Stock Exchange offered Steve a job with the opportunity to trade their excess capital. It was an offer Steve could not refuse, and I supported his decision to go. I found myself back in the same predicament that I had been in a year earlier. Rather than try to find someone else who understood the Point and Figure method of technical analysis that I had become accustomed to, I decided it was time to learn it myself.

Steve explained the basics to me and recommended I read his closely guarded copy of the book by A. W. Cohen. That weekend I started reading the book, and after the first three pages, my life changed. All the years of operating in a fog, searching for the Holy Grail and believing it was all too complicated to learn, came to an end. What I had found in the first three pages made all the sense in the world to me.

It took me back to my economics education in the university. The concept that I found in those first pages was the irrefutable law of supply and demand. All of a sudden, the workings of the stock market made sense. If there are more buyers than sellers willing to sell, the stock will rise and if there are more sellers than buyers willing to buy, the stock will decline. If buying and selling pressure are equal, the stock will remain the same. There is nothing else. Fundamental reasons cause the shifts in supply and demand, but in the end it is the supply-and-demand relationship that affects the price of the underlying stock.

From that day on, I read every book I could find on the subject even though most of the books available were manuscripts dating back 30 years and more. I continued to manage the options strategy department for nine years. In 1987 I saw an opportunity to start my own company. Dorsey, Wright & Associates, Inc. began business on January 2, 1987. It was learning the Point and Figure method of technical analysis that gave me the confidence and strength in my conviction to start this new enterprise. Our company now advises over 100 broker dealers and numerous money managers throughout the world. We have a money management arm in Beverly Hills and operate several trading partnerships.

This book was written so that just about anyone can understand it. If you have been looking for a logical, sensible way to approach your investment endeavor, you've come to the right place.

2

POINT AND FIGURE
FUNDAMENTALS

Many investors are familiar with charts of some kind or other, whether it is from school or reading newspapers or magazines. Point and Figure charts were developed over 100 years ago and have stood the test of time. This is one of the things that attracted me to them in the first place. I have taught this method of technical analysis in many seminars and classes. I have even taught it to schoolchildren as young as 12 years old. The law of supply and demand governs the movement of price in stocks, or anything for that matter: If there are more buyers than sellers willing to sell, prices rise; on the other hand, when there are more sellers than buyers willing to buy, prices decline. It is these imbalances in supply and demand that cause prices of stocks to move up and down and nothing else. Fundamental changes in the underlying company's outlook can cause this imbalance, but it is the imbalance nonetheless that causes the stock to move. The Point and Figure method of analyzing stock movement was designed simply as a logical, organized way of recording this battle between supply and demand. The word "organized" is the key. A basic road atlas would be very difficult to use if the actual lines depicting the roads and interstates were missing. It is the same in the stock market business. Looking at an endless list of High-Low-Close quotations on any particular stock would be equally confusing. When these quotations are organized in a logical fashion, however, the battle between supply and demand becomes much more clear. The Point and Figure chart simply shows whether supply or demand is winning the battle. We use various chart patterns and trend lines to guide our buy-and-sell decisions. These patterns will be covered in detail in later chapters.

A tennis match is a helpful analogy to illustrate what happens in this battle between supply and demand. Consider a match between tennis greats, Jimmy Connors and John McEnroe. Let's call demand Jimmy Connors and supply John McEnroe. The tennis match is made up of various sets. The sets played in a tennis match are similar to the Point and Figure chart moving back and forth, changing columns of alternating X's and O's. This seemingly random movement in the Point and Figure chart is similar to the seemingly random changes in sets won during a tennis match. Eventually one of the players wins enough sets to emerge victorious in the match. Likewise, it is only when the match is completed that we have a handle on which way the stock is likely to move. The Point and Figure chart considers the sets that are played as market noise and not worthy of inclusion in the decision-making process. In the short run, stock prices move about randomly but eventually demand or supply takes control and a trend begins. In this book, I will refer to tennis and football in explaining many of the market indicators and stock chart patterns you are about to learn. The football analogy comes from Mike Burke, my mentor, who is the editor of *Investors Intelligence.* One day I was visiting him with an important client of mine from Paris, and Mike mentioned how the market indicators reminded him of a football game. Since then, I have found the analogy most aptly describes the stock market indicators we follow that were created by Chartcraft decades ago. My analogy of the tennis match is the easiest to use when learning the fine points of the Point and Figure chart itself. Let's play ball!

We will begin with the basics of maintaining your own chart. It only takes a few minutes each day to update 20 or 30 charts. All you need is a financial page providing the high and low prices of stocks each day on the major exchanges. If you have a computer with a phone modem, many on-line computer services also will update the charts for you for a nominal fee.

The Point and Figure chart uses only the price action of the stock—volume is not a consideration. Remember, we are only interested in the battle between supply and demand. Two letters of the alphabet are used in this method of charting, "X" and "O." The X represents demand. The O represents supply. The key to this method is how the chart moves from one column to the next. For the purposes of this book, we will use the 3-point reversal method. As you become more adept at this method, you may want to choose other reversal points. At my company, however, we never deviate from the three-box method described in this section. Remember, keep it simple. Take a look at Figure 2.1, which shows a basic chart, so you can get an idea of what the Point and Figure chart looks like.

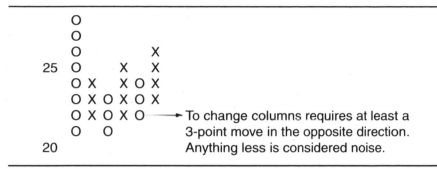

Figure 2.1

As you can see, the chart pattern is formed by alternating columns of X's and O's. The only way a column of X's can change to a column of O's is by reversing three boxes. The same three-box reversal method applies to the column of O's. This moving back and forth from one column to the next is what causes the chart pattern to form.

Before we go any further, let's look at the values of the boxes in relation to the price of the stock. The box sizes change as the stock moves through certain levels. This is why we call this method a *three-box* reversal method rather than a 3-point reversal method. Between 20 and 100 the box size is 1 point per box. The box size changes below 20 and above 100. If a stock were trading between $5 and $20, the box size would be ½ point. If the stock were trading at $100 or higher, the box size would be 2 points. Therefore to change columns from X's to O's when the stock was between $20 and $100 would require 3 points. We established that between $20 and $100 the box size was $1, so 3 boxes equals $3. The same three-box reversal would only be 1½ points if the stock was between $5 and $20. If the stock were trading below $5, the same three-box reversal would only be ¾ of a point. Think in terms of box reversals.

Figure 2.1 illustrates how much the stock must rise or fall to create a reversal on the chart. You may think I am being redundant, but that's OK—I intend to be redundant in this chapter to help you catch on to the basics of maintaining your own chart. The rest of the book will flow easily once you understand this concept. If you don't catch on after the first reading, go back and reread this chapter.

When I lecture on this subject I use the flowchart shown in Figure 2.2 to demonstrate how to update a chart. The basic concept is as follows. Whichever column the chart is in, you will remain in that column as long as the stock continues moving in that direction. So, if the chart was in a column of O's and declining, your first question of the flowchart at the

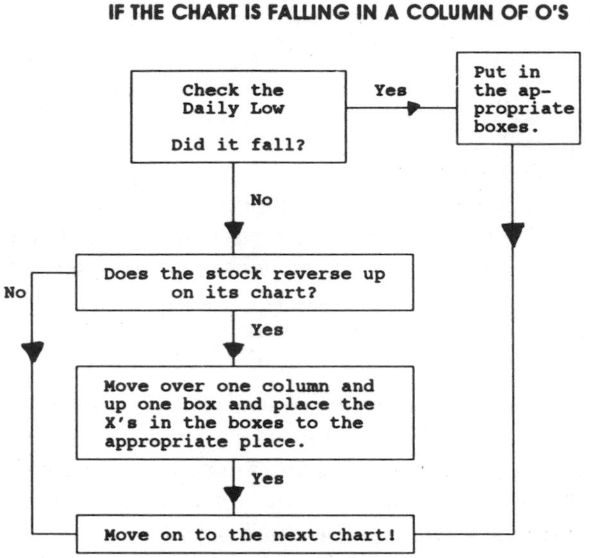

IF THE CHART IS FALLING IN A COLUMN OF O'S

Figure 2.2   The flowchart for charting. When charting a stock, the updating process is essentially like one of the old flow charts you have seen.

close of the business day would be, Did the stock decline one full box or more on the chart? If the stock did decline one more box, let's say from $45 to $44, then record that move by making an O in the $44 box and stop—go no further that day. Don't think about the chart again until the close of business the following day. At the close of business the following day, you must ask the same question again. Since the stock is still in a column of O's, did it decline another box or more? Answer the question by looking at the low price for the day. If the stock in this case hit $43 or lower (declined one more box or lower), record the move by making an O in the box and stop. I don't care if the stock reversed later in the day and went to $100. You'll deal with that move tomorrow. You are only concerned with one direction per day. OK, at this point, the stock is at $43 in a column of O's. Since the stock is still in a column of O's, the next day at the close of trading you ask the same question again. Did the stock decline one more box or lower? Today, the answer is no to flowchart question 1.

Because the stock did not decline enough to close one more box, you go to the second and last flowchart question. Since the stock did not decline any further, or at least enough to close another box, did the stock reverse up three boxes? Well let's find out. Count up three boxes from $43, that would be $44, $45, $46. OK, did the stock hit $46? Let's say it hit \$45⅞. Not good enough. That was only a 2⅞ reversal, not 3. What do you do? Nothing. The next day, you go through the same process again. Since the stock is still in a column of O's, the first flowchart question that must be answered is, Did the stock go down one box or more? Get the picture? If over time, the stock does reverse up three boxes to \$46 by following these two flowchart questions, you will find the chart now one column over to the right and now represented by X's. The chart is now rising. The same process starts over again, only this time the first flowchart question is, Did the stock move up one box or more? That is really the whole ball of wax.

Once again, it takes three boxes to reverse from one direction to the other. For example, if a stock were trading in a column of X's with a top of 45, it would take a move to 42 to reverse this chart to a column of O's. Anything less than three boxes would be considered market noise, not worthy of recording. Conversely, if the stock in question was trading in a column of O's with a current low at 45, it would need a rise to 48 before a reversal into a column of X's could be recorded; as before, anything less than three boxes would be considered market noise. This is as difficult as it gets to update a chart. Figure 2.3 shows some examples of reversals.

There is one exception to the preceding pattern. If a stock reversed, for example, from \$21, the required number of points would only be 2. This is because the stock will be moving through a *level*, where the box size changes. For example, if a stock is moving up (in a column of X's) through the upper teens and has a high of 21, a reversal would take place at 19, a move of only 2 points. The three boxes in this case were at 20, 19½, and 19 as the box size below 20 is ½ points per box rather than the 1 point per box above 20. Keep break points in mind when you are charting at levels where the box size changes. If you just price the vertical axes properly, you need deal only with the boxes. Prices will take care of themselves. Keep it simple. Just assign the proper point value to the box, ½, 1, and so on and then count three boxes.

This brings you to the actual charting. The daily high and low quotations for a stock are all that you will need. Most newspapers have a financial section. The only prices you are concerned with are those that

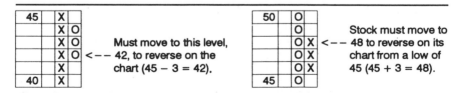

Figure 2.3 Examples of reversals.

cause changes in the chart. For example, a stock is in a column of X's and has a high of 28⅞. For charting purposes, we would read this as 28 because ⅞ is not enough to close the box of 29. To add another X, the stock must reach a price of 29—28⅞ is not 29. To the Point and Figure chartist, ⅞ is simply market noise when the box size is 1 point. When a stock is in a column of O's and you're looking at a stock's low, you go up to the next whole number. Using the same example, a stock has a low of 28⅞. You read this as a low of 29. The stock must move to 28 to add another O to the chart. When you get a reversal of three or more boxes on a chart, you plot the reversal one column over and one box up or down depending on the direction of the reversal. If the stock reverses down, you will plot an O one column over and one box down. If the stock reverses to the upside, you will plot an X one column over and one box higher. When reversing up or down, your count does not begin equal to the last number. Up means begin counting up one box. A reversal down suggests you begin counting down one box.

The only record of time in the Point and Figure chart is the replacing of the X or O with the number of the month when the chartist makes the first entry of that month. Placing the month in the chart has no significance except as a reference point. As the stock moves about, it alternates back and forth from one column to the next, X to O, O to X, and so on. At no time will you have an O in a column of X's nor an X in a column of O's. As previously mentioned, the first action point on the chart in any given month is represented by the number of the month. For example, if a stock rises one box, you would add another X to its chart. If that X, or plot, is the first one for July, you would use a 7 instead of an X in that box. This also holds true on down moves. For example, if a stock declined one box, and that is the first action point in August, you would put an 8 in the box instead of an O.

Let's cover it again. If the chart is rising, first check the daily high, and add an X if the stock has risen enough to close the next open box or boxes. You would add as many X's as needed to represent the stock's move. If the stock rose 4 points during the trading session, and each box equaled $1, you would put four X's in the chart. If the same stock moved up 5 points, you would add five X's. Flowchart question 1 would have been satisfied and at that point you stop charting for that day. If, on the other hand, the stock did not move high enough to add another X, you go to flowchart question 2 and check the daily low to see if it has declined enough to reverse on the chart. The reversal is the key feature of the Point and Figure chart. If it did reverse, move one column over and one box down, then add the three O's representing the reversal. If the stock did not decline enough to warrant a reversal, then there is no action on the chart for the day. Remember, the three-box reversal means all three boxes must be filled before you fill any of them (2⅞ points is not 3, and 3 is the requirement for a reversal if the point value of a box is 1). You cannot begin filling one box then the next until you get three. The chart will remain in its current column until it closes (hits) all three boxes on the reversal.

By using a three-box reversal method, we eliminate the minor moves that often occur in the market and look for moves that are significant enough to warrant representation. This is why the Point and Figure chart has it all over the bar chart. If a stock is declining, use the same process in reverse. Look first to see if the stock has moved down enough to add another O. If it has, add the O or O's. If the stock did not decline enough to close another box, then look at the daily high to see if the stock has rallied enough to reverse the chart up. If it has, move one column over and one box up and add the three new X's. If it has not moved up enough to reverse, there is no action on that chart for the day. Some stocks can sit for months without any change. In volatile markets, there are times when the chart could continue in its present direction and then reverse. In other words, the stock rose enough to close another box with an X, but the last 20 minutes of trading that day, the stock declined 8 points on earnings news. You would simply stick to the flowchart, close the box with an X and forget the reversal at the end of the day. You will deal with that reversal tomorrow. It is a good idea to be aware of the stock's reversal at the end of the trading session, even though you don't record it on the chart that day. This can happen when earnings reports are released. The stock rises one box on the day, but late in the session the earnings are released. Let's say they are much less than Wall Street expected. This could have the effect of immediately collapsing the stock price thus producing what might seem like a reversal back down the chart. A chart can only move in one direction a day. In this case, you update the chart by moving it up in the column of X's. If the stock has moved enough late in the day to reverse, you will more than likely chart that reversal the following day.

If you have already gotten the hang of updating your chart, you can move along to the next section; if not, let's recap for a moment. If a stock is rising in a column of X's, you will record any subsequent up-moves as long as that up-move equals or exceeds the next highest box. If the stock does not move up enough to equal the next higher box, then you look to the low to see if the stock reversed columns. To reverse into a column of O's from X's, the underlying stock must reverse three boxes to be significant enough to warrant a change in columns. Thus, the action points in a stock that is rising and has the $50 box closed with an X will be 51 for another X, or 47 to qualify for a reversal into a column of O's. The opposite is true for a stock declining. The easiest way to chart is to determine your two action points before you seek the high and low for the day. In the preceding example, your action points

DATE	HIGH		LOW		LAST	
20-APR-94	16	5-8	16		16	
21-APR-94	16	1-4	16		16	1-8
22-APR-94	16	7-8	16	3-8	16	5-8
25-APR-94	16	3-4	16	1-2	16	5-8
26-APR-94	17	3-8	16	1-2	17	3-8
27-APR-94	17	3-8	17	3-8	17	3-8
28-APR-94	18	1-8	17	1-2	17	3-4
29-APR-94	18	1-8	17	5-8	17	5-8
2-MAY-94	18	3-8	17	1-2	18	
3-MAY-94	18	1-4	17	7-8	18	
4-MAY-94	18	1-4	17	7-8	18	1-8
5-MAY-94	18	1-4	17	1-2	17	1-2
6-MAY-94	17	3-4	17	1-2	17	5-8
9-MAY-94	17	3-4	17	1-8	17	1-8
10-MAY-94	17	5-8	17	1-8	17	1-8
11-MAY-94	17	5-8	17	1-8	17	3-8
12-MAY-94	17	1-2	17	1-8	17	1-4
13-MAY-94	17	1-2	17	1-8	17	3-8
16-MAY-94	17	3-8	17	1-8	17	1-4
17-MAY-94	17	1-2	17	1-8	17	1-4
18-MAY-94	17	5-8	17	1-4	17	3-8
19-MAY-94	17	5-8	17	3-8	17	1-2
20-MAY-94	17	5-8	17	1-4	17	3-8
23-MAY-94	18		17	1-2	17	5-8
24-MAY-94	18	7-8	17	5-8	18	7-8
25-MAY-94	19	5-8	18	5-8	18	7-8
26-MAY-94	19	3-4	18	3-8	18	1-2
27-MAY-94	19	1-8	18	1-2	18	7-8
31-MAY-94	19	3-8	18	7-8	19	
1-JUN-94	22	1-4	19	5-8	21	3-4
2-JUN-94	20	1-2	19	1-2	19	3-4
3-JUN-94	21		19	7-8	20	1-2
6-JUN-94	21	3-4	20	7-8	21	
7-JUN-94	21	1-2	20	3-4	20	3-4
8-JUN-94	21	1-8	20	1-2	20	5-8
9-JUN-94	20	3-4	20	1-2	20	1-2
10-JUN-94	21	5-8	20	1-2	21	1-2
13-JUN-94	23	1-8	21	1-4	22	7-8
14-JUN-94	23	1-4	22	1-4	22	5-8
15-JUN-94	22	7-8	22	1-2	22	3-4
16-JUN-94	24	1-4	22	3-4	23	7-8
17-JUN-94	24	5-8	23	3-4	24	
20-JUN-94	23	1-4	22	1-4	23	
21-JUN-94	23	1-8	21	7-8	21	7-8

Figure 2.4   U.S. Surgical historical data.

DATE	HIGH		LOW		LAST	
22-JUN-94	22	1-4	21	1-8	21	5-8
23-JUN-94	21	5-8	20	3-4	20	3-4
24-JUN-94	21	3-4	20	1-2	21	3-8
27-JUN-94	21	1-2	21		21	1-2
28-JUN-94	23	5-8	21	1-4	23	5-8
29-JUN-94	24	1-8	23	1-4	23	7-8
30-JUN-94	23	7-8	22	1-8	22	3-8
1-JUL-94	23	1-4	22	1-2	22	7-8
5-JUL-94	23		22	1-2	22	3-4
6-JUL-94	22	5-8	22		22	
7-JUL-94	24		22		23	5-8
8-JUL-94	24	1-4	22	7-8	23	1-2
11-JUL-94	23	3-4	23		23	1-8
12-JUL-94	23	3-4	23	1-4	23	3-8
13-JUL-94	23	5-8	23	1-4	23	1-4
14-JUL-94	23	5-8	23	3-8	23	1-2
15-JUL-94	23	3-8	22	5-8	22	3-4

Figure 2.4   *(Continued)*

were $51 or $47. That's all you look for in the high and low for the day. Did the stock hit $51? If the answer is no, then did it hit $47? If one of those action points was hit, record the correct price and *stop*. Once you understand the concept of the reversal, you have mastered the nuts and bolts of this method.

Now it's time to construct a chart based on prices taken from *The Wall Street Journal* (see Figure 2.4).

CHARTING U.S. SURGICAL

We have used the price quotations shown in Figure 2.4 to construct the chart that appears in Figure 2.5. Take a look at that chart now. Notice how the last box closed in the chart in April is at the price of $16. We begin updating the chart from that point. Remember the easiest way to maintain a Point and Figure chart is to determine where your actions points are. In other words, if the chart is in a column of O's, the first action point would be one box lower than the last one recorded. If the stock does not decline low enough to record the lower box, then your second and last action point would be a three-box reversal up. In the case of U.S. Surgical, the first action points from the bottom at $16 in April would be $15½ (one box lower) or $17½ (a three-box reversal up). From the $16 level, there are no other action points. Whichever action point is hit first, record it, then determine your next action point. That

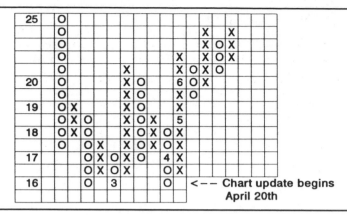

Figure 2.5   U.S. Surgical.

basically is all there is to updating a chart. Always think of your two action points. We update 1,400 Point and Figure stocks charts per day by hand. We also update those same charts and another 5,000 by computer later in the evening. This is exactly how we do it each day.

Using Figures 2.4 and 2.5, let's update U.S. Surgical stock beginning at the $16 in April. As discussed earlier, there are numbers on the chart that correspond to the months of the year and provide a convenient reference point.

1. On April 20, determine action points for $16. They are $15½ and $17½. Let's explain how we get these numbers one more time. Since we begin with the stock in a column of O's, the $15½ action point is simply one box lower than the last one recorded at $16. The $17½ action point corresponds to a three-box reversal up. Remember that each box below $20 and above $5 equals ½ point. Three boxes represents 1½ points, thus $16 + 1½ = $17½. In this case $17½ is hit before $15½. Notice how, on April 28, $17½ is hit as well as $18. This action causes the reversal plus one box. Now go up to $18 in a column of X's.

2. On April 28, determine your action points. They will be $18½ for a one-box rise or $16½ for a three-box reversal. Record whichever comes first. It takes until May 24 for the stock to move enough to be considered significant enough to record. The stock rose to $18⅞ closing the $18½ box. This is a good example of why the Point and Figure chart is so important. The bar chartist would have been recording moves in the chart every day. The Point and Figure chartist would have done nothing from April 28 until May 24

because nothing significant happened between those dates. The Point and Figure chartist is not interested in noise.

3. On May 24, determine your action points. They are $19 on the up-side and $17 for a three-box reversal. Now you wait to see which one is hit first, then establish your next action points. Easy huh? On May 25, the next day, U.S. Surgical hit a high of $19⅝. This closed the action point box of $19 as well as the next box above it at $19½.

4. On May 26, determine your action points. They are $20 and $18. If the stock rises one more box and hits $20 make an X. Instead of rising, if it falls three boxes to $18 or lower, reverse into a column of O's and represent the move. On June 1, the stock hit $22¼. You can now move up in X's to the $22 box. Notice how the box size has changed. It was ½ dollar (point) per box below $20, now it is 1 dollar (point) per box above $20 up to $100.

5. One June 2, establish your action points. They are $23 and $19½. The $23 one is easy, the $19½ action point might confuse you a little. Remember the breakpoints in box size. Three boxes down from $22 would be $21, $20, $19½. Below $20 is ½ point per box. (I know you are aware of that, but I want to drive it home.) The very next day the stock declines to $19½ so you will reverse into a column of O's. Supply had taken control for the time being. Your action points will now begin with one box lower to continue in the same direction, or a three-box or more reversal into a column of X's.

6. On June 3, establish your action points. The chart is now in a column of O's at the $19½ level. Your action points are $19 and $22 for a three-box reversal. Once again, we cross the equator, the point where the box size changes from ½ to 1, so a three-box reversal up from $19½ is ½ point to $20 then 1 point to $21 and 1 point to $22. Note how the box size changes when you cross the $20 mark. OK, let's see which one is hit first. On June 13, the stock rises to $23, so the stock reverses up into a column of X's and the $23 box is closed.

7. On June 14, establish your action points. Since you are in a column of X's, your first action point is one box higher than the last one closed. That number is $24. A three-box reversal would be $20. So we are looking for $24 and $20. On June 16, $24¼ is hit closing the $24 box.

8. On June 17, establish your action points. I'm sure you get it by now. We are looking for $25 or $21. $25 represents a one-box rise and $21 the three-box reversal. On June 23, the stock declines to $20¾. This reverses it back down the chart and into a column of O's. The $21 box is now closed with an O.

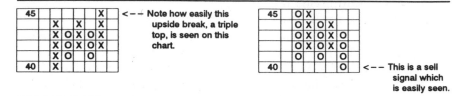

Figure 2.6   Buy and sell signals.

9. On June 24, establish your action points. We are looking for $20 and $24. On June 29, the stock hits a high of $24⅛. The stock now reverses back up into a column of X's. The reversal forms a double top.

10. On June 30, establish your action points. They are $25 and $21 for a three-box reversal.

This has been an interesting exercise because the stock crossed the equator a couple of times demonstrating three-box reversals using ½-point and 1-point box sizes.

One of the reasons Point and Figure charts are so practical is that the chart formations stand out because we move over and down a box when making a reversal. This is easily seen by looking at a chart that has just broken out. By moving down a box when the stock reverses down, the tops, or resistance areas, stand out. By moving up a box when the stock reverses up, the lows or support areas stand out. Figure 2.6 provides examples of such movements.

TREND LINES

Trend lines are one of the most important guides you have in Point and Figure charting. I am always amazed how a stock will hold a trend line on the way up or down. Trend lines are very easily drawn using the Point and Figure method, whereas bar chart methods involve a lot of subjectivity. Two basic trend lines are used in Point and Figure charting: the Bullish Support line and the Bearish Resistance line. We will discuss each of these separately as well as two other trend lines, the Bullish Resistance line and the Bearish Support line. For long-term investors, a stock is always bullish if it is trading above the Bullish Support line. Conversely, a stock is always bearish if it trades below the bearish resistance line. That is for long-term investors. Traders are much more flexible and find the truth somewhere in between most of the time.

The Bullish Support Line

The Bullish Support line is a major component of a stock's chart pattern. It serves as a guide to the underlying securities uptrend. Typically these lines are like brick walls. It is uncanny how so many stocks will hold the trend line as they rise in price. Investors should not buy stocks that are not trading above their Bullish Support lines. Drawing the line is very simple and has not changed since the inception of the Point and Figure method. Once a stock has formed a base of accumulation below the Bearish Resistance line and gives the first buy signal, we go to the lowest column of O's in the chart pattern and begin drawing a trend line starting with the box directly under that column of O's and diagonally connecting each box upward in a 45-degree angle. Unlike bar charts, which connect prices, the Point and Figure chart never connects prices. The angle for a Bullish Support line will always be a 45-degree angle. The Bearish Resistance line will always be the reciprocal of the 45-degree angle or a 135-degree angle. We will typically give a stock the benefit of the doubt if it gives a sell signal while it is trading close to the Bullish Support line. Once a stock rises significantly above this trend line and gives more buy signals, you can go to the bottom O of that new distribution and draw another trend line. The first Bullish Support line will always serve to be the long-term trend line and may very well come into play years later. These shorter term trend lines serve as visual guides for you. The short-term trend lines can also be valuable to the trader in identifying the direction of stocks. Traders often initiate a long trade when the stock has declined

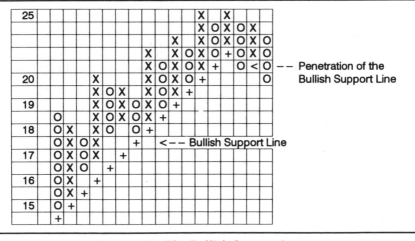

Figure 2.7   The Bullish Support Line.

near the Bullish Support line because the stock is then close to the stop-loss point. The most important characteristic of the Point and Figure method is its clear guidelines for entering and exiting a trade. One of the main keys to successful investing is avoiding the big hit. These guidelines will help you do that.

When the stock penetrates the trend line and simultaneously gives a sell signal, it is a critical event and a strong sign to sell the stock. To qualify as a penetration, the trend line must be violated and not just touched. There is no such thing as the line being a little penetrated. It is or it isn't. In Figure 2.7, the stock maintained the trend line all the way up from $15 to $25. Soon after, supply took control of the stock. When the stock hit $21, it not only gave a double bottom sell signal but also violated the Bullish Support line. The violated support line was the key sign there was a high probability that the trend had changed.

The Bullish Resistance Line

The Bullish Resistance line is drawn by moving to the left of the last buy signal and going to the first wall of O's. Remember, it is not the first column of O's but the first wall of O's. A wall of O's is usually that last down move in the stock from which it begins to bottom out.

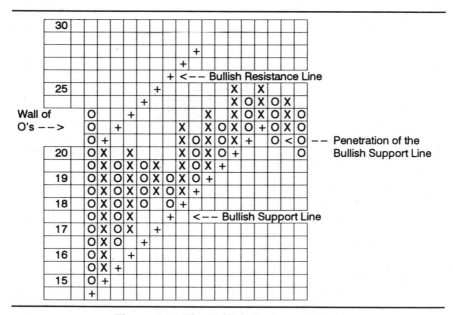

Figure 2.8   The Bullish Resistance Line.

This is the point where demand begins to take the upper hand. Figure 2.8 best demonstrates this. Then go to the column of X's right next to the wall of O's and begin drawing your trend line, beginning with the empty box above that top X. This line will be a 45-degree angle as is the Bullish Support line. Typically, a stock will encounter resistance as it moves to the Bullish Resistance line though this line may have to be drawn a number of times. The boundaries of the Bullish Support line and the Bullish Resistance line form a trading channel. In Figure 2.8, the Bullish Resistance line is drawn from the wall of O's beginning at the $21 level.

The Bearish Resistance Line

The Bearish Resistance line, which is the exact opposite of the Bullish Support line previously discussed, is shown in Figure 2.9. When a stock forms an area of distribution above the Bullish Support line and gives the first sell signal, you can go to the top X and begin drawing the trend line in the box directly above that X. Next connect the boxes diagonally down in a 135-degree angle, the reciprocal of the 45-degree angle of the Bullish Support line. Actually, all you need to do is connect the boxes and the angle will be 135 degrees. The same principles and trading tactics apply in reverse to the Bearish Resistance line. We

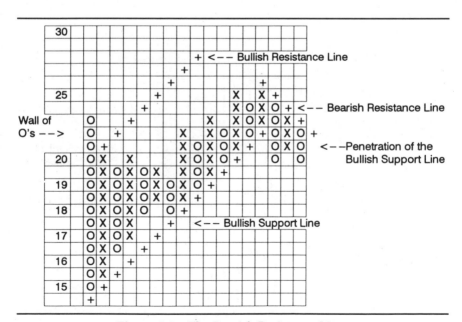

Figure 2.9 The Bearish Resistance Line.

typically prefer not to go long when below the Bearish Resistance line. This line, like the Bullish Support line, can be as strong as a brick wall. We say a stock is bearish when it is on a sell signal and below the Bearish Resistance line. Be wary of buy signals that come from just below this resistance line as they tend to be false or best suited to traders. Stocks that are moving up to this line typically find formidable resistance there. Also, a stock must be on a buy signal to penetrate the Bearish Resistance line. Short sales can be initiated in weak stocks when the underlying stock rallies up to the resistance line but is still below it. This is the optimum point to sell short on any of the bearish chart patterns.

The Bearish Support Line

As shown in Figure 2.10, the Bearish Support line is the reciprocal of the Bullish Resistance line and is drawn by moving to the left of the Bearish Resistance line to the first *wall* of X's. Again, not to the next column of X's but to the first wall of X's. Then move to the first column of O's next to it and begin drawing your support line down from the empty box below the last O. The line, which will automatically be a 135-degree angle by connecting the diagonal boxes, can be used as a guide to identify where any decline might be contained. The Bearish

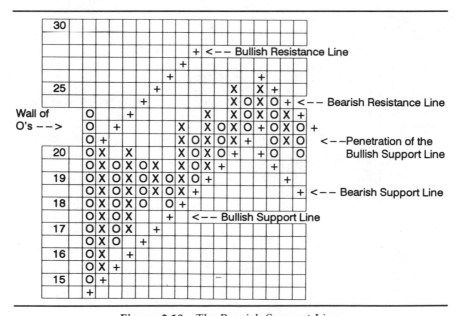

Figure 2.10   The Bearish Support Line.

Resistance line and the Bearish Support line in combination form a channel that the stock can be expected to trade in. Movement down to the Bearish Support line is likely to cause bottom fishing as investors create demand supporting the stock at that level. As the stock rises to the resistance level, investors who have been stuck holding the declining stock will elect to sell on rallies.

Price Objectives

Price objectives in Point and Figure technical analysis are derived through two methods called the horizontal count and the vertical count. These methods of determining price objectives come from the science of ballistics and have been used in Point and Figure analysis for many decades. The distance a bullet will travel can be calculated if the following factors are known—the size of the powder keg that will propel the projectile, the length of the barrel, the resistance the projectile will experience traveling through the barrel, the air temperature, and the attitude of the rifle. The best definition describing this science was written in an *Encyclopaedia Britannica* article in the 1920s. The following passage is from the book *The Point and Figure Method—Advanced Theory and Practice* (distributed by Morgan, Rogers, & Robertson, Inc., New York, copyright 1934).

> Exterior ballistics is that part of the science of ballistics in which the motion of the projectile is considered after it has received its initial impulse. The factors involved are the pressure of the powder or gas in the chamber of the gun from which the projectile secures its initial velocity, resistance of the bore before the projectile leaves the barrel, the resistance of the air, and the influence of gravity, all must be calculated in order to determine the probable objective of the projectile.

These same principles have been applied to stock and commodity trading to arrive at a rough estimate of the price objective following a breakout of a consolidation area. The vertical count is the most reliable and should be used whenever possible. We don't tend to use the counts much in our daily business because we are investment oriented rather than trading oriented. The trader is more interested in how far the stock is likely to move in relation to the distance to his stop. For investment purposes, we are more interested in relative performance rather than a close stop. Still, it won't hurt to take a moment and determine how far the underlying stock you are considering for purchase or sale might move.

Speaking of the trader, let's digress for a moment and talk about trading bands. We typically use statistical analysis to determine the relative overbought-oversold nature of the underlying stock. This calculation is simply the bell curve you learned in Statistics 101. If we find that a stock is 2 or 3 standard deviations above trend we know that the probability is high the stock will pull back a little. In such cases, we would normally enter an order to buy on a reversal back down the chart. If the stock has pulled back and is on the oversold side of the bell curve, we would typically recommend the purchase at the market. Keep in mind that just because a stock is overbought doesn't mean it can't become more overbought. Conversely, a stock can become even more oversold. This is the major drawback to using statistics as your primary method of analysis. We find it useful but only as a secondary consideration. Now let's get back to actually calculating the vertical count.

The Vertical Count

When a stock finally bottoms out and begins to move up, it will give a simple buy signal at some point. A buy signal comes when a column of X's exceeds a previous column of X's. Once a buy signal is given, the stock will rise to a certain level where supply again takes over. When the stock reverses into a column of O's, the first column of X's off the bottom is finished. There can be no more X's placed in that column. At this point, count the number of boxes in the column of X's, and multiply times 3 (if you are using the three-box reversal method). Then multiply that figure by the value per box. When that is done, add the result to the bottom of the line of X's (where that column began). This will give you a rough estimate of the stock's price objective on that move. Remember, the price objective is a guide, not a guarantee. It is not set in concrete, as many stocks meet their first price objective and continue on up, so keep the chart formation and trend lines in mind when deciding whether to sell the stock. Just because a stock has met its expected price move, it does not mean you must sell. It does, however, suggest you reevaluate its potential from that level.

Notice that in the example of the vertical count shown in Figure 2.11, box sizes change. You must first count the boxes below $5 as each box represents ¼ point. Then count the boxes above $5 as they represent ½ point per box. There are four boxes representing ¼ point. Multiply them times 3 and then multiply that number by ¼ ($4 \times 3 = 12 \times \frac{1}{4} =$ $3). Now count the boxes above $5 and ending at $8. There are six boxes at ½ point per box ($6 \times 3 = 18 \times \frac{1}{2} = \$9$). Now add the two counts together, and you get ($3 + $9) = $12. OK, here's the last step. Add the $12 to the dollar value at the first box in that column. The potential move is $4¼ + $12 = $16¼. This example helps you understand how to use the count at breakpoints.

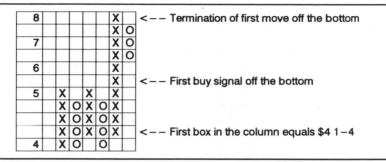

Figure 2.11 The vertical count.

Vertical Count for Short Sale

Calculating the vertical count for a short sale is similar to that of a long position with one exception. Instead of multiplying the move by 3, you multiply by 2. In Figure 2.12, we count the number of boxes in the first move off the top, which creates the first sell signal. There are seven boxes in that column. Multiply 7 times 2 and that comes to 14. Now multiply 14 times the box size which is 1. That comes to 14. Now the last step is to subtract 14 from the level of the first O in the column, which is $30. The price objective is $30 − $14 = $16.

The Horizontal Count

A horizontal count is taken by counting across the base a stock has built, multiplying by 3 and then multiplying again by the value per box. This is similar to the vertical count except you count horizontally across the formation as opposed to the vertical move off the bottom. I look at the horizontal count as an exercise in counting the size of the powder keg that will propel the projectile. In ballistics, the powder keg is the amount of gunpowder in the shell casing, and the projectile is the

		X		X		X			
30	O	X	O	X	O	X	O		
	O	X	O	X	O	X	O		
	O	X	O	X	O		O		
	O		O				O		
							O		
25							O		
							O		

Figure 2.12 The vertical count for a short sale.

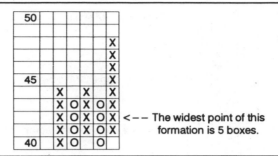

Figure 2.13   The horizontal count.

bullet that will fly when the charge is detonated. I associate the vertical count with the distance the projectile travels before gravity takes control and pulls the bullet back to earth. This analogy always helped me understand the concept of the count when I was learning this method many years ago. Try to keep this as simple as possible because the count is only a guide. It is far more important to consider the market, sector, relative strength, and chart pattern when initiating a long or short position. This book will place more emphasis on these variables than the count.

In Figure 2.13, you would simply count the number of boxes horizontally at the widest point of the formation. That number is multiplied by 3 and the product of that multiplication is again multiplied by the box size. In this example, the box size is $1 (5 × 3 = 15 × $1 = $15). Then add the product of this multiplication to the lowest point of the formation, which is $40. The expected move is thus $15 + $40 = $55. Where the count really comes into play is in determining your risk-reward relationship. You should have at least two points potential profit for each point potential loss before initiating a trade. Keep in mind there are 10,000 stocks to trade. Don't get hung up on one stock for any reason. There is always another train coming down the track. All you have to do is watch for it.

3

CHART PATTERNS

Recording the Battle between Supply and Demand

The backbone of the Point and Figure analysis is the chart pattern. The beauty of this method is its ability to form simple chart patterns that record the battle between supply and demand. The reason this method is so credible is it is founded on the irrefutable law of supply and demand, which affects our life on a daily basis. Although just about everything we come in contact with has some association with supply and demand, it wasn't until my first course in college-level economics that I really thought about and came to understand this basic law. It was this introductory course that led me to get a degree in economics. While many of the concepts I learned are outmoded now, one remains unchanged—supply and demand. The driving force behind price change of all kind is supply and demand. If there are more buyers than sellers willing to sell, then the price will rise. On the other side of the coin, if there are more sellers than buyers willing to buy, then the price will decline. This is as true for the price of watermelons as it is for the price of stocks. These price changes affect our lives on a daily basis but rarely do we think much about the law that governs these changes.

In the stock markets, prices change daily. Buyer and seller battle it out for control of the stock. Eventually one side wins the battle, and the stock begins to take on a trend. I have taught this method of stock analysis to children in grade schools by using the analogy of a tennis match. In a singles tennis match, two players use rackets to hit a fabric-covered, hollow rubber ball back and forth over a net stretched across a

27

marked, level, rectangular area each trying to cause the other to fail to hit the ball back over the net. The match consists of games and sets; there are a certain number of games in a set and a certain number of sets in a match. The contest sometimes continues for an extended period until eventually one player wins the match. Virtually the same thing happens with stocks. Over the near term, stocks seem to move back and forth randomly the same way players may win alternate sets of a tennis match. Eventually, however, either demand or supply will win out and establish a trend. In the Point and Figure method, a particular pattern will form signaling that either demand or supply has taken control of the stock. We are not interested in making commitments in the stock market on the evidence of the sets. We are only interested in making commitments on the evidence of a completed match. The Point and Figure chart patterns tend to repeat themselves and thus provide a high degree of predictability about the future move of the underlying stock. All too often, investors buy stocks that are clearly being controlled by supply simply because they never venture past the fundamentals of the company. What we try to accomplish is to stack as many odds as possible in our favor before we make a stock commitment. That includes fundamentals and technicals.

A good friend of mine, Jim Yates, has used the following analogy when explaining profits and probabilities. Consider a basketball game in which one player is dribbling the basketball down the court. Along the way, he receives a personal foul from an opposing team player. A personal foul simply means the player can go to the foul line and shoot two shots (free throws) at the basket, unencumbered by the opposing team. Each shot he attempts is independent of the other. Prior to his shooting, the television commentator says that this player is a 70 percent free-throw shooter. This means that he will make 7 out of 10 baskets when he attempts a free throw. Keep in mind that he has two opportunities to make a basket, each one independent of the other. What is the probability that he makes both shots? When I present this problem at seminars, most people will answer 70 percent, whereas the actual probability of making both shots is 49 percent ($.7 \times .7 = 49\%$). What this suggests is this basketball player, over time, will be less than successful at completing two free-throw shots.

You, as an investor, have the same problem. You must perform two tasks correctly, each one independent of the other. You must buy the stock right and you must sell the stock right. Have you ever bought a stock, had it go up, and—before you sold it—watched it go right back down again? If you haven't, I have. I have also had the distinct displeasure of buying a stock and having it go right down without the benefit of a rise first. In the latter case, I never even made the first basket. This whole book is designed to help you increase your odds of success. We'll outline the whole game plan as we go along.

Right now, let's deal with chart patterns and their probabilities of success. Keep this factor of probability in your mind as we discuss each pattern in depth. These chart patterns are like road maps. They are really not any different from a map you might study to find the best interstate for a vacation trip to New York from Richmond, Virginia. If you were to choose I-95 South instead of I-95 North, it would take you to Key West, Florida, first. Selecting the wrong route is a common mistake most investors make. They set out on a trip to New York from Virginia and choose I-95 South to get them there. As a broker, I did this many times simply because I didn't know any better. We emphasized the "What" question and never considered "When."

Stockbrokers typically sell a stock on the fundamentals because it is usually the only form of analysis investors understand. It's the story that catches the investors' interest and that is exactly what is sold to them. I'm in no way suggesting fundamental analysis isn't important. It is essential in answering the question *what* stock to buy; it is the first line of defense. Fundamentals is, however, provide only half the equation. Once the stock has been selected and is determined to be fundamentally sound, the next task is to determine whether it has a high probability of going up or down. This is the point where technical analysis comes in to play.

The best results in investing are achieved when fundamental and technical analysis are used together. At Dorsey, Wright & Associates, we use many filters to help us answer the *what* question. One of the best ways to find lists of fundamentally sound stocks is simply to call your broker and ask for his firm's recommended list. There are many other purveyors of this information. What is difficult to find is good technical research on the supply-and-demand relationship of the underlying stock. By the time you finish this book, you will have all the technical tools you need to be consistently successful in investing in the stock market.

Before I begin explaining the chart patterns, I want to present the results of a study done many years ago by Professor Earl Davis of Purdue University. It concerns the profitability associated with the different chart patterns, and we have found the results to be accurate. The study was first published as part of the manuscript *Profit and Probability—Technical Analysis of the Price Fluctuations of Common Stocks*. Mike Burke, the editor of Chartcraft permitted us to use the study. The following tables based on that study are from the book *How to Use the Three-Point Reversal Method of Point and Figure Stock Market Trading*, by A. W. Cohen (published by Chartcraft, Inc., Larchmont, NY) 1968.[*]

---

[*]Adapted from *Profit and Probability—Technical Analysis of the Price Fluctuations of Common Stocks by Point and Figure Method*, by Robert Earl Davis, Associate Professor of Chemistry, Purdue University, copyright 1965 by R. E. Davis.

Chartcraft Inc. is now located in New Rochelle, New York. Professor Robert Earl Davis of Purdue University is the person that actually did the study.

STATISTICAL PROBABILITIES OF CHART PATTERNS

Bull Market Results

We will discuss many chart formations—both bullish and bearish. We can look at these patterns and see which ones are the most profitable, which ones take the longest to play out, and which are the most reliable. The following are the bullish formations:

Formation	Profitable	Average Gain	Time
Double Top	80.3%	38.7%	11.5 months
Triple Top	87.9	28.7	6.8 months
Spread Triple Top	85.7	22.9	7.7 months
Bullish Triangle	71.4	30.9	5.4 months
Bullish Signal	80.4	26.5	8.6 months
Bearish Signal Reversed	92.0	23.2	2.5 months
Combinations	79.5	36.0	8.0 months

As you can readily see, there is a variation in these formations—in percentage of times profitable, in average gain, and in average time. All of these elements are important and different traders may find one item more important than another. This will be for each to determine. If you average the above patterns, you see:

1. Profitability of 83.7%.
2. Average gain of 29.5%.
3. Average time of 7.2 months.

Bear Market Results

Here are the bear market results. Remember you can make money on each side of the market if you are willing to play both sides. Again, with the proper use of Point and Figure analysis, the following results might be achieved:

Formation	% of Time Profitable	Average Gain	Average Time
Double Bottom	82.1%	22.7%	4.7 months
Triple Bottom	93.5	23.0	3.4 months
Spread Triple Bottom	86.5	24.9	4.6 months
Bearish Triangle	87.5	33.3	2.5 months
Bearish Signal	88.6	21.9	4.9 months
Combinations	83.3	22.9	3.4 months

Averaging the above shows:

1. Profitability of 86.9%.
2. Average gain of 24.8%.
3. Average time of 3.9 months.

Bull Market versus Bear Market

Comparing the results from both the bull and the bear markets by putting them side by side will allow us to draw several conclusions:

	Bull Market	Bear Market
Profitable	83.7%	86.9%
Average Gain	29.5%	24.8%
Average Time	7.2 months	3.9 months

The first conclusion to be drawn from this table is that there is less risk in selling short in a bear market than in buying in a bull market. The average gain in a bear market is 4.7 percent less than in a bull market, but this is more than compensated by the fact the average time for the gain in a bear market is 3.3 months shorter than for a bull market. Therefore traders who do not sell short in a bear market are acting contrary to their own best interests. In a lesser period of time, at smaller risk, selling short in a bear market will actually make more money than being long in a bull market. The bull market profit is at the rate of 4.09 percent per month while the bear market profit is 6.36 percent per month. Traders cannot afford to lose such a profitable opportunity. They must learn to adjust their thinking to play both sides of the market.

Losses

What about losses? The trading formations with all the ramifications of the proper conditions under which a trade should be established still do not guarantee a profit every time. The trader and investor should also consider the probability of losses and how they should be handled. The loss probabilities are as follows:

Formation	Unprofitable	Average Loss	Time
Double Top	15.3%	13.1%	4.6 months
Triple Top	12.1	8.3	2.2 months
Spread Triple Top	14.3	7.3	2.5 months
Bullish Triangle	24.6	5.4	3.0 months
Bullish Signal	16.9	10.4	4.9 months
Bearish Signal Reversed	8.0	10.0	1.5 months
Combinations	15.4	8.1	3.8 months

Averaging these shows:

1. Not profitable 15.2% of the time.
2. Average loss of 9.0%.
3. Average time of 3.0 months.

Two rules can be deduced from the preceding statistics:

1. Never let your losses go beyond 10%.
2. Give your trade about three months to work in your favor. If it does not work in that time, close the position.

These are general rules for cutting your losses short and switching to trades that might prove more profitable.

You can see from this study that the probabilities are in your favor if you wait for the right chart pattern to form before making a stock commitment. In our day-to-day operation evaluating and trading the markets, we have found that sticking to the bullish chart patterns when going long stock and the bearish chart patterns when going short usually produces superior results. The probabilities outlined in the study are pretty much on the money. While there are no guarantees in the market, you can certainly increase your probabilities of success.

Had I known about this during my broker years, I would have been able to save a lot of heartache. We always tried to recommend stocks that were fundamentally sound, but we never knew if we were on I-95 North or South. It is such a simple concept, yet most brokers and investors never get a handle on it. Once a good client of mine called to discuss possible trades in the market. I had just learned about an option strategy called "covered writing" that involves buying a stock and simultaneously selling a call option against the position. The client and I talked at length about the stock. We discussed how Burlington Industries was a great company (the leader in the textile business at the time). He liked the covered-writing concept, so we did the trade, bought the stock, and sold the call option against the position. I sold it as a conservative strategy. I was really thrilled that I was able to explain the concept of a covered write on the phone.

After the close of business, I went with my broker buddies to the Bull and Bear club as we did every evening to have a beer and discuss the day's business. I mentioned to them that I had done a covered-write trade that day and the underlying stock was Burlington Northern. One of the fellows responded "oh, the railroad." I broke out in a cold sweat. I said no, I had bought the textile company not the railroad.

As it turned out I had in fact bought the client the railroad despite talking textiles the entire time. The names Burlington Northern and Burlington Industries are close, right? Well, the names might be close but their businesses are like the North and South Poles. The trade turned out fine and I was probably better off with the railroad than with the sock company. In fact Burlington Industries didn't even have listed options at that time. Talk about stacking the odds in your favor, I shut my eyes and took a shot in the dark.

OK, let's begin with the chart patterns. Study these carefully, as they will become your most important tool.

Double Top

In the previous chapter, you learned how to maintain your charts. The most basic chart patterns are the Double Top and Double Bottom. The Double Top requires 3 columns: two columns of X's and one column of O's. The key to interpreting the chart patterns is to determine where the stock exceeds a point of resistance or support. A feature of Charles Dow's charts that caught the eye of some astute turn-of-the-century investors was the charts' accurate identification of levels of distribution and accumulation. Distribution corresponds to a top (resistance) and accumulation corresponds to a bottom (support). Resistance is the point at which a stock reaches a particular price and encounters selling pressure. Back to the supply-and-demand scenario. This is the point where supply exceeds demand. For example, IBM rises to $60 and meets selling pressure. This selling pressure exceeds the demand at that price and the stock retreats back a few points. Remember, it requires a three-box reversal to change columns. In this example, if the selling pressure was enough to force IBM back to $57 or lower, the chart would revert to O's from X's. In the tennis match analogy, supply would have won one set. The match continues. Let's say over the next few weeks demand once again creeps back into the stock at $57 and causes the price to rise to $60 per share. This is another three-box reversal back up into a column of X's, and IBM now sits at the same price level that previously found supply.

The question now is whether the sellers that forced the stock back before are still there. I have seen stocks hit resistance numerous times over many months until the selling pressure was finally exhausted. The only way to find out if the sellers are still operating at that price is to see how IBM negotiates that level. If it is again repelled, then the sellers are still there. If it instead is able to move to $61, then we can say that demand has prevailed at this price by exceeding the level where supply was previously in control. By exceeding this level of resistance the Point and Figure chart gives its most basic buy signal, the

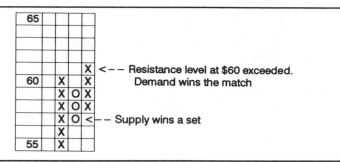

Figure 3.1   The Double Top.

Double Top. Naturally, other things must be considered before the stock is purchased but in this most simple pattern, we can say demand is in control. If you could give me no other information on IBM, my decision would be to buy the stock. By IBM exceeding that point of resistance, we can say that demand won the match. The chart pattern would look like the one shown in Figure 3.1.

Let's cover the Double Bottom. In this pattern, supply wins the match. Let's say instead of IBM exceeding the previous point of resistance, it instead reversed and exceeded the previous level of support. You can see in Figure 3.2 that the stock declined to $56, at which point demand overtook supply and the stock reversed back up into a column of X's. At $59, the stock encounters selling pressure which drives IBM back down the chart to the $56 level where demand previously took the upper hand providing support. This time, however, the buyers are not there as before, and the selling pressure persists until the stock exceeds that level of support. The match is over. Supply wins and the probability is lower prices. The reason supply overtook demand is not important. How the stock reacts to the supply and demand is all that matters, for in the end, supply and demand cause stocks to move up and down and nothing else.

You can now see why we call the pattern Double Top and Double Bottom. The stock rises or declines to the same level twice. You can

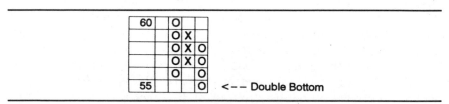

Figure 3.2   The Double Bottom.

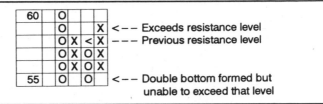

60	X		X			<-- Double top formed but unable
	X	O	X	O		to exceed that level.
	X	O	X	O		
	X	O	<	O		--- Previous level of support
	X			O		<-- Exceeded previous support level.
55	X					Double bottom sell signal.

Figure 3.3 Double Bottom with resistance.

60	O				
	O			X		<-- Exceeds resistance level
	O	X	<	X		--- Previous resistance level
	O	X	O	X		
	O	X	O	X		
55	O		O			<-- Double bottom formed but
						unable to exceed that level

Figure 3.4 Double Top with support.

probably already guess what we might call the pattern if it rose or declined to the same level three times.

In Figure 3.3, you can see that when the stock rose back to $60, it was repelled for the second time. This clue suggests to us that there is formidable resistance at that level and the sell signal is that much more important. Looking at this chart, we can tell that the upside potential is only $60. Naturally, things can and do change, but this is all we have to go with for the time being. Short sellers always want to know points of resistance because a penetration of these levels might signal a reversal in trend.

Figure 3.4 shows us that there is good support at $55 simply because that is the price where the stock stopped going down on two separate occasions. For some reason, there are buyers at that level. We consider this a level of accumulation or support. This Double Top buy signal is more important than the previous one because there is more information available with which to make a decision. The fact the stock found support twice at the $55 level suggests to us the stock will hold there in the event it experiences further weakness—just a little clue the chart in Figure 3.1 did not have.

The Bullish Signal

We add one more dimension, an added clue, to the pattern this time. Notice in Figure 3.5 how the last column of O's does not extend down as low as the previous column of O's. We call that a rising bottom. It

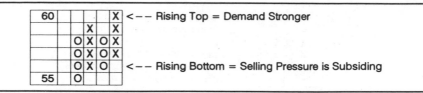

Figure 3.5   Double Top with a rising bottom.

signifies that supply is becoming less a factor in driving the stock. On the other side of the coin, demand is getting stronger as the last column of X's exceeds the previous column of X's. The rising bottom is not a major revelation but does provide added guidance when evaluating the supply-demand relationship of the underlying stock. Of the three double tops we have discussed thus far, this one is the strongest and would warrant the largest commitment.

The best way to understand these patterns is to take a legal pad and pencil and simply write down in 50 words or less exactly what you see (no different from the composition 7-year-olds sometimes have to write for homework, describing their room). What I see in Figure 3.5 is

1. A tennis match that only took four sets (columns) to complete.
2. I see two sets where McEnroe won (columns of O's) and two sets where Connors won (columns of X's).
3. The last column of X's exceeded the previous column giving a Double Top buy signal.
4. The second column of O's did not decline as low as the previous column of O's suggesting McEnroe is losing strength.
5. The last column of X's exceeds a previous column of X's suggesting Connors is gaining strength.

Breaking the pattern down to its lowest common denominator, simplifies analysis.

The Bearish Signal

The Bearish Signal is the opposite of the Bullish Signal. Figure 3.6 shows that demand in this case is becoming less strong as the last column of X's fails to reach the previous level. Selling pressure however is increasing as evidenced by the lower column of O's. These clues simply suggest demand is losing strength and supply is gaining strength. All too often, investors buy stocks in this condition only to see them erode further.

60	X				
	X	O	X		
	X	O	X	O	
	X	O	X	O	
		O		O	
55				O	

<-- Lower Tops = Buying Pressure is Subsiding

Figure 3.6   Double Bottom with a lower top.

So far, we have discussed the Double Bottom and Double Top. All other patterns we will cover are expansions of this basic form. By now, you can see how simple this method is to grasp. Let's go on to the Triple Top buy signal.

Triple Top

The Triple Top is exactly what the name suggests—a chart pattern that rises to a certain price level three times. The first two times the stock visits that level, it is repelled by sellers. The third time the stock rises to that level, it forms the Triple Top. The buy signal is given when the stock exceeds the level that previously caused the stock to reverse down. This pattern is shown in Figure 3.7.

There are many reasons why a stock will encounter supply at certain levels. Think back to a time when you bought stock thinking it was the bottom or at least an opportune price level to buy and instead of rising the stock immediately declined. We have all had one or two experiences like that. The thought that probably crossed your mind as you saw the stock lose value was to call your broker and tell him to get you out if the stock got back to even. This is a perfectly normal human reaction. When your broker places that order to get you out at your break-even point, you are in essence creating supply at that level.

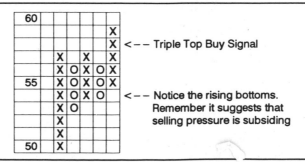

Figure 3.7   The Triple Top.

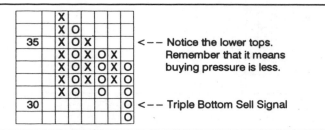

Figure 3.8   The Triple Bottom.

If more sellers are willing to sell their stock at that level than buyers are willing to buy, the stock will decline. The only way we know whether the selling pressure has been exhausted at a particular level is by the stock exceeding that price. If the stock is repelled again, the sellers are still there. I have seen stocks bounce off certain prices for as long as 18 months. In fact, Coca-Cola could not get through the $45 level for over 1½ years. Finally in September 1994, the stock was able to exceed $45 and it went right up to $50 without a breather demonstrating that the upside potential on a stock is constrained if this selling pressure remains overhead.

The more times a stock bounces off a resistance level, the stronger the breakout will be when it comes. It was said years ago that the degree to which a stock will rise is in exact proportion to the time the stock took in preparation for that move. In other words, the wider the base from which a stock breaks out the higher the stock will rise.

Triple Bottom Sell Signal

The Triple Bottom sell signal, like the Triple Top, has a high degree of reliability. When I teach seminars on this subject, I use Figure 3.8 as an example of how dangerous it can be for investors to exclude technical analysis when buying a stock. Consider an investor who buys this stock at $31 per share and then leaves on vacation for one month. He checks the financial papers frequently and notices that his stock is still around the price he paid for it, only down a point. Not bad for a market that had been volatile for the past month. He feels comfortable with the stock. The fundamentals are all in place. What is he missing in this puzzle? What he is missing is that a whole tennis match between supply and demand has been completed with supply winning the match.

The probability of lower prices is very high. The Triple Bottom does not mean that the stock will cave in immediately, it suggests that the risk in that position has increased tremendously. Whether this investor chooses to do anything about the signal or not, he should at least be aware of it. If the investor does nothing other than increase his awareness of a potential decline, he is far ahead of the investor who holds the same position without any warning. Other considerations, such as relative strength, sector bullish percent, overall market condition, and trend lines, will all be discussed in later chapters.

In analyzing the Triple Bottom pattern, keep a close watch for rising bottoms and declining tops. Think back to the Double Top formations. When the stock declined but was unable to decline as far as it previously did, it implied that selling pressure was drying up. Conversely, if the tops or columns of X's are making lower tops, it suggests that demand is drying up. These two clues make the chart more bullish or bearish respectively. This will hold true with any chart pattern.

In the 1980s, the Triple Top was particularly effective. Breakouts typically did well as all stocks had a tendency to rise during that period. Following the crash of 1987, the Triple Top has best been used on pullbacks. Expansions on the triple top are merely patterns that take longer to complete. Patterns like the Quadruple Top or Quintuple Top are rare. The more tops a pattern has the more bullish, and the faster the pattern develops, the more bullish. Some patterns in stocks like utilities take longer to form because of the inherent low volatility in that type of stocks.

Keep in mind that other factors must be taken into consideration when evaluating a chart. We'll put it all together in the chapters ahead.

The Bullish and Bearish Catapult Formation

The Catapult (Figure 3.9) is simply a combination of the Triple Top and the Double Top. This pattern is a confidence builder. The Catapult comprises a Triple Top buy signal followed by a pullback producing a rising bottom. Following the pullback, the stock resumes the trend giving a

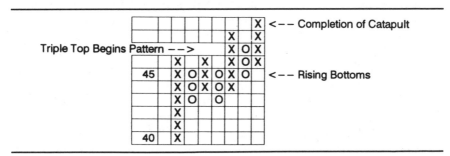

Figure 3.9   The Bullish Catapult formation.

Double Top buy signal. Take a look at the pattern in Figure 3.9. Notice the Triple Top buy signal followed by the pullback into a column of O's. Notice how the column produces a higher bottom. The resumption of trend completes the Catapult by giving a Double Top buy signal.

Let's look at the Catapult in pieces to better understand what it is saying to us. The Triple Top is saying that the stock has a very high probability of rising in price, assuming the market is in a bullish mode. In fact, this type of pattern has a success probability of 87.5 percent in bull markets. The subsequent reversal producing a higher bottom suggests that supply is beginning to dry up or become a less significant factor. The resumption of trend and subsequent Double Top buy signal simply confirms the Triple Top. I said before that the catapult is a confidence builder. This is the pattern that you should be most aggressive with when the overall markets are in a bullish mode, the underlying sector is in a bullish mode, and the fundamentals are superior in the stock.

The steps involved in stock selection resemble the steps involved in taking the previously mentioned automobile trip from Virginia to New York City. Before you begin the trip, you need to take care of a number of tasks such as gassing the car up, checking the oil, and checking the water in the radiator. Then you must select the most direct route to New York (I-95 North). Gassing the car, checking the oil, and so on are similar to checking the fundamentals of the underlying stock. Selecting the proper interstate to embark on is similar to evaluating the technical (supply and demand) picture of the underlying stock. Many investors are diligent in doing the fundamental work on a stock they want to buy but ignore evaluating the probability of it rising in price. Buying a fundamentally sound stock that has just completed a chart pattern that suggests lower prices not higher is like doing all the preparation for a trip to New York, then embarking south on Interstate 95 toward Florida. The idea is to stack as many odds in your favor before you begin the journey. There still isn't any guarantee. As much as people try to make investing a science, it remains an art.

I have taught numerous classes on this subject to grade schoolers, and it only takes 30 minutes of instruction for them to make the right selection when evaluating a bearish and bullish chart together. The beauty about teaching children is that you don't have to deprogram them. Adults have preconceived ideas about how the market is supposed to work mostly derived from watching TV programs about finance. All we are trying to ascertain with these chart patterns is whether supply or demand is in control of the underlying stock. If you go any farther than that, you've gone too far. Keep it simple. The law of supply and demand causes prices to change whether it's in the supermarket or the stock market.

Trading Tactics Using the Catapult

The Catapult is a confirmation pattern—the final double top that completes the Catapult simply confirms the previous Triple Top. It's a confirmation that demand is in control at this point in the stock's trend. The first part of the pattern is the basic Triple Top. I mentioned before that in the 1990s market buying on the pullback or reaction from breakouts offers a higher probability of success in the trade. Once a Triple Top has exceeded the previous column of X's and then pulls back, the potential for a Catapult exists. Investors might consider buying half their position on the three-box reversal from the Triple Top. This gives them a good entry point for the first portion of the position and gets them in close to their stop point. Let's talk about the stop for a second. At what point will investors have to stop out of the position if they are wrong in their assumption that the stock will rise? In this case, with the only information being the chart pattern, the only logical stop would be the Triple Bottom. At that level, the pattern would suggest that supply was in control. If the stock is selected using strong fundamentals, has strong relative strength, and is trading above the Bullish Support line, the probability of a failure in this pattern is low. Remember that in a bull market the Triple Top has an 87.5 percent success rate as suggested by the previous study. Still, investor must consider what to do when things go wrong. There needs to be a plan of action if the trade begins to go sour. Remember, this is not an exact science, it's an art.

Once half the position is bought on the three-box reversal and the mental stop is in place, investors can begin to execute the plan to buy the other half of the position on the completion of the Catapult by placing that order with their broker. Traders can then raise their stop to the new Double Bottom sell signal that is formed when the stock reverses back up to complete the Catapult. Long-term investors will keep their stop on the violation of the Bullish Support line, otherwise known as the trend line. In Figure 3.10, we would have to assume that supply had taken control if the stock violated the trend line and simultaneously gave a double bottom sell signal. The stop-loss point would come at the $42 level once the Catapult formation was complete. Just keep in mind that as long as a stock trades above the bullish support line, we consider it bullish. Long-term investors will only stop out on violations of the trend line. Traders will take every sell signal regardless of the trend line.

So far on our order entry using the Catapult, we have bought ½ the intended position on the pullback to $43 and entered a mental stop-loss point at $40. Now for the second half of our intended position. An order called a "Good until Cancel" (GTC) order can be placed with your broker. The GTC order simply allows you to select a price you are willing

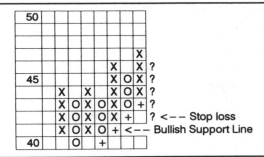

Figure 3.10

to pay for your stock, and your order remains on the specialist's books until the stock reaches that price. In this case, you would place an order with your broker to buy the remainder of your position at $47, the level where the bullish Catapult formation will be completed.

You can now see where you bought the second half of your intended position. Notice how the stop has risen now to the new Double Bottom sell signal that has formed at $42. This new stop allows us to protect profits should supply suddenly take control of the stock. It is important that long-term investors only use the trend line to stop out of a position. Traders are much shorter term in nature and may select a percentage of the entry price as their stop. A. W. Cohen, who wrote the book *How to Use The Three-Point Reversal Method of Point and Figure Stock Market Trading* always suggested that investors risk no more than 10 percent in a stock. In today's more volatile markets, a 10 percent decline can happen fast. We find it more useful to carefully select your entry point and then give the stock some room to perform.

By looking at the Catapult formation, you can see many other combinations of entry points that you can use. The key is you have an

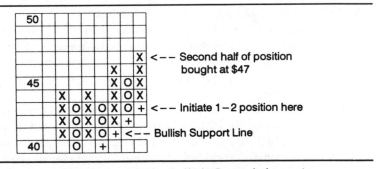

Figure 3.11 Trading with the Bullish Catapult formation.

organized and logical guide to assist you in finding entry and exit points when investing. No other charts that I am aware of can do this. The Point and Figure charts are without a doubt the best and most accurate guides an investor can use.

Bearish Catapult Formation

The bearish Catapult formation can be interpreted exactly opposite the bullish Catapult formation and is particularly useful in timing short sales. Entry and exit points would be selected the same way we did with the bullish Catapult. Stop points are particularly important in selling short. The risks in short selling are theoretically unlimited. In reality, that is not probable, but I have seen situations where stocks received buyout offers that significantly increased their price. The problem with being short in these unusual situations is that the stock stops trading and opens at a higher price without anyone being able to get out. These situations, however, are few and far between. It is very important however, to plan your entry point so you have a palatable stop price. A short seller might plan to sell half his intended position short on the first reversal back up in the chart pattern following the Triple Bottom sell signal. This will allow him to initiate the short relatively close to his stop point. Trend lines are even more important in short selling. The second half of his intended short position can be initiated when the stock reverses back down and completes the bearish Catapult formation. Let's look at Figure 3.12.

You can see that this pattern is the exact opposite from the bullish Catapult. Watch carefully for this pattern as it clearly suggests lower prices in the underlying stock. Whether you understood Point and Figure charting or not, if you looked at two fundamentally sound stocks, both in the same group, one with a bearish Catapult formation and one

50	O						
	O						
	O						
	O	X		X			
	O	X	O	X	O		
45	O	X	O	X	O	X	
	O		O		O	X	O
					O	X	O
					O		O
							O
40							

Figure 3.12   The Bearish Catapult formation.

with a bullish Catapult formation, it wouldn't take long for you to determine which stock you wanted to buy.

I would like to divert the discussion a moment from stock to options. These same patterns are used to assist the investor in using the options market. I have always looked at puts or calls as being surrogates for the underlying stock. We only use in-the-money calls or puts because the delta (the amount the option will move in relation to a 1-point move in the underlying stock) is much closer to 1 for 1. If an in-the-money long call is used as a substitute for buying the underlying stock then use the same entry and exit points as you would use if you were buying the underlying stock. The same goes for put purchases as substitutes for outright short selling. Another school of thought in options buying is to let the premium be your stop: Never buy more options than you would otherwise have an appetite for round lots of the underlying stock either long or short. In other words, if you were normally a 300-share buyer, then only buy 3 options. If you allow the premium to be your stop, then you have the staying power to hang in the position until expiration. I have seen numerous times where a stock declines substantially early in the trade only to come back strong a few months later. We could devote a whole book to this subject, but let it suffice for now that Point and Figure chart patterns can be very useful in assisting the investor with entry and exit points for options trading as well as stock trading (see Chapter 9 for additional information about options). Let's go on to one of my favorite option trading formations, the Triangle.

The Triangle Formation

The Triangle formation is a combination of patterns we have seen before. The key to understanding chart patterns is being able to sit down with a pencil and paper and write down exactly what you see. Don't look at the pattern in total and try to decipher it. Evaluate the parts making up the pattern, and you will then understand the pattern in total. In Figure 3.13, you can readily see the rising bottoms and lower tops in the pattern. To qualify as a Triangle, the pattern must have five vertical columns. The rising bottoms suggest that supply is drying up, or becoming less of a factor. You will also see the series of lower tops. The lower tops suggest that demand is becoming less of a factor in driving the stock. In our tennis analogy, the two players are getting more tired after each set, and the players have equal ability. Something will eventually have to give. One player or the other will get a second wind or begin to take the upper hand. It is at this point that we want to make a commitment in the underlying stock. There is nothing to do but wait and watch the match. If the pattern resoles itself up, it will

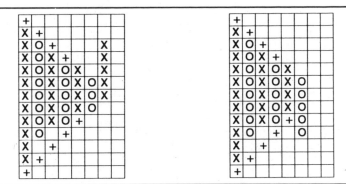

Figure 3.13   The Triangle formations.

give a double top buy signal. The Double Top buy signal simply suggests that demand has won the match and the probability is higher prices in the stock. Now look at the Bearish Triangle in Figure 3.13. Notice how the match is won by supply. The Double Bottom sell signal suggests that the probability is lower prices in the stock. These patterns are simply road maps. They are not crystal balls.

Going back to the probabilities found in A. W. Cohen's book, we find that the Bullish Triangle has an average gain of 30.9 percent. The average time for the gain is 5.4 months. This pattern lends itself to option trading very well. The potential gain is the highest of any pattern, which helps overcome the premium paid for an option. The time frame of 5.4 months is well within the expiration months available on most option series. It's just a very solid pattern. You will usually find a Triangle formation taking place as a stock is trending up or down. It suggests a period of confusion for supply and demand. The rising bottoms suggests supply drying up and the lower tops suggests demand is also becoming less significant. Keep your eye out for this pattern. One of the best ways to evaluate lots of stocks is to buy Chartcraft's monthly chart book. It has about 10,000 charts in it—all the listed stocks and many of the over-the-counter stocks. We use this book ourselves. I highly recommend Chartcraft as a source of Point and Figure charts.

The excerpt from our daily *Equity Market Report* shown in Figure 3.14 points out how potentially profitable the Triangle can be.

Variations of the Triple Top

I usually call this pattern the Diagonal Triple Top, but I hesitate to use the name because it sounds too difficult. Possibly a better name would be a Bullish Signal. I have said many times if investing gets too difficult

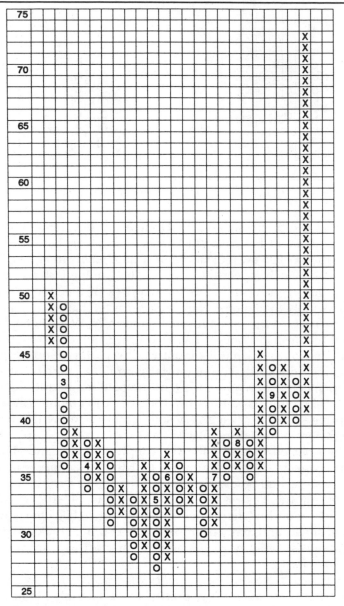

[INTU] INTUIT broke a double top at 45. This breaks the stock out of a triangle pattern; such patterns typically lead to quick, explosive moves. The main trend is up with the stock trading above the bearish resistance line. Will test chart highs at 50. Ok to buy INTU here with a stop loss of 38 which violates the uptrend line.

Figure 3.14   Intuit (INTU).

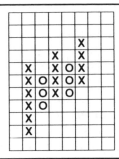

Figure 3.15   The Diagonalized Triple Top.

for a seventh grader to understand, the system is needlessly complex. It is important to keep it simple especially in technical analysis. We don't usually use this pattern as a Triple Top, but older publications classify it as one. This variation is simply two Double Top buy signals, one right after the other. This is the sign of a good strong uptrend. A stock in a strong uptrend will produce rising bottoms and rising tops, and that is exactly what this pattern demonstrates. Notice in Figure 3.15 that you simply have two consecutive Double Tops with rising bottoms.

Variations on the Triple Bottom

This pattern is simply the reverse of the above Diagonal Triple Top or Bullish Signal. We can simply call this the Bearish Signal. It has a series of lower tops followed by lower bottoms. Just looking at Figure 3.16 suggests that supply is in control. This is all you want your chart pattern to alert you to. Another way to look at it is two consecutive Double Bottom sell signals. We almost never evaluate this pattern as a Triple Bottom although A. W. Cohen clearly classifies it as such.

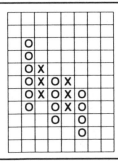

Figure 3.16   The Diagonalized Triple Bottom.

The Spread Triple Top and Bottom

This pattern is simply a Triple Top that takes a little more space on the chart to complete. You will notice the gaps between the tops in Figure 3.17. This is where the spread comes in. The normal Triple Top has no gaps between the tops. The same philosophy applies in this pattern as the Triple Top. In each case, the stock rises to a certain price level and is repelled two times. The third attempt at that price is successful by the stock moving through the level shown by a column of X's exceeding the point of resistance. Since the stock was repelled twice at that same level, there are apparently sell orders there. The reason is not important. What is important is there are sellers at that particular level. The only way to know if demand can overtake the selling pressure is to see how the stock negotiates the level again. Simply stated, if the stock is repelled again at this level of resistance, the sellers are still there. You need not know any more. If the stock exceeds that level, then demand has overcome the supply that previously caused it to reverse. This is why we always wait for a particular level to be exceeded before we make a long or short commitment in the stock. In the 1980s, we typically just bought or sold the breakouts. In the 1990s, we have found out that it is best to buy on the pullbacks. For most of the 1980s, stocks went up. So far in the 1990s, we have seen a more normal market in which stocks go up and down. It's been a stock picker's environment and likely to remain so for the foreseeable future. Figure 3.17 shows what the pattern looks like for both the Spread Triple Top and the Spread Triple Bottom.

Notice that in these two patterns, the stocks are trading at the same price. Consider that both stocks are fundamentally sound and each is being recommended by a major firm on Wall Street. Both stocks

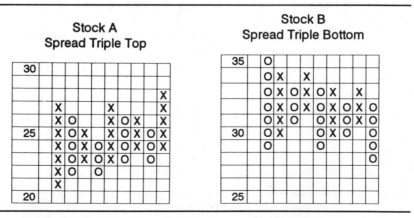

Figure 3.17 The Spread Triple Top and Bottom formation.

are in the same industry group and pay about the same dividend. You have studied the fundamentals of the two stocks and are now trying to determine which stock to buy. It's the moment of truth. Which stock do you select? Without the chart patterns shown here, you would be in a quandary. Looking at the fundamental data alone, both stocks are equal, therefore both stocks should do about as well in the future. Not so. If you had the benefit of evaluating the Point and Figure charts in Figure 3.17, the selection process would become much easier. With the information I have just given you, which stock do you select? It doesn't take an in-depth understanding of this method to determine stock A is in an uptrend with the probability of higher prices and stock B is in a downtrend with lower prices likely. I have shown this same example to seventh graders I have taught, and in almost every case, they have picked stock A over B for purchase.

This simple exercise shows why charts are so important and why you can achieve the best results in the market when you use both fundamental and technical analysis. The fundamental work answers the question *what,* and the technical side of the equation answers the question *when.* Both are equally important. The first question, *what,* is easily answered because fundamental research is everywhere on Wall Street. There are some great firms on Wall Street that specialize in providing all the fundamental research you could want for a nominal fee. Value Line is one of the best known. Anyone doing business with a broker of a major firm on Wall Street has access to all the fundamental ideas that the firm produces along with its related research. Good technical analysis is much harder to come by, but once you have finished this book, you will be perfectly capable of performing that task yourself.

One thing I would like to add to this discussion is that 75 percent of the risk in any particular stock is the market and sector. The problem most investors have is that they concentrate 75 percent of their effort on evaluating the fundamentals. It is extremely important to buy stocks when you are in possession of the ball (the market is in a bullish mode). We will cover the market indicators in later chapters. Once again, stack as many odds in your favor as possible before you make a commitment in the stock market. I don't know how many times acquaintances have come up to me and asked what I think about a stock tip they just got from a friend. They usually say it's a very reliable source. My answer is always the same, and I will repeat it for you: If it's inside information, you won't have it. The second you have it, it's outside information and those who are really in the know have already acted on it. In almost every case, you can look back on the Point and Figure chart and see clearly where the insiders were operating. Once you get the handle on this method, which has remained true to form for over 100 years, you will see why the Point and Figure chart is as good as inside information. The Triangle pattern (see Figure 3.13) is an excellent example of the method's effectiveness. You must follow a sequence of events before you make a stock commitment. Step 1 is to evaluate the overall market, step 2 is to evaluate the sector you are investing in, and finally step 3 encompasses stock selection.

Bullish Shakeout Formation

This is one of my favorite patterns. We keep a strong eye out for these patterns because they have a high degree of reliability. The Shakeout was not one of the patterns studied at Purdue University, but we have found it very useful in real-life application. Mike Burke, the editor of Chartcraft brought it to our attention a few years ago, and we've been profitably using it since. Whenever we come across one of these patterns we try to feature it in our daily *Equity Market Report*. It is called the Shakeout because the pattern easily deceives investors when the sell signal is given.

There is a big difference between the chartist and the technician: Many chartists operate on chart patterns alone without any other input whereas technicians will use a number of other indicators to assist them in evaluating stocks. Don't get too hung up on the patterns themselves; there are other considerations when making a stock selection. The chart patterns should be used to determine whether supply or demand is in control of the underlying investment vehicle. Because so much risk is associated with the market and sector, it is imperative to thoroughly evaluate both factors before considering the underlying stock. If you are buying stocks in a down market, you will surely lose money. If you are selling stocks short in an up market, you will surely lose money. This is why we have devoted so much time in this book to understanding broad market indicators and sectors.

The Shakeout pattern should only be used in a bull market. We have not had much success, as one would imagine, using this pattern in a bear market. For the pattern to be a true Shakeout formation, it must have the following six attributes:

1. The stock must be in a strong uptrend.
2. The stock should be trading above the Bullish Support line.
3. The stock must rise to a level where it forms two tops at the same price.
4. The subsequent reversal of the stock from these two tops must give a Double Bottom sell signal.
5. This sell signal must be the first in this uptrend.
6. The relative strength chart must be on a buy signal.

Sounds like a lot doesn't it? It's not really. In our day-to-day operations, we fudge these parameters a little but in general the Shakeout has these characteristics. You can adjust many of these patterns to suit your style of investing. Remember, the whole idea in using chart patterns is to determine whether supply or demand is in control. Don't forget that, and don't read too much into it because you will usually overthink the position, which in turn results in losses. The best machine is the one with the fewest moving parts.

We usually use the pattern shown in Figure 3.18 for trading purposes. The reason for that is that to qualify for a Shakeout, the stock must already be in a strong uptrend. Other patterns would have gotten investors in earlier. The Shakeout begins by giving the Double Bottom sell signal. We never know what level the sell signal will carry the stock down to so our action point for entry into this stock is on the first three-box reversal back up the chart (see Figure 3.19). This is the only point where we know demand is back in control. Once the stock reverses back up into a column of X's, the position can be taken. The next consideration is, what to do if things go wrong? Where is the stop-loss point? We always use the Double Bottom that is formed when the stock reverses back up as our exit point. Normally this is 4 points' risk. We

19						
		X		X		<-- Double Top at the same price
18		X	O	X	O	
		X	O	X	O	
17		X	O		O	
		X			O	<-- Shakeout begins
16		X			O	
		X				
15		X				

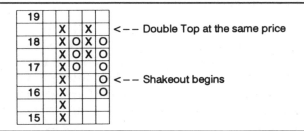

Figure 3.18 The Shakeout formation.

19							
		X		X			
18		X	O	X	O		
		X	O	X	O	X	<-- Action point to buy
17		X	O		O	X	
		X			O	X	
16		X			O		
		X					
15		X					

Figure 3.19 Action point on the shakeout.

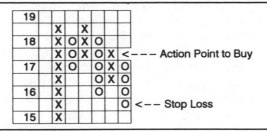

Figure 3.20   Stop loss on the shakeout.

have many clients that don't wait for the reversal. They initiate the trade when the Shakeout begins. That's fine, as long as they understand they are jumping the gun. The reliability of this pattern, and any other bullish pattern, diminishes when the overall market is in a bearish mode. Look at Figure 3.20 to see how entry and exit points are established. If the trade was established at the action point, and the stock immediately reversed, the stop point would be the first sell signal the stock gives. The stop is at $15½.

Remember, this is primarily a trading pattern. In-the-money calls might be used as a stock substitute.

Reverse Shakeout Formations

This is a pattern that I named simply because it is the exact reverse of the bullish Shakeout. My assumption was that since the Shakeout formation worked so well for bullish trades, why not evaluate the opposite side of the coin? It turned out that this pattern has merit and thus should be mentioned in this book. The pattern is constructed in the same way only in reverse (see Figure 3.21). A stock should have the following characteristics.

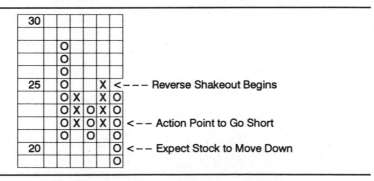

Figure 3.21   The reverse shakeout formation.

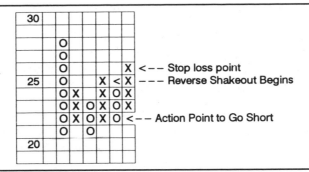

Figure 3.22   Stop loss on the reverse shakeout.

1. The stock should have negative relative strength.
2. The stock should be trading below the Bearish Resistance line.
3. The stock should be in a strong downtrend.
4. The chart pattern should have formed two bottoms at the same level.
5. The buy signal the stock gives should be the first in the downtrend.

This is a trading pattern and as such should work well with puts as short sale substitutes. The requirements to qualify for this pattern should be used for any stock you consider selling short.

Let's talk for a moment about the stop—what do we do if things go wrong. The stop on the short sale would initially be the Double Top buy signal formed when the stock reversed down initiating the action point. If things go wrong, you will need a logical point to stop the loss. The Double Top buy signal will simply suggest that demand is back in control of the stock.

The Long Tail Down

This is one of Chartcraft's favorite bottom-fishing patterns. To qualify for a Long Tail Down, the stock must have declined 20 or more boxes without a reversal. After such a decline, the first reversal up usually provides a good trading opportunity. We have used these patterns very successfully recommending these plays in our daily *Equity Market Report*. I remember a time we thought the pattern was infallible. It had worked for a string of trades, so we decided to pound the table on the next one we came across. It seems that Murphy is always hanging around when you alert the world to a particularly lucrative situation (You know Murphy's Law: If anything can go wrong it will). One day we came across a Long Tail Down in Apple Computer. Apple is a great trading stock as the volatility is high and it seems everyone has played it at sometime or another. Apple had just gone through one of these 20-box down patterns. We knew we had a winner. This time we pounded the table with the recommendation to buy on the first three-box reversal back up the chart. I mean we pounded the table. When the reversal came, I think most of our customers took the trade and many of our customers are large institutions. You guessed it, the stock struggled up a point or so and then caved in. The first one in many moons that didn't work. It always seems to work out like that. The one you get everyone in fakes you out. On balance, this is a good trading pattern. The idea is simple. When a stock has declined 20 boxes or more, you take the first three-box reversal back up the chart as your action point. The stop-loss point is the Double Bottom sell signal that is set up when the stock reverses up into a column of X's. The longer it takes for the stock to decline 20 boxes the less reliable the pattern is. This is for trading purposes only and not for investors. A stock that has declined 20 boxes or more usually has something wrong with the fundamentals. One of the better ways to play the trade is through the call market. This will give you staying power to expiration, and you need not worry about your stop point being hit. If the stock rises from your entry point, you can raise your stop to each subsequent sell signal that forms. This will allow you to get the full ride if no sell signals are given. It also prevents

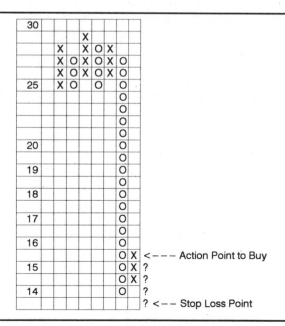

Figure 3.23   The Long Tail Down.

you from taking a profit too quickly. Always allow your profits to run as much as possible and take as much subjectivity out of the equation as possible. Figure 3.23 shows the Long Tail Down pattern.

The same philosophy can be applied to a long run of X's up but with a much smaller degree of success. As a stock rises, the fundamentals are coming to fruition and there are no dissatisfied investors. For this reason, we just don't see enough selling pressure to warrant a trading commitment in a stock that rises 20 boxes without a reversal. Pullbacks in strong stocks like these appear as opportunities to buy not to sell and can easily generate demand. Remember, there are no dissatisfied investors at tops. Still the very nimble can take advantage of it. I usually don't. I am much more apt to attempt a trade on a 20-box down move.

The High Pole Warning Formation

This pattern was pioneered by the late Earl Blumenthal. Mike Burke, the editor of Chartcraft, has done a lot of work with this pattern as well. The few times that we have actually taken action on this pattern, however, we have always used it as a warning. This pattern is most reliable in bear-configured markets. To qualify for a High Pole, the Point and Figure chart must have exceeded a previous column of X's by at least 3 boxes. Following the rise in X's, the stock must pull back at least 50 percent of that last up-thrust on the chart. The thought behind the formation is that there must be something wrong with the supply-demand relationship if the stock subsequently gave up 50 percent of the last move up. It's a warning that supply might be taking control of the stock. I will usually give the stock some room and place more emphasis on the trend line as my guide for a potential stop. The High Pole does, however, increase my awareness of a potential change in the supply-demand relationship of the underlying stock. Figure 3.24 is an example of a High Pole Warning formation.

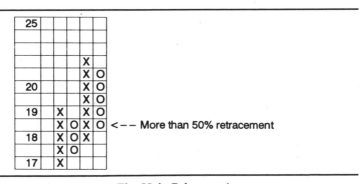

Figure 3.24 The Hole Pole warning.

The Low Pole Formation

The Low Pole formation was pioneered by Mike Burke of Chartcraft. I find this pattern more useful than the High Pole simply because investors are more apt to make a commitment in a stock that appears to be a bargain than to sell a stock that has done well for them. The Low Pole simply means the selling pressure that had been driving the stock down is probably over to a great degree. This does not mean that you jump on the stock with unbridled enthusiasm. The company probably still has problems. Remember, you want to buy stocks that are fundamentally sound. That is your first line of defense. Traders, on the other hand, can attempt to make money on a bottom-fishing expedition. The trader's best play is to wait for a pullback following the Low Pole and enter the stock there (see Figure 3.25). Buying on the pullback will establish the entry point closer to the stop level. It also sets up the potential for a nice Double Top buy signal on the next reversal back up the chart. It is usually best to allow the stock to come to you if possible.

The Broadening Top Formation

The Broadening Top formation is simply a variation on the Shakeout formation. The primary difference between the two is that the Broadening Top gives a buy signal prior to the sell signal being given. Let's look back for a moment. If you don't have the Shakeout firmly in mind go back and look at the pattern (Exhibits 3.18–3.20). You will see that the underlying stock has risen up to a certain level two times but was unable to exceed that level the second time. The stock in essence formed a Double Top. Subsequently, it reversed and gave that first sell signal in the uptrend. In the case of the Broadening Top formation, the stock exceeds that previous top the stock made. In other words, it gives a Double Top buy signal. The subsequent reversal gives the sell signal.

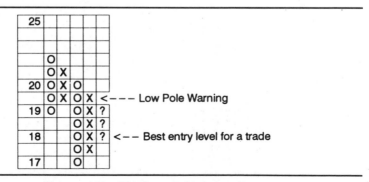

Figure 3.25   The Low Pole warning.

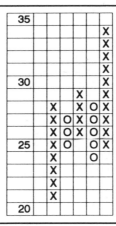

Figure 3.26   The Broadening Top formation.

The combination of the higher top and lower bottom has the appearance of broadening the pattern. To complete the pattern, the stock then reverses back up the chart to give another Double Top buy signal (see Figure 3.26). If you look at those two consecutive Double Tops you will see the same pattern as the Diagonal Triple Top described in the section Variations on the Triple Top, the only difference is the sell signal in the pattern. I always think in terms of economics when I evaluate a Point and Figure chart. What is it telling me in economic terms? The forces that cause price changes in anything are supply and demand. Since these patterns are nothing more than a logical, organized method of recording supply and demand, the answer must lie in basic economic principles.

The Broadening Top formation usually takes place after a stock has run up nicely. What the formation is basically saying is that supply and demand had equal power at the point the pattern was broadening out. The Double Top buy signal was suggesting that demand was still in control. The Double Bottom was suggesting that supply had taken the helm and the uptrend was in question. The subsequent buy signal clearly showed that demand was still in control and that the stock had found enough sponsorship to move higher.

The Bearish Signal Reversed

We almost always play this pattern. It is seldom seen, but when it is, you should pay close attention. Investors can detect the pattern while it forms, which allows them to plan their trade. Oftentimes, we will show the pattern and discuss the underlying stock in our report days before the pattern is complete. In this great chess game, it helps tremendously to be able to plan your moves. The pattern must have seven columns in it to qualify. Each column of X's must be lower than the one before and each column of O's must carry lower than the one prior to it. In the tennis match analogy, the player symbolized by X is clearly underperforming the player symbolized by O. You can easily see this. Remember keep it simple. Look at the pattern in the context of a tennis match where each column in the pattern represents a set within the match. You can see that when a column of O's takes control of a set it carries lower than the previous column. Action like this demonstrates supply is getting stronger. When the column of X's takes control, it is unable to carry up as high as it previously did. By evaluating a pattern in this context, you can easily see supply is stronger than demand and the probability is lower prices. Now for the reversal. The reversal up into a column of X's with the subsequent Double Top buy signal clearly shows a change in this supply-demand relationship. Something has happened to cause demand to not only win a set by reversing up but to win the match by exceeding a previous top and thus giving a buy signal. What makes this buy signal more important is that it exceeds a series of lower tops. In essence it breaks the spell. Figure 3.27 shows this pattern.

The reversal is often caused by some sort of news that is not widely disseminated or understood by Wall Street. Insiders are usually operating at this point. Ask yourself a question. Why would such a negative pattern clearly being controlled by supply change abruptly midstream? Is it possible that an upcoming earnings report is likely to be better than Wall Street expects? Usually there is some fundamental change in the stock that is not widely known. The Bull Market Results table shown early in this chapter indicates that this pattern has the highest probability of success.

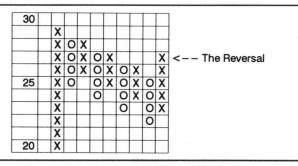

Figure 3.27   The Bearish Signal Reversed.

The Bullish Signal Reversed

This pattern, which is the reverse of the Bearish Signal Reversed, was not included in the Purdue University study on probabilities. This pattern shows seven columns of rising bottoms and rising tops—the exact opposite the Bearish cousin (see Figure 3.28). When the last top is made in the seventh column, the stock reverses and without a period of distribution declines to give a Double Bottom sell signal as well as break the series of rising bottoms. We have seen this happen in drug companies where FDA approval of a particular drug was not forthcoming. Someone usually knows of this before Wall Street does. There are many other reasons for the quick reversal, but it usually is brought on by insiders. When I say insiders, I don't necessarily mean the management of the company, simply any investor who has information that is not widely known on Wall Street. I can truly say that I have never made money on so-called inside information. When anyone calls you with a tip, the whole street usually knows it. Whenever someone gives you a tip, ask yourself what the person has to gain from telling you. In the final analysis, you will find that frequently the reason for clueing you in was that the tipster had stock to sell.

In *Barron's* recently I saw an interview with a well-known money manager. The interviewer asked him for some of his best picks, and he generously named some stocks that he thought were great values at current prices. I looked in the back of the paper for the list of stocks that the mutual funds are buying and selling and, lo and behold, his fund was selling a stock he had named—from the front page to the back page, a 180-degree turnaround. If this analyst was buying the stock, why would he publish it? So investors could compete with him in the market and possibly drive the price up? Not likely. What is likely is that he had bought the stock earlier at much better prices. Be wary of tips, especially at cocktail parties. I could go on for chapters on this subject.

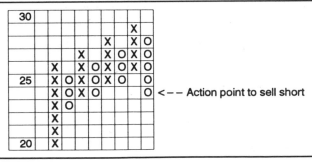

Figure 3.28 The Bullish Signal Reversed.

Before we leave the Bullish Signal Reversed let's look at Figure 3.28 and discuss the pattern using the tennis match analogy. The rising tops clearly shows that demand is in control of the match. Each time the X wins a set (rises in a column), it does it more convincingly by exceeding the level it previously hit. Each time the O wins a set (declines in a column), it does so less convincingly as it is unable to decline as low as it previously did. Then, without the stock moving back and forth at the top (distribution), it declines in a straight column to give the sell signal and break the series of rising bottoms. In terms of economics, supply has taken control of the stock at $24. This is the point where you should enter your short position. The stop is a little more difficult. In Figure 3.28, your stop point would be the Double Top buy signal at $30 which would be $6 risk. Since this pattern usually carries the stock down quickly, a stop point of the first three-box reversal back up the chart would be sufficient for a good trade. For example, if the stock reverses and moves up to $27 from your entry point of $24, you should probably consider stopping the position out simply because the pattern is not performing as expected. We could go through all kinds of examples of stops, but in the real world of investing it just isn't cut and dried. Many factors come into the equation, not the least of which is the investor's temperament. In most cases, long-term investors will only use the trend lines as stops. Traders have different problems. Watch for this pattern. It won't show up often but when it does, take action.

The Bullish Triangle Formation

The Triangle formations are simply variations of the Bullish and Bearish Signal formations. We frequently use this pattern to signal option buying opportunities. This pattern shown in Figure 3.29 indicates that supply and demand have gone into a period of equilibrium, each having equal weight at that point in time. This can be seen by the declining

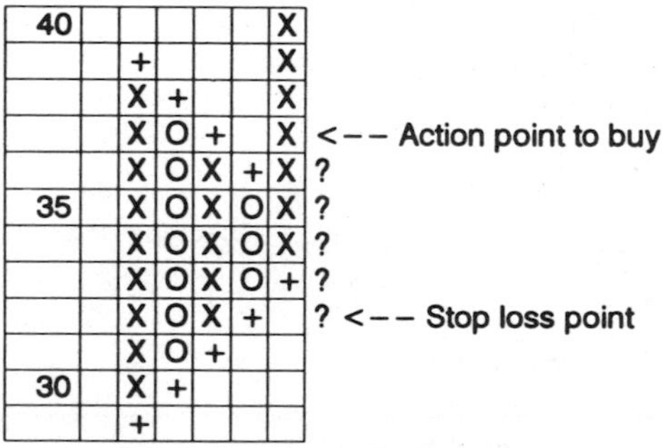

40					X	
		+			X	
	X	+			X	
	X	O	+		X	< – – Action point to buy
	X	O	X	+	X	?
35	X	O	X	O	X	?
	X	O	X	O	X	?
	X	O	X	O	+	?
	X	O	X	+		? < – – Stop loss point
	X	O	+			
30	X	+				
	+					

Figure 3.29   The Bullish Triangle formation.

tops and the rising bottoms. In fact, both are losing strength at about the same rate. As the tops decline, demand is becoming less strong. On the other hand, as the bottoms rise supply is becoming less of a factor. Something has to give. The pattern declines to a point where the trend line developed by the lower tops meets the trend line that is formed by the rising bottoms. The stock will then go one way or the other. When a stock has been in an uptrend and then forms this triangle it is said to be bullish. The probability is that the stock will regain sponsorship and break out of that triangle on the upside. The pattern should have five vertical columns to qualify. We often see triangles with many more columns. The action point to buy is when the Double Top buy signal is given. What makes this different from the basic Double Top is the stock is also breaking a series of lower tops. This clearly shows that demand is back in control and higher prices can be expected. The triangle is not always broken on the upside however, which is why it is important to wait for the signal. This pattern reminds me of two boxers slowing down in the seventh round, each one hanging on the other in an attempt to regain strength. In the eighth round, one fighter comes out and has clearly found his second wind. The next three rounds go to him. This is a good pattern for options because the breakout leaves a good close stop if the stock fails. The Bull Market Results table suggests that the probability of success is 71.4 percent for an average gain of 30.9 percent and should take 5.4 months.

The Bearish Triangle Formation

The same parameters apply to the Bearish Triangle as to the Bullish Triangle. This one has a higher probability of success and happens faster. Referring to the Bear Market Results table, the Bearish Triangle is profitable 87 percent of the time for an average gain of 33.3 percent and the average time for the pattern to work out is 2.5 months. It seems

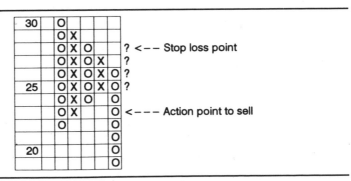

Figure 3.30 The Bearish Triangle formation.

that on bearish patterns, gravity takes hold. This pattern is very well suited to put option trades because of the speed with which the pattern typically works. The same triangle is formed but in this case the stock breaks out on the downside by giving a sell signal at the $23 level (see Figure 3.30).

Mike Burke's Bull and Bear Traps

Mike Burke developed these patterns. I have often referred to Mike as the Sherlock Holmes of investing. He is constantly searching for new clues to help further develop the art of technical analysis. He is a true pioneer in this business. Mike had a tremendous opportunity to learn under the great A. W. Cohen, the first editor of Chartcraft. Mike is the current editor of the service. He also puts out a great newsletter called *Investors Intelligence*. After reading this book, you will want to subscribe to that publication as many of the indicators discussed here can be found in that letter.

The Bear Trap is a pattern that often suggests a stock's bottom. When a stock has had a long decline and is trading at a level where it has found a bottom in the past, we watch for the Bear Trap. It is characterized by a stock giving a Triple Bottom sell signal that only penetrates the bottom by one box (see Figure 3.31). The stock then promptly reverses up into a column of X's. What this pattern suggests is the last hangers-on in the stock have finally given up. It is usually associated with some news article about the stock. Possibly the company cuts its dividend or a magazine has a negative feature article. The last investors have ridden the stock down finally giving up. They have thrown the towel in at the last minute: "*XYZ Magazine* must be right, it's all over for the Auto's." At this point, there is no more supply left in the stock. No one left to sell. The supply-demand relationship of the stock changes. The pendulum switches to the demand side. At this point, all it takes is a few buyers and the stock rallies up, leaving Mr. Jones, the investor, bewildered once again.

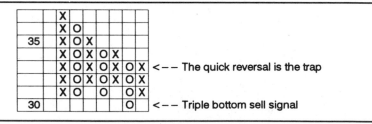

Figure 3.31   The Bear Trap.

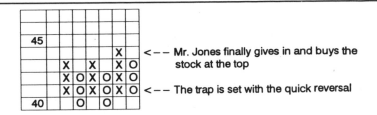

Figure 3.32   The Bull Trap.

The Bull Trap is the exact opposite (see Figure 3.32). The news that drives the last person in is some favorable article or news release that causes Mr. Jones to jump aboard. The stock gives a Triple Top buy signal and promptly reverses. Again the supply-demand relationship changes. There are no buyers left, everyone who wants to get in is in. All it takes at this point is a few sellers and the stock caves in. The Bull Trap is most effective at levels where the stock has topped out in the past.

4

CONSTRUCTING AND MANAGING THE TRADE

The easiest thing to do in the stock market is buy stocks. Anyone can do it. What most investors lack is the game plan, what to do when things go right and what to do when things go wrong. This chapter will deal with finding a good entry point, determining the price objectives, and using stops. I also want to discuss when to take a profit. Taking profits is often the hardest thing an investor can do. This is why so many investors ride stocks up and ride them right back down again.

Let's begin with constructing the trade. My assumption in this chapter is that we have already evaluated the market, sector, and fundamentals and are now down to finding an entry point for the security selected for purchase. Let's look back to the 1980s for a moment. Back then, we simply bought the breakouts without paying much attention to the risk/reward ratio. Most stocks just rose during that period. It was an easy time for investors, an easy time to become complacent. During the 1980s, we primarily operated with the offensive team on the field. The 1990s have been quite a different game. The defensive team has seen a substantial amount of action thus far.

Buying stocks on pullbacks can offer substantial advantages over just buying at the prevailing market price. One of the uncertainties an investor must consider when buying a stock is the risk/reward ratio in the position: How great is the risk versus how high is the stock likely to rise? I recommend that you seek a risk/reward ratio of at least 2 to 1—be sure you have the potential to make $2 for each $1 you risk. Two calculations are necessary before you buy a stock. The first calculation you must perform is a count, whether it be a horizontal count or vertical count, to determine how high the stock is expected to go. We covered these calculations in Chapter 3. The second calculation is the determination of your stop-loss point if things go wrong. In general, traders will take the first sell signal the chart produces, and investors will stop on a trend-line break. If your risk/reward is greater than 2 to 1, you can continue.

One way to increase the risk/reward is to buy a stock on pullback. This does two things: It increases the potential percentage gain in the stock and it moves the stock closer to the stop point. Figure 4.1 illustrates this principle. It depicts a stock that has made a bottom at $30 and subsequently risen to give a buy signal at $35. On first observation, buying the stock on the breakout at $35 might seem like the most logical thing to do, but on closer inspection we see that there are $6 (points) at risk to the trible bottom sell signal stop loss point at $29. Our upside potential is calculated using a vertical count to ascertain the number of boxes in the column of the first move off the bottom that produces the breakout. In this case, there are five boxes in that column. Multiply 5 by 3 (we are working on a three-box reversal method), then multiply that figure by 1 (the box size). The math is as follows: ($5 \times 3 = 15 \times 1 = 15$). Now add the 15 to the bottom X in that column. That would come out to be $15 + 31 = 46$. If we bought the stock on the breakout at $35, the potential gain would be $11 ($46 - 35 = 11$). With a risk of 6 and a potential gain of 11 the risk/reward relationship is less than 2 to 1.

If you still wanted to buy the stock for whatever reason, you would have to change this ratio. One way to do that is to buy the stock on a pullback. You might miss the trade because nothing guarantees the stock will pull back but that's OK. There is always another train coming through the station. What you would do is enter a Good Til Cancel order to buy at $32 if the stock pulls back to that price. It is important to place the order and wait. Say you bought the stock on a three-box reversal at $32 from the breakout at $35. Now your potential gain would be 14 points and your stop-loss would be 3 points. The ratio has changed to better than 4 to 1. Four points possible gain for a single point of risk, very good odds. By having patience and entering an order to buy on the first three-box reversal, you would have set up a trade

35					X		<-- Buying on the Breakout yields a price objective of 46
			X		X	O	
		O	X	O	X	O	
		O	X	O	X	O	<-- Waiting for a pullback yields a reward of 14 points and a risk of just 3 points
		O	X	O	X	?	
30		O		O		?	
						?	<-- Stop loss at 29

Figure 4.1 Buying on Pullbacks.

with good potential profit. Remember there are 10,000 stocks that trade. Let the stock come to you, there is no rush.

THE BULLISH CATAPULT FORMATION

The Bullish Catapult formation shown in Figure 4.2 illustrates how an investor might average in a position by averaging down or by averaging up.

1. This signal is a Triple Top buy signal. Investors might choose to purchase their whole position at the breakout. They might also consider buying half their position at the Triple Top buy signal and averaging in the other half on the first three-box reversal at (2).

2. Notice the three-box reversal following the Triple Top buy signal. Investors who purchased half their position on the breakout at (1) might fill their order by buying the other half on the reversal. Other investors might consider initiating their purchase only on the pullback. I prefer this method. By doing this, investors move closer to their stop-loss point and increase their potential gain. In the case of averaging up, investors might consider buying the first half of their position on the pullback at (2) and adding the other half on the first three-box reversal back up the chart at level (3), when they are sure demand is back in control.

3. Some investors might not consider buying the stock at all until the catapult is actually completed at level (4).

There are many ways to enter a trade; you don't have to go into it blindly. The Point and Figure method gives you a clear road map to guide your decisions. Don't forget that before you even get to this point you must evaluate the market, sector, fundamentals, and relative strength. Finding a good entry point can make the difference between a successful or unsuccessful trade. I prefer to buy stocks on pullbacks

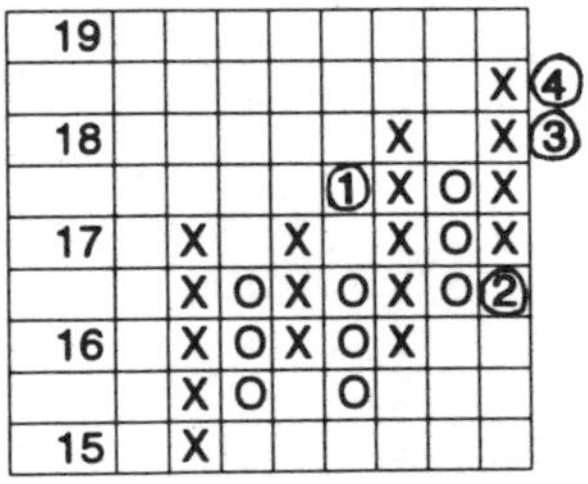

Figure 4.2   The Bullish Catapult formation.

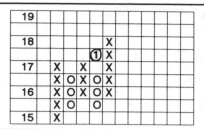

Figure 4.3   The Triple Top.

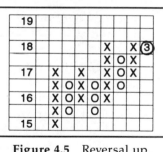

Figure 4.4   Pullback.

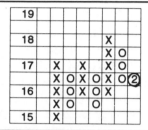

Figure 4.5   Reversal up.

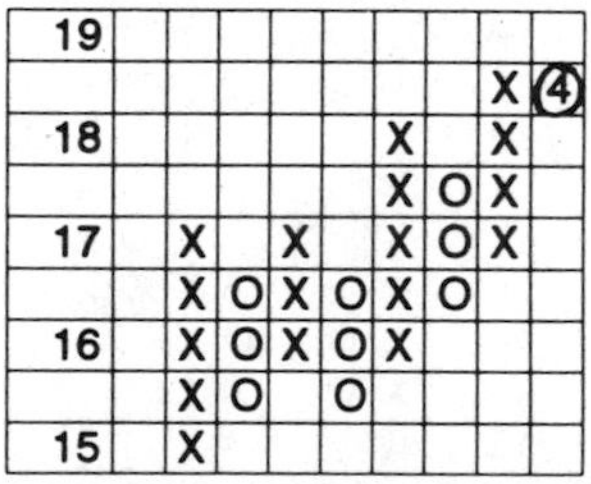

Figure 4.6   Catapult completed.

to support as I've mentioned. If you will just have patience, most stocks will come to you. You will miss some trades, but on balance you will be able to call the shots. Be sure you act rather than react. Use Good-Til-Cancel orders as they take the emotion out of the buy decision. Figures 4.2 through 4.6 are snapshots of the different levels of a Bullish Catapult an investor might choose to begin averaging in his position.

THE BEARISH CATAPULT FORMATION

Investors should construct a short sale a little differently than they would a long trade as previously illustrated. It is always best to sell short as near your stop point as possible. I have found that it is best to enter a short sale on a reversal back up the chart as close to the Bearish Resistance line as you can get. For short sales, the underlying stock should be trading below the Bearish Resistance line. The stock should have negative relative strength and preferably have turned negative within the past year. The entry point should be on a reversal back up the chart. At least the initial or partial position should be initiated on the reversal back up the chart. Your stop loss point will be a penetration of the trend line. Your stop should be lowered on each subsequent sell signal the stock makes. The first half of the short sale is put on at $17\frac{1}{2}$ when the stock reverses up to the trend line. In the event the stock continues to rise, a stop of $19 is placed. The second half of the position is put on when the stock reverses down to $16. The stop can then be lowered to $18 now. The new level a double top buy signal is formed.

MANAGING YOUR STOP IN A SHORT SALE

When you initiate a short sale, you must make the usual risk/reward calculation. In the vertical count for short sales, we count the column of

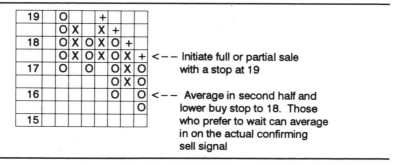

Figure 4.7   The Bearish Catapult.

O's on the first move off the top when that column has ended. You know the first column of O's has been completed when the chart reverses back up into a column of X's. In Figure 4.8, (1) shows the first move off the top, which culminates in a Double Bottom sell signal. This is the point at which the trend changes from up to down. A vertical count would be calculated by counting the number of boxes in that column, multiplying that number by 2, then multiplying again by the box size (6 × 2 = 12 × 1 = 12). Now subtract 12 from the price level of the first O in that column (29 − 12 = 17). Our initial count suggests the stock has a price objective of $17. Now it's time to calculate the potential risk by counting the boxes up to the first buy signal the stock will give. In Figure 4.8, the first buy signal will come at $31. Don't get lost now. Think about this for a second. If you sold short on the sell signal created at $24 (see (1)), your risk to the stop point of $31 is 7 points. Your potential gain as suggested by the vertical count $24 minus the price objective of $17 is 7 points. Your risk reward is less than 2 to 1. The short sale is not a go.

Now, let's calculate the risk reward if you initiate the short sale on a reversal back up to the trend line (2). You would enter a sell stop order at $28, at level (2). A sell stop order simply instructs the specialist in the stock to awaken your order and sell at $28 and execute at the market on the next uptick. In the case of a short sale, you must sell on an uptick. Let's say these requirements are fulfilled and you get your short off at $28. Your risk to the stop point of $31 is 3 points. Your potential gain now is the $28 entry point minus the vertical count objective of $17 or 11 points. Your risk reward is now greater than 3 to 1. This short is now a good play.

Notice the levels (3), (4), and (5) shown on Figure 4.8. These are points where the chart is producing subsequent Double Bottom sell signals. Each time another sell signal is given in the stock, you can

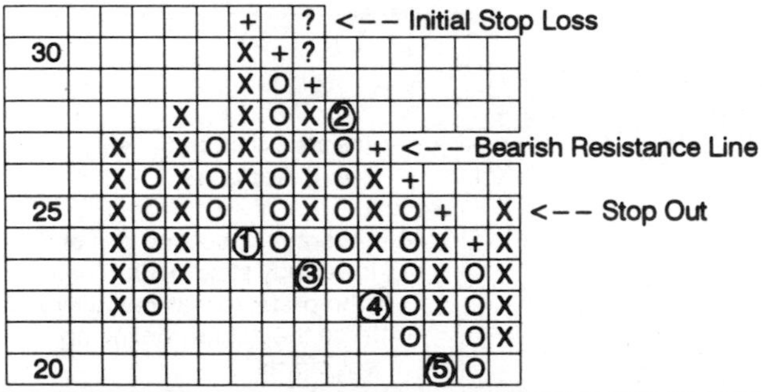

```
                      + |  ? | <-- Initial Stop Loss
 30               X  + |  ?
                  X  O |  +
            X     X  O |  X ②
      X     X  O  X  O |  X  O  +    <-- Bearish Resistance Line
      X  O  X  O  X  O |  X  O  X  +
 25   X  O  X  O        O  X  O  X  O  +     X   <-- Stop Out
      X  O  X   ① O     O  X  O  X  +  X
      X  O  X        ③ O     O  X  O  X
      X  O            ④   O  X  O  X
                         O     O  X
 20                   ⑤ O
```

Figure 4.8   Managing your stop in a short sale.

lower your stop to the next buy signal that the chart will give. Notice the level "Stop Out." Finally the stock reversed up giving a Double Top buy signal as well as penetrating the Bearish Resistance line. The short sale is over and the profit was $28 entry level and $25 stop point = 3 points gain. No great trade but profitable nonetheless. Had you taken the short on the sell signal at $24, since it was on an uptick, you would have lost 1 point on the trade.

It is important for a short sale to work out as soon as possible because the short sale is done in a margin account and the investor will be liable for any dividends paid by the underlying stock. Remember the short seller is only borrowing the stock from some other investor and has no rights to the dividend.

This short sale assumes the overall market condition is in one of the three bearish modes, the sector is above 50 percent and in one of the bearish modes, the relative strength chart is negative, and the stock is trading below the Bearish Resistance line. It also helps if the stock has negative fundamentals. *Value Line* has a very good ranking system to help you determine which stocks have negative fundamentals. *Investors Daily* newspaper also has some very good numbers that you can use effectively. In Chapter 9, I will discuss how you might use puts as a substitute for a short sale.

MANAGING THE TRADE

Now that you have found the optimum entry point and own the stock, what do you do? We have found it profitable to take money off the table as the stock rises. Remember the basketball example of the guy who received the personal foul. He had two shots to make, each one independent of the other. As a 70 percent free throw shooter, he has only a 49 percent chance of making both shots ($.7 \times .7 = .49$). You have that same problem. To be successful at buying stock, you must buy the stock right and you must sell it right. Many investors buy the stock right, watch it go up, then watch in disbelief as the stock goes down. It is much less nerve-racking when you have a plan.

In our discussion of trend lines, we said that as long as a stock is trading above its long-term Bullish Support line, it is bullish and long-term investors should hold the stock. Long-term players should ignore sell signals that come from above this Bullish Support line. For such players, the trend line is the most important guide. The short-term traders will sell on any sell signal. Once the position is put on for short-term traders, they will place a stop-loss order one box below the previous column of O's. They will be taken out of a position more frequently but will also avoid the severe hit. A trader who suffers a 50 percent loss of capital needs a 100 percent gain to win it back. This is why preservation of capital is the most important thing to a trader. Stops can be a trader's best friend. Figure 4.9, a Time Warner chart, illustrates these points. Remember, the numbers in the chart represent the months of the year. A, B, and C represent October, November, and December.

Let's take a look at the expected move in this stock from the entry point. The vertical count off the bottom is taken by counting the first column of X's up following the bottom in the stock. Notice how Time Warner bottomed at $19½ in December. The subsequent rise carried the stock up to $27 in the column of X's that has the 1, 2, and 3 in the column. It's always good to review. Count the number of X's in the column (there are 8). Now multiply times 3 (remember we are using the three-box reversal method): $3 \times 8 = 24$. Now multiply times the box size ($1 per box): $3 \times 8 = 24 \times 1 = 24$. Now add 24 to the level of the first X in the column. The potential move is $20 + $24 = $44. Now look at where Time Warner went before the trend line was broken. The stock topped out at $46.

Taking a subsequent count can provide more guidance. Here's how to do it. We did a count on the first move off the bottom. Once the stock starts to move up, it invariably will give another sell signal somewhere along the rise. Once this subsequent signal is given, a potential new

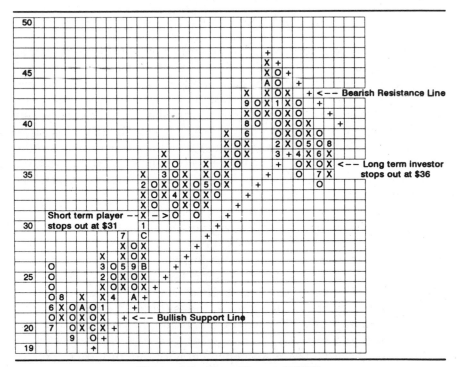

Figure 4.9 Time Warner (TWX).

bottom is in the making. We know the bottom is made when the stock regains sponsorship and rises to give another buy signal off that bottom. Look at Figure 4.9. Notice how Time Warner gives a sell signal at $31 where the trader stops out. The next buy signal comes at $36 (column of X's with the 5 in it exceeds the previous column of X's by one box). You can now count the X's in that column and multiply by 5. There are 5 X's in that column. We multiply times 3 then again times the box size of 1 and get 15. Now add that to the first X in that column and you get $32 + $15 = $47. The second count still suggests a move in the vicinity of the first count of $48. The long-term investor could have chosen to sell when the stock came near one of those price objectives. In either case, the chart did not suggest the play was over. When the trend line was broken, the stock had declined 10 points from its top. The trader made a 29 percent return on this play while the investor made 50 percent (if you consider that both entered the trade at $24 on the pullback in April). This brings us to the question of when to sell.

WHEN TO SELL

In our money management subsidiary, we try to take profits as the stock rises and the outlook is still good. After we have determined the price potential of the stock and feel confident it has adequate room to exceed the average gain for bullish patterns, we sell ⅓ of the position if the stock rises 30 percent and another ⅓ if the stock rises 50 percent; we hold the last ⅓ until the underlying stock does one of three things: It breaks the uptrend line, the relative strength chart turns negative, or the stock falls back to the point where we took the first profit (up 30 percent). As long as the stock holds its trend, we will stick with it. By holding the last ⅓, you maintain a position in stocks that just continue to perform such as Wal-Mart, Home Depot, Coca-Cola, and many others.

TAKING A PROFIT—WHAT TO DO
WHEN THINGS GO RIGHT

The following discussion of when to sell is adapted from an article from our *Daily Equity & Market Analysis* report of September 15, 1994. The discussion goes over some ideas on what to do when things go right. We seem to devote so much time protecting ourselves in the event things go wrong we fail to cover the other side of the equation.

One of the hardest things to do is take a profit. One of our clients called the other day and was wondering about taking profits and mentioned that 3 points profit which he had in a position was not enough to take for this person's clients. With the short-term indicators going on hold, I asked, "How would a 3 points loss fit with this customer?" What do you

35					+						
			X		X	+					
		X		B	O	X	O	+			
		A	O	X	O	X	O		+		<-- Bearish Resistance Line
		X	O	X	O		O		+		
30		X	O				O			+	
		X					O				+
		X					O				
		X					C			X	
		X					O			X	
25		X					O			X	
		X					1			8	
							3			X	
							O			X	
							O			6	
20							O		X	X	
							O		X	O	X
19							O		5	O	X
							O		X	O	
18							O	4	X		
							O	X	O	X	
17							O	X	O	X	
							O	X	O	X	
16							O		O		

Figure 4.10 Mylan Labs (MYL): Taking profits at the Bearish Resistance line.

do? Here's a way to gauge taking a profit. Look at the chart of Mylan Labs (MYL) (Figure 4.10). We recommended the stock for traders on the first buy signal off the bottom on a Double Top buy signal at $18½. The stock has since gone to $27. Notice on the chart how the stock is right up against the Bearish Resistance line. This is the point where the stock will probably konk out. Profits should be taken here. Another way to do it is to take profits off the table as the stock rises. If the stock rises 30 percent, (in this case it would have been $24), you might consider taking ⅓ of your position off the table. When the stock rises 50 percent, take another ⅓ off the table. In this case that would be in the $27 area. You could then set a stop for the last ⅓ at the point you took the first profit. What you don't want to do is ride it back down. That's like getting a personal foul in basketball which gives you two free throws at the basket. You make the first basket but hit the rim on the second.

Cheyenne Software (CYE)

Figure 4.11 shows a recent recommendation which was a play on a 20 unanswered box down move. We went in on the first three-box reversal back up the chart with a stop on the first sell signal. Taking ⅓ off the table as the stock moves up does two things: (1) It allows you to take profits while still having a position in the stock should it continue up; (2) it gives you cash to reemploy elsewhere.

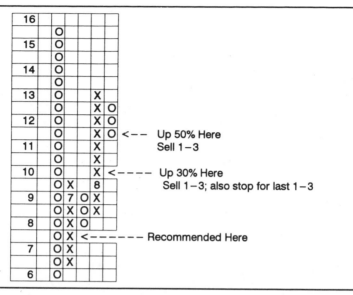

Figure 4.11   Cheyene Software (CYE): Scaling out.

LONE STAR STEAKHOUSE (STAR)

Another possible profit-taking spot is the Bullish Resistance line. This line is drawn by going to the left of an uptrend and connecting the boxes at the first wall of O's. If this line is broken you can move out to the next wall. The Bullish Resistance line gives you some perspective on how far a stock might run on its current move. Traders are well advised to take profits at this level. Traders can reenter on a pullback to the center of the channel.

```
25 |                                                              X | <-- Take Profits
   |                                                            + X |
   |   X                        Bullish Resistance Line -- + : X |
   |   X O      X                                        +    X |
   |   X O X    X O X                                  +      X |
20 |   X 5 X O X O 6 O X                             +      X   X |
   |   X O X O X O X O X O X                       +  X    X O X |
19 |     O X O    O X O X O X O X                +    X O X O X |
   |     O        O    O X O X O X O +    X    X O X O +       | <-- Bullish Support Line
18 |              O    O X O X O X    X O 7 O    +            |
   |                   O    O X O X O X +                    |
17 |                        O X O X O X +                    |
   |                        O    O X O +                     |
16 |                             O    +                      |
```

Figure 4.12   Lone Star Steakhouse (STAR): Taking profits at the Bullish Resistance line.

General Datacomm (GDC)

GDC is a stock which has been on our Best Page since $16⅜. As you can see from Figure 4.13, the stock has done well to say the least. The point of this discussion is we have a twenty box up move that has been unanswered with a reversal. We always recommend taking profits on the first 3-box reversal after a 20-box move up. This is simply another way to take profits. Although the chart pattern has not yet suggested there is any problem, it is in dire need of some sort of relief. You can always go back in on the next buy signal.

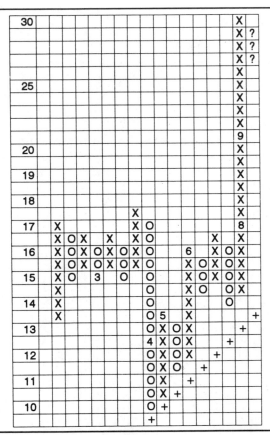

Figure 4.13 General Datacom (GDC): Taking profits on the three box reversal.

SOME HELPFUL GUIDELINES IN MANAGING A TRADE

1. The first line of defense is the underlying stock's fundamentals. Be sure the stock you buy has strong fundamentals. This information is available just about anywhere on Wall Street.

2. Select stocks that have just turned positive on their relative strength charts within the past 9 months. This will help ensure positive relative performance for a long time. Remember, these charts last 2½ years on average.

3. Buy stocks in sectors that are below the 50 percent level on their Bullish Percent charts and are in one of the three buy modes. Sectors will be covered in later chapters. Sell stocks short in sectors that are above the 50 percent level and in one of the three bearish modes.

4. Protect profits in stocks whose underlying sector has risen above the critical 70 percent level and subsequently reversed down. This is a high-risk condition for the sector and profits must be hedged or protected in some way.

5. Only buy a stock that is trading above its Bullish Support line. Stocks tend to take the path of least resistance and that is to follow a trend line.

6. Only sell a stock short that is trading below its Bearish Resistance line. Stocks trading below the Bearish Resistance line will tend to rise to that line and then fall again. This is the path of least resistance for a stock in a downtrend.

7. Diversify your portfolio, spread the risk. Some stocks will decline and some will rise. If all the stocks in the portfolio have positive relative strength, the bad stocks that decline will not underperform as much as the good stocks outperform.

8. Keep an eye on the percentage of stocks in the sector that have changed to positive relative strength over the past 6 months. This can tell you a lot about the longevity of any rally in that sector. In other words, if a sector goes on a buy signal but is showing that the number of stocks with positive relative strength in that sector has declined over the past 6 months, the rally in that sector is likely to lose steam quickly. We like to see sectors that have an increasing percentage of stocks on relative strength buy signals over the past 6 months. Mike Burke, the editor of *Investors Intelligence* brought this idea to our attention.

5

USING RELATIVE STRENGTH CALCULATIONS

RELATIVE STRENGTH—THE CHARTCRAFT METHOD

One of the most important tools investors have at their disposal is the relative strength calculation. The basic objective of all investors is to outperform the broad averages. The best way to tell whether your stock is outperforming is to evaluate its performance relative to a market average. In this case, we will use the Dow Jones Industrial. Consider the following example. Your stock is trading at $80 per share and Dow Jones is at the 1000 level. To determine how your stock is trading relative to the Dow, you would simply divide the price of the stock by the Dow and then plot the resulting number exactly as you would a normal Point and Figure chart. If we divide $80 by 1000 and move the decimals away to make a more manageable number, we get a figure of .08 or 80. This can then be plotted on a graph similar to the one we use for plotting the actual price of the stock. Let's say next week the Dow declines to 800 and the stock declines to $72. Once again, perform the same calculation, divide the price of the stock by the current price of the Dow, and move the decimal. The resulting number is .09 or 90. You would then plot this number on the graph you had started the previous week.

In this example, the stock declined from $80 to $72, the Dow declined from 1000 to 800 and the relative strength chart rose 12.5 percent from 80 to 90. In this case, it is clear the stock is down only because the broad averages are down. Previously, we discussed how 75 percent of the risk in a stock is the market and the sector. When the tide goes out in the marina, all boats go down and those with structural damage stay down. Never lose sight of that fact.

Relative strength charts are very long-term, lasting 2 to 2½ years, and are only updated once a week. These charts don't speak often, but when they do you should listen. In many cases, the market is in a condition where the defensive team should be on the field and you should not be buying stocks of any kind. In such markets, relative strength really comes in handy as these charts clearly show those stocks which are outperforming the averages even though they might be declining as in the preceding example. In down markets, it pays to keep lists of stocks that are demonstrating superior relative strength versus the broad averages. These strong stocks will be your buy list when the offensive team comes back on the field. Have patience. There is no need to overtrade. Make long stock commitments only when the odds are in your favor.

Relative strength calculations help investors choose between stocks that superficially appear to be similar. Let's say you were evaluating three stocks in the same industry group. Each stock is fundamentally sound and the Point and Figure trend charts are similar. The only difference between the three stocks is that only one has a positive relative strength chart. Which one do you choose? The logical selection would be the stock with the positive relative strength chart. Stocks with positive trend charts and negative relative strength charts usually tread water.

It wasn't until October 1990 that I gained total respect for the relative strength chart. In one week in October, we noticed the relative strength charts of Dominion Resources, Houston Industries, Scana Corp, and Texas Utilities turned positive for the first time in four or more years. What were the relative strength charts telling us? Think about it for a second. It gets your attention when you see a number of stocks in the same group go from negative to positive relative strength. Since these are all utility stocks, the message was interest rates were about to begin coming down. Utility stocks are interest rate sensitive. The message was clear. This in turn spoke volumes about the prospects of the stock market in general, as it too has a tendency to follow interest rates. Only one month later, the first week of November, we received a major buy signal from the market in general. The utility stocks' relative strength charts timed it perfectly. The market is always giving clues. You must be astute and aware. Yogi Berra said it best: "You can observe a lot just by watching."

A similar case happened in November 1991. In one week, we saw Hercules Corporation, Briggs & Stratton, and Cummins Engine turn positive on their relative strength charts after being negative for years. The message or clue was the cyclical stocks were ready to take the lead. Since I started in the brokerage business in 1975, I had never seen anyone make money in Hercules Corporation (HPC). When the relative strength chart turned positive, it got my attention. We immediately recommended these stocks to our clients and they were absolute home runs and I mean grand slams. We were probably one of the first on Wall Street to uncover the change in sectors from consumer goods to cyclical stocks. It was through no brilliance on our part, we just observed. Because of this recommendation, we gained a large hedge fund as a client and I am proud to say they remain clients to this day.

One more example of how relative strength helped us uncover a stock early in the move was Chrysler Corporation in 1992. In March 1992, the relative strength chart of Chrysler turned positive for the first time since August 1987. This change got our attention fast. The trend Point and Figure chart had already begun to give major buy signals off the bottom. The stock had been in a strong downtrend for many years. With the positive trend chart and the change in relative strength, we pounded the table on the stock. In fact, at every talk I gave for the next couple of years I said that the change in relative strength suggested that Chrysler would soon have more orders for cars than the company could produce. In April 1994, I was watching the "Nightly Business Report" on CNN, and the commentator actually said Chrysler was getting more orders than it could fill. This was just about at the top. The relative strength change in 1992 was on the nose again. I have said before the key to success in investing or anything for that matter is confidence. The relative strength chart can give you the confidence to act rather than react.

Let's take a look at the relative strength chart for Chrysler as shown in Figure 5.1, and you will see why we became so aggressive on the stock. Remember, the relative strength chart was constructed by dividing the price of Chrysler by the price of the Dow Jones. Let's look at the trend chart at the same time, and you will see the strong buy signals the stock was giving off the bottom of its long decline.

There are many other stories about how relative strength calculations can help uncover changes in sector sponsorship, but I think you get the idea now. Stocks with positive relative strength have a tendency to outperform those with negative relative strength.

When making new stock commitments, try to find stocks with relative strength charts that have turned positive within the past six months to a year. This helps ensure you have a stock with lots of life left. Stocks whose relative strength has been positive for a long time might be close to turning negative. This is why it is important to evaluate the relative strength chart itself rather than simply accepting a positive or negative reading generated by a computer. Investing is still an art, not a science. The best place to get relative strength charts is from Chartcraft of New Rochelle, New York. It is the best purveyor of Point and Figure charts in the world. This company has everything

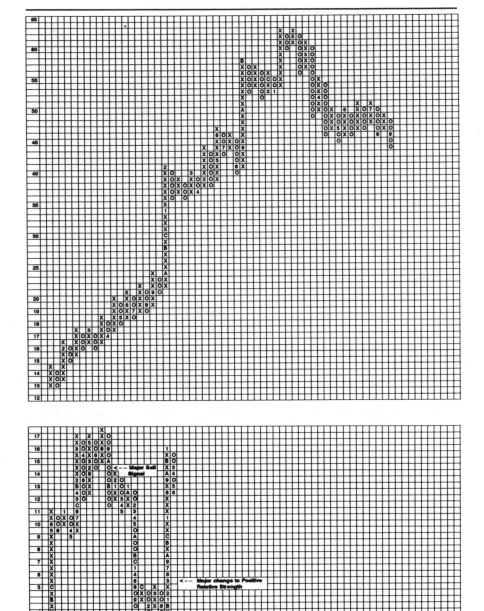

Figure 5.1 Chrylser (C) trend chart (top) and Chrylser relative strength chart (bottom).

the average investor could possibly want. Mike Burke, the editor, is without a doubt one of the best technicians and investors on Wall Street.

We need to cover a couple of the relative strength calculations before we leave the subject. Some stocks are so strong that their relative strength charts go straight up in a long column of X's without the first reversal. For the stock to turn from positive to negative relative strength, the chart would have to decline to a point where it exceeded a previous bottom. When the relative strength chart has a long column of X's up, the underlying stock would have to absolutely collapse to turn the relative strength chart negative by exceeding its previous bottom. In this case, we typically call the first three-box reversal in the chart negative until a pattern can form. This is the only time we act without an actual signal. It simply makes common sense. Evaluating the relative strength chart in such a way allows you to take proper defensive action before things get out of hand.

In the example shown in Figure 5.2, you can see that if we had waited until the relative strength chart actually declined enough to exceed a previous bottom and give a sell signal, it would have been too late and of no use. The reciprocal would be true in a chart that was so negative that it showed a very long tail of O's down. We would call the first three-box reversal back up the chart as turning positive.

One of the things I found most difficult to do when I was a stock-broker was face a loss in a client's portfolio. I had a tendency to be eternally optimistic. Human nature causes us to hang on to any thread of hope that the stock we bought was the right one. Once all the technicals break down, we tend to look to the fundamentals to bail us out. It has happened all too often, and a broker has a natural tendency to focus on the stocks that are doing well and shove the losers back in the corner of the account, where they get wished up on a daily basis in the

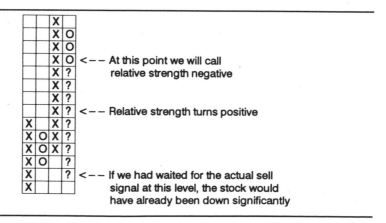

Figure 5.2   High poles up in relative strength.

hope that one day someone will realize the stock is undervalued. Don't hold your breath. Wall Street knows the fundamentals and, for reasons you are not aware of, has chosen to avoid that stock. Only when the stock seriously tanks will the real story come out. It is said that investors are simply traders holding a losing position. Rather than take a loss, most investors will hold on for the long term in the expectation the stock will come back. In many cases, they just don't. The long and short of it is by ignoring the losers and taking profits in the winners, you eventually end up with a portfolio of losers.

When I was a broker, what never occurred to me was to swap bad stocks for good ones. Let's say you bought a stock at $30 in the software sector. Over time, the stock declines to $24 and the relative strength chart turns negative. Rather than sitting with the stock and wishing it back up, why not find another stock around the same price in the same industry that has recently turned positive on its relative strength chart and is both fundamentally and technically sound? Sell the bad one and buy the good one. You have a much better chance of getting your money back with the good stock.

Whenever a stock's relative strength chart turns negative, you should sell the stock. When your stock is no longer outperforming the averages, you must find a new one. You are much better off letting your good stocks run while weeding out the bad ones. It's difficult to do but it is a must. The late A. W. Cohen had a rule that if a stock had not performed as you expected in 90 days, kick it out. This philosophy has merit because you must keep your capital working for you. Your money might as well be in passbook savings if it is tied up in a dead stock.

It is important to establish rules that you follow religiously. I have given many speeches on the subject, but one time in the past I failed to follow my own advice. For a period I was in a slump. It seemed that nothing I did worked. I couldn't understand what was wrong. We were using the tools, but something wasn't clicking. The more I tried to figure it out, the more elusive the answer became. I was at wits' end when, almost miraculously, I received a call from a friend, who was also a client of ours. His name is Mike Moody. He and Harold Parker are now vice presidents of my company and senior portfolio managers in our money management operation in Beverly Hills, California.

The story I am about to relate happened before they came aboard. Mike had been a client of ours for many years and had been implementing these principles very successfully in his money management business. I told him I was in a slump and couldn't figure out what was wrong. With a chuckle, he told me I hadn't been practicing what I preach. Although I was a strong advocate of relative strength, I had been buying stocks with negative relative strength. Although I am a strong believer in sector rotation, I had been buying stocks in bearishly configured sectors. My stop points were too close, and I had no money management rules. I had forgotten the basics and was virtually out-thinking myself. Mike brought me back to earth, and everything has been fine since.

When you try to make investing too complicated, confusion sets in and you make major mistakes. Bernard Baruch said you should always write down why you bought a stock. If that reason ever changes, sell the stock. If I had been writing down why I was buying any particular stock, I would have had to stop and think about what I was doing and would not likely have made those mistakes. Write down why you are buying a particular stock.

Here are some ideas on managing money that should help you become more successful. You will undoubtedly come up with a few of your own, just be sure to stick to them. Thanks to Mike, I was able to climb out of my slump and again begin practicing what I preach. Sometimes it's difficult to follow our own judgment—we tend to try to out-think ourselves. Keep it simple, whatever you do. I have added some of our other house rules to Mike's list:

1. The first line of defense is the underlying stock's fundamentals. Be sure the stock you buy has strong fundamentals. This information is available just about anywhere on Wall Street.

2. Select stocks that have just turned positive on their relative strength charts within the past six months to a year. This will help ensure positive relative performance for a long time. Remember, these charts last about 2 to 2½ years.

3. Buy stocks in sectors below the 50 percent level on their Bullish Percent indexes and in one of the three buy modes. Sectors will be covered in Chapter 8. Sell stocks short in sectors above the 50 percent level and in one of the three bearish modes.

4. Protect profits in stocks whose underlying sector has risen above the critical 70 percent level and subsequently reversed down. This is a high-risk condition for the sector and profits must be hedged or protected in some way.

5. If you buy a stock and it rises 30 percent, take ⅓ of the position off the table. If it rises 50 percent, take another ⅓ off the table. Hold the last ⅓ until the stock's relative strength chart turns negative or the stock declines to the level where you took the first ⅓ off.

6. If you buy a stock and it immediately declines 15 percent, sell it if the stock is underperforming the broad averages. If it is not under-performing the averages, then hold on. I also like A. W. Cohen's rule of not risking more than 10 percent. A portfolio of 10 stocks only risks 1 percent of the portfolio if only 10 percent is risked on

any one stock. There is a low probability all your stocks will all fall at once.

7. Only buy a stock that is trading above its Bullish Support line. Stocks tend to take the path of least resistance and that is to follow a trend line.

8. Only sell a stock short that is trading below its Bearish Resistance line. Stocks trading below the Bearish Resistance line will tend to rise to that line and then fall again. This is the path of least resistance for a stock in a downtrend.

9. Diversify your portfolio, spread the risk. Some stocks will decline and some will rise. If all the stocks in the portfolio have positive relative strength, the bad stocks that decline will not underperform as much as the good stocks outperform.

10. Keep an eye on the percentage of stocks in the sector that have changed to positive relative strength over the past 6 months. This can tell you a lot about the longevity of any rally in that sector. If a sector goes on a buy signal but is showing that the number of stocks with positive relative strength in the sector has declined over the last 6 months, the rally in the sector is likely to lose steam quickly. We like to see sectors increasing the number of relative strength buy signals over the past 6 months.

MOODY AND PARKER'S RELATIVE STRENGTH STUDY

Mike Moody and Harold Parker did a study on Point and Figure relative strength calculations that was published in *Stocks & Commodities Magazine*. They selected the 20 largest capitalization stocks in the Standard & Poor's 100 Index as of October 1988 and examined the period running from October 1988 to October 1990. This period was chosen because it included various types of markets—rising, falling, and stable. Their goal was to determine if there was a meaningful performance difference for individual stocks versus a market index as a function of the relative strength signal. If the signals given by a relative strength Point and Figure chart are valid, their sample test should show meaningful and reasonable, consistent, incremental performance improvement from using relative strength as a filter to select trades.

Figure 5.3 shows how they did it. The 20 stocks they tracked fell into three broad groups. Groups 1 and 2 held their relative strength readings throughout the study. Group 3 stocks switched between relative strength signals one or more times.

You can see the Group 1 stocks with positive relative strength had an astounding gain of 59.3 percent while the Group 2 stocks with negative relative strength turned in a loss of 19 percent. The performance

GROUP 1

POSITIVE RELATIVE STRENGTH	PERFORMANCE
ATLANTIC RICHFIELD (ARC)	+62.5%
AMERICAN TELEPHONE TELEGRAPH (T)	+21.4
COCA COLA (K)	+119.0
MERCK (MRK)	+37.5
MOBIL OIL (MOB)	+40.5
WALMART STORES (WMT)	+75.0
Average Performance	+59.3%
S&P 100 Performance	+13.3%

GROUP 2

NEGATIVE RELATIVE STRENGTH	PERFORMANCE
DIGITAL EQUIPMENT (DEC)	−47.8%
DUPONT (DD)	+20.7
EASTMAN KODAK (EK)	−13.0
SEARS ROEBUCK (S)	−35.9
Average Performance	−19.0%
S&P 100 Performance	+13.3%

GROUP 3

SWITCHED BETWEEN RELATIVE STRENGTH SIGNALS			PERFORMANCE	
			+RS	−RS
AMOCO (AN)				
10/88–6/90 Buy	6/90–8/90	Sell	+45.7%	+9.8%
8/90–10/90 Buy			−5.3	N/A
BELL ATLANTIC (BEL)				
10/88–10/89 Sell	10/89–7/90	Buy	−7.8	+41.7
7/90–10/90 Sell	10/90	Buy	+8.3	+2.1
DOW CHEMICAL (DOW)				
10/8–6/89 Buy	6/89–10/90	Sell	+6.8	−30.6
EXXON (XON)				
10/88–5/89 Buy	5/89–8/90	Sell	0.0	+20.5
8/90–10/90 Buy			−5.7	NA
GENERAL ELECTRIC (GE)				
10/88–3/89 Buy	3/89–10/90	Sell	+2.2	+4.0
FORD (F)				
10/88–10/89 Buy	10/89–10/90	Sell	−3.8	−44.0
GENERAL MOTORS (GM)				
10/88–5/89 Buy	5/89–10/90	Sell	+2.6	−5.0
HEWLETT PACKARD (HWP)				
10/88–5/89 Buy	5/89–10/90	Sell	+5.9	−51.9
INTERNATIONAL BUSINESS MACHINES (IBM)				
10/88–9/90 Sell			+1.9	−10.2
9/90–10/90 Buy				
MINNESOTA MINING (MMM)				
10/88–10/89 Buy	10/89–10/90	Sell	+17.7	+8.2
Average performance with positive relative strength			+5.4%	
Average performance with negative relative strength			−5.0%	

Figure 5.3 Relative strength study by Mike Moody and Harold Parker.

differential was 78.3 percent. Group 3 stocks that moved back and forth between positive and negative turned in a less impressive return; however, the average performance for positive relative strength stocks was a gain of 5.4 percent and the stocks with negative relative strength turned in a loss of 5.0 percent.

Although the sample size would preclude the experiment from being statistically valid, it clearly shows relative strength makes a difference and should be used as an integral part of the stock selection process.

RELATIVE STRENGTH AS A SHORT-TERM INDICATOR

In many cases, the actual change in the relative strength chart has a tendency to be a lagging indicator. As mentioned earlier, these charts tend to last 2 to 2½ years. During that time, there can be numerous tradable moves within the confines of a long-term trend. As daily practitioners of this methodology, we watch these charts very carefully. Over many years we have noticed that changes in direction in a relative strength chart can be a leading indicator of a change in trend in a stock. Since these charts are long term, simple reversals in trend can last many months. It is very important to evaluate the relative strength chart along with the trend chart. The easiest way to do this is order the *Option Stock Relative Strength Chart Book* from Chartcraft of New Rochelle, New York. There are now over 1,400 optionable stocks. Chartcraft pioneered the concept of relative strength Point and Figure charts. We have found that simple reversals in the relative strength charts can significantly increase your odds of success in a trade. Think about this for a second. The relative strength Point and Figure charts are made up of up moves and down moves within the confines of a long-term trend. Reversals in that trend are clearly demonstrating a change in the underlying stock's relative performance to the broad market at that very moment. This change can last for months on end, while the overall relative strength chart might be suggesting something entirely different for the long term.

These reversals in the chart can signal multiple point moves in the underlying stock. So-called long-term investors aren't concerned with a 20 percent change in their stock's direction, they are only worried about the long-term implications of the move. The short-term trader is happy to pick up a 20 percent move here and there. Changes in actual relative strength signals begin with the first reversal. Since these charts are so long term, reversals in trend can be very profitable to the trader. Traders need every edge they can get.

We have found the reversals to be so important we list them in our research reports every week. A recent recommendation was on

AMGEN with the stock at $42. The stock had been beaten up pretty thoroughly over the previous year. The sector had been wiped out as evidenced by its Bullish Percent Index declining below the 30 percent level. Bear Stearns had just upgraded the stock to "Buy," and what clinched it for us was that the relative strength chart had just reversed up into a column of X's. Not a buy signal, but a reversal up. This reversal up, along with the other pieces of the puzzle coming together, caused us to make a major recommendation in that issue. Bear Stearns's recommendation of the stock answered the fundamental question "What" for us. Our job is to answer the question "When." The stock rose 20 percent very rapidly. You can see through the sequence of events in Amgen how reversals in the relative strength chart might be used. It is an integral part of the decision process.

6

THE NEW YORK
STOCK EXCHANGE
BULLISH PERCENT

The Most Important Market Indicator

INTRODUCING THE NYSE BULLISH PERCENT INDEX

This chapter on the New York Stock Exchange (NYSE) Bullish Percent covers a critical area of investment strategy (see Figure 6.1). It is of paramount importance that you grasp this concept thoroughly. This index is our main coach and dictates our general market posture. It wasn't until January 1987 that I fully understood what the Bullish Percent Index was all about. That was the month my partner and I started Dorsey, Wright & Associates. Before that, I was Director of Options Strategy at a large regional brokerage firm. Although my department was self-contained, in that we did our own research and never piggy-backed off the firm's recommendation, we did use another outside service for our intermediate-term market outlook.

During the 1980s the market outlook was pretty easy. Stocks just went up. This was the decade that made many investment advisors. We primarily focused on the option stock universe and, to a lesser degree, on the market and sectors. As I mentioned before, stocks generally rose during this period so the focus was on catching the next train out of the station. The decade of the 1980s was wild indeed. Things were popping, and the listed derivatives market was only about 6 years old, having debuted in April 1973. By the time the 1980s rolled around, options derivatives were the fastest game in town. If I were asked to

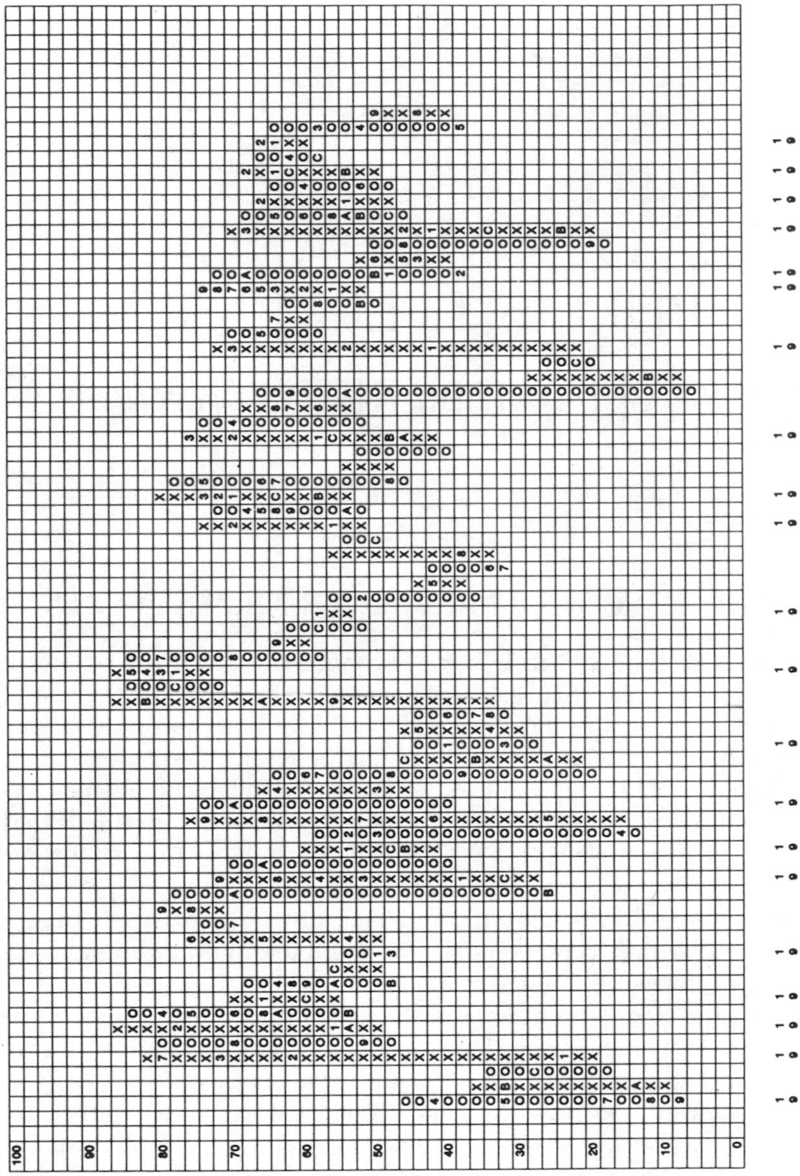

Figure 6.1A NYSE Bullish Percent—1974–1994.

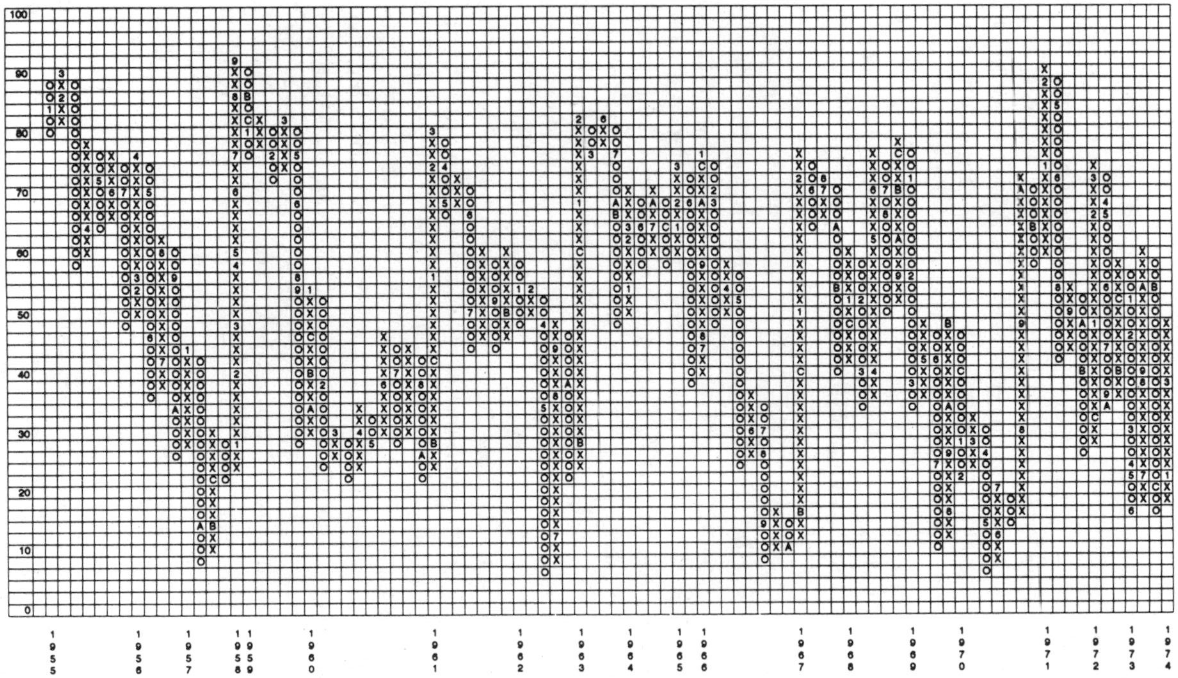

Figure 6.1B NYSE Bullish Percent—1955–1974.

define that period with one word, it would be *overleverage*. It seemed everyone had a stake in the game. By 1987, the game had gotten easy and everyone, it seemed, had become comfortable with the state of the market. Rising prices translated into easy money in options. Until October 1987, that is.

Misuse of put options had a dampening effect on the options market. Put options can be viewed as insurance products. Buyers of puts are typically seeking insurance to hedge some market risk they feel unable to accept. The seller of puts on the other hand is contracting to provide the insurance the buyer is seeking. A put seller stands ready to purchase stock at a certain price for the life of the contract, no matter how far below that price the stock declines. This is similar to an insurance company insuring your car for the life of the contract. The insurance company will make you whole if you have an accident. If no cars ever had any accidents, the insurance business would be the greatest business of all. Good premiums and no risk. Because stocks rarely had accidents during the early 1980s, investors decided to enter the underwriting business. You know what happens when everyone thinks some investment is too good to be true—it generally is. Well, in October 1987, every automobile in the country had an accident the same day. The Aetna Life & Casualty companies of the stock market (put sellers) all went bankrupt. I am referring to the investors who sold those puts that, up until October, usually expired worthless. This expiration month, they didn't. From that day on, the investment business changed.

The point of the discussion of the crash of 1987 is that the NYSE Bullish Percent Index saved our company. We were only 10 months old and had just begun to get some clients. We had decided when we started the company that our main market indicator would be the NYSE Bullish Percent Index. We simply went with what had apparently worked for many decades prior to 1987. Chartcraft, the creator of this index must have been doing something right, having been in business since the early 1950s. Mike Burke, the editor of Chartcraft, told me once that if he was only allowed to use one market indicator and nothing else, he would select the NYSE Bullish Percent Index as his guide. That was good enough for me. I learned everything I could about it that year.

On September 4, 1987, the indicator suggested we put the defensive team on the field as it reversed over into a column of O's, giving a sell signal. The only thing we knew to do was follow it, no questions asked. From that day forward, our feature article in our daily *Equity Market Report* had to do with how to hedge a portfolio with options. The following month the crash came, and I'll be the first to tell you we had no idea the decline would be so severe. Nonetheless those who chose to follow our recommendation were prepared. The crash took no prisoners.

By the first week in November, the same indicator that had suggested defense on September 4 now suggested offense. Once again, we knew of nothing else to do but follow it. Those who followed our recommendation got back in right at the bottom. I must add there was no brilliance on our part for those calls on the market, it was the NYSE Bullish Percent that did it. Ultimately, the most credit should go to the late A. W. Cohen for creating this index in 1955 and to the late Earl Blumenthal for refining it.

After the crash we put together a marketing piece consisting of excerpts from our report pre- and postcrash. This marketing piece in essence opened doors for us. From that day forward, the NYSE Bullish Percent has been the mainstay of our market indicators. I have written many articles on it, and each time I write about it I learn a little more. We have used this index to guide our intermediate market action for 8 years now. We have seen it work in bull, bear and neutral markets. The more you learn about this index, the more confidence you will have in your day-to-day market operations. Let's now discuss how it works. Read carefully, and reread it again and again if necessary.

If I could impress on you one fact concerning the markets it would be that 75 percent of the risk in any stock is the market and sector. If the overall market is not supporting higher prices, very few stocks you own, if any, will do well. I recently spoke at the Yale Club's annual Wall Street Night with Merrill Lynch's Director of Investment Strategy, PaineWebber's Director of Investment Strategy, and the Economist for Herzog, Heine, Geduld, Inc., who are some of the brightest people on Wall Street. Once they had finished their discussion on the market's outlook, it was my turn. The first chart I put up was a typical outline of a football game you might see on *Monday Night Football.* You know, when John Madden writes on the TV with his grease pencil showing what just happened on the last play. The chart looked like Figure 6.2.

In a football game, two sides operate on the field at any one time, offense and defense. The same forces act in the marketplace. There are times when the market is supporting higher prices, and times when the market is not supporting higher prices. When the market is supporting higher prices, we can say that you have possession of the ball. You have the offensive team on the field. When you have the ball, your job is to take as much money away from the market as possible; this is the time you must try to score. During times when the market is not supporting higher prices, you have in essence lost the ball and must put the defensive team on the field. During such periods, the job of the market is to take as much money away from you as possible. Think for a moment about your favorite football team. How well would they do

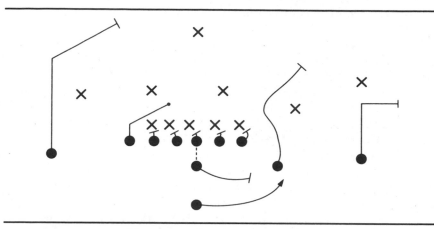

Figure 6.2   Bootleg option right.

this season if they operated with only the offensive team in every game. They might do well when they had possession of the ball, but when the opposing team had the ball, your team would be scored on at will. The net result is your season would be lackluster at best. This is the problem most investors have: They don't know which team is on the field, much less where the game is being played. Let's face it, most American investors only buy stocks, they never sell short. The NYSE Bullish Percent clearly signals when the environment is ripe for offense or defense. I want to make it absolutely clear that *there is a time to play offense and a time to play defense.* You must know which is which.

The first question that you must ask and find a way to answer before you make any stock commitments is, "Who's got the ball?" The NYSE Bullish Percent Index was created by the late A. W. Cohen in 1955. He was the first editor of Chartcraft and partners with Lee Gray in that operation. Lee Gray, by the way, is still the head of Chartcraft/Investors Intelligence. What Mr. Cohen was trying to create was a market indicator that was bullish at the bottom and bearish at the top. Normal trend charts of indexes like the Dow Jones and the S&P 500 are always bullish at the top and bearish at the bottom. Trend charts of market indexes invariably lead investors to buy at the top and sell at the bottom.

The NYSE Bullish Percent is simply a compilation of the percent of stocks on the NYSE on Point and Figure buy signals. Think back for a moment to Chapter 3. A bullish chart is one where the last signal was a column of X's that exceeds a previous column of X's. If you simply thumbed through all the Point and Figure chart patterns of the stocks on the NYSE and counted the ones that were on buy signals, then divided by the total number of stocks evaluated, you would have the NYSE Bullish Percent Index. A sixth grader could do it. We have computers that do the counting for us. Let's say, for instance, there were 2,000 stocks on the NYSE and 1,000 of them were on Point and Figure buy signals. The Bullish Percent would be at 50 percent (1,000 / 2,000 = 50 percent). We use the same three-box reversal to shift columns in this index as we do in the normal Point and Figure chart. Each box constitutes 2 percent, and the vertical axes runs from 0 to 100 percent. I look at that as the football field we are playing on. When the index is rising in a column of X's, more stocks are going on buy signals. Think for a moment what actually takes place if the index is at 50 percent this week and over the next two weeks rises to 52 percent. Changes in the index can only come from *first* signals that are given, not subsequent signals. Let's say XYZ stock bottoms out after declining and then gives that first buy signal off the bottom. That signal turns the stock from bearish to bullish (see Figure 6.3). It is this first buy signal that is recorded. All subsequent buy signals are not counted. One stock, one vote. To be sure you understand how this index moves, let's theoretically cut the number of stocks trading on the NYSE down to 100. Over the next week, 12 stocks experience a new buy signal like the one shown in Figure 6.3, and 10 stocks experience new sell signals. The net result of the action for the week is two new buy signals or 2 percent more stocks are on buy signals. Remember that each box on the chart represents 2 percent, so a 2 percent net change in new buy signals allows the chart to rise one box.

Remember the only way to switch from one column to the next is through a three-box reversal. It would take a sum total of 6 percent net buy or sell signals to cause a reversal. Reversing from one column to the next is tantamount to losing or gaining possession of the ball.

The chart is made up of columns of X's and O's with the vertical axes running from 0 to 100 percent. We think of this as a football field consisting of 100 yards. There are two things we try to ascertain with

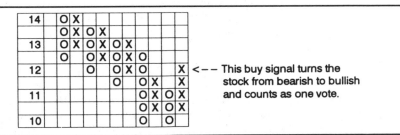

Figure 6.3   Bearish to Bullish.

this chart: (1) Who has the ball? (2) What is the field position? If you colored the area above the 70 percent level red and the area below 30 percent level green, these would represent the two extremes much like the end zones of a football field. The higher the index climbs, the more overbought it becomes. The lower it drops, the more oversold it gets. When the index is rising in a column of X's, we say you have possession of the football. When you have possession, you must run offensive plays. This is your time to attempt to score against your opponent, the stock market. When the index is declining in a column of O's, we say the market has the ball and your job is to try to keep it from scoring against you. The numbers in the boxes on the chart represent months of the year, so you can see the time spent in a column of X's or O's is generally a number of months, not weeks.

It is important to fully understand this index so let's go back to our discussion about how the index rises and falls. It takes a net change in buy or sell signals to move the index. The minimum percentage move in the index is 2 percent. It requires a 6 percent net change to change columns. This 6 percent change is the critical part of the index. Typically, I look at the index as a gauge of how many players are on the field. In July 1990, the Dow Jones was making all-time highs with the NYSE Bullish Percent Index at 52 percent. This showed that the Dow might have been at a new high but only 52 percent of the NYSE players were on the field. In other words, the NYSE Bullish Percent was at 52 percent and in a column of X's as you can see from the chart. One would have expected to see more than 52 percent of the stocks participating in the rally when the Dow was at new highs. A few weeks later, Iraq invaded Kuwait, and the same day the NYSE Bullish Percent reversed over into a column of O's signaling investors had lost the ball once again. Those who heeded the signal avoided a major crunch in the market. The net result was the index declined to the 18 percent level in October 1990 which was the bottom. The first week in November the index reversed into a column of X's signaling investors had once again taken possession of the ball. Those who were willing to listen bought stocks right at the bottom. Those who preferred to listen to the news media were expecting a depression or worse. I am continually amazed with the accuracy of this index. It helps the investor understand the most important question in investing, "Who's got the ball?"

NYSE BULLISH PERCENT RISK LEVELS

There are six degrees of risk in the index similar to the different signals a traffic light can give. The late A. W. Cohen felt if the index was rising in a column of X's and above the 50 percent level the market was bullish. Conversely, if the index was declining in a column of O's and below the

50 percent level the market was bearish. The late Earl Blumenthal fine-tuned the NYSE Bullish Percent to include 6 degrees of risk:

1. Bull Confirmed.
2. Bull Alert.
3. Bull Correction.
4. Bear Confirmed.
5. Bear Alert.
6. Bear Correction.

The following sections discuss each of them in detail.

Bull Confirmed Market

This is the strongest of markets and one that should be aggressively played on the upside. You have possession of the football so you must run plays and attempt to score against your opponent. This type of market occurs when the Bullish Percent gives a buy signal by exceeding a previous column of X's, as illustrated in Figure 6.4. Single buy signals on the trend chart of common stocks and the S&P can be followed here. It is equally important to evaluate the relative field position of the index. Bull Confirmed at the 70 percent level is very different from Bull Confirmed at the 30 percent level. Bull Confirmed at 70 percent puts the index in overbought territory where you must use hedged strategies for any commitment in which you buy stock. Bull Confirmed at 30 percent has the index in oversold territory. With this field position, you would want to simply buy stock outright.

Bull Alert Market

This market occurs when the Bullish Percent reverses up into a column of X's from below 30 percent. The index does not have to exceed the 30 percent level, simply reverse up (see Figure 6.5). At the 30 percent or

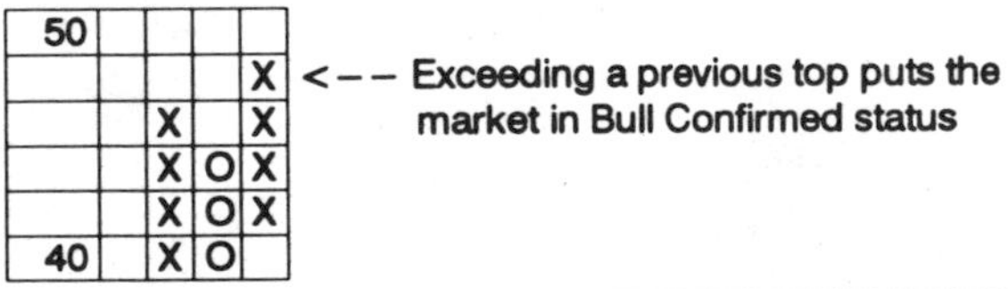

Figure 6.4 Bull Confirmed status.

30	O	
	O	X
	O	X
	O	X
	O	
20		

O X <– – A simple reversal up from below 30%
O X   puts the market in Bull Alert status

Figure 6.5   Bull Alert status.

lower level, many stocks are making their lows. The actual reversal to the upside suggests most lows have been made and the probability is up from there. A long trading posture should be established here but with caution. Trading profits of 10 to 15 percent should be taken as many stocks will have a tendency to retest their lows before establishing an extended bull trend. Stocks giving sell signals should be avoided; the same action happens at tops: Stocks have a tendency to retest their highs before an extended bear trend is established. This risk level change is tantamount to a red light changing to green. If I could institute another traffic signal to help you better understand this risk level, it would be flashing green—basically the opposite of flashing red. It is not as bullish as steady green but is close to it.

Bull Correction Market

The bull market is getting a little extended at these levels, and the market is currently digesting its excesses. The bull trend is likely to resume shortly. It is characterized by a 6 percent reversal down from a Bull Confirmed status that takes place below the 70 percent level, or a 6 percent reversal from above the 70 percent level that does not decline below that critical 70 percent level. It is telling us that the market leaders will likely drop in price due to profit taking. Defensive option strategies can be taken at this point. Selling call options or purchasing

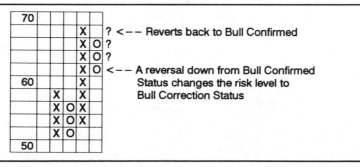

Figure 6.6   Bull Correction status.

puts as insurance against a potential decline in the broad averages might be a desired strategy here. Traders should be prepared to buy the stock on the next 6 percent (3 box) reversal to the upside in the Bullish Percent Index. The bull market is still intact; it's just taking a breather. The traffic light would have changed from green to yellow in Bull Correction status. The next reversal back up into a column of X's reverts the risk level back to Bull Confirmed as shown in Figure 6.6 by the column of questions marks (?).

Bear Confirmed Market

This market is characterized by the Bullish Percent Index penetrating a previous bottom as shown in Figure 6.7. We never second-guess this market. Traders can establish short positions in the S&P or common stock. All other long stock positions should be hedged in some way. Field position is important to consider in this risk level. Bear Confirmed at 30 percent is not as dangerous as Bear Confirmed at 70 percent. Always keep the field position in mind. The traffic light is red in this risk level.

Bear Alert Market

When the Bullish Percent drops below 70 percent without penetrating a previous bottom a Bear Alert occurs suggesting the market is in a corrective phase (see Figure 6.8). These corrections usually bring the

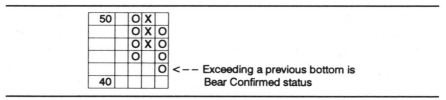

Figure 6.7   Bear Confirmed status.

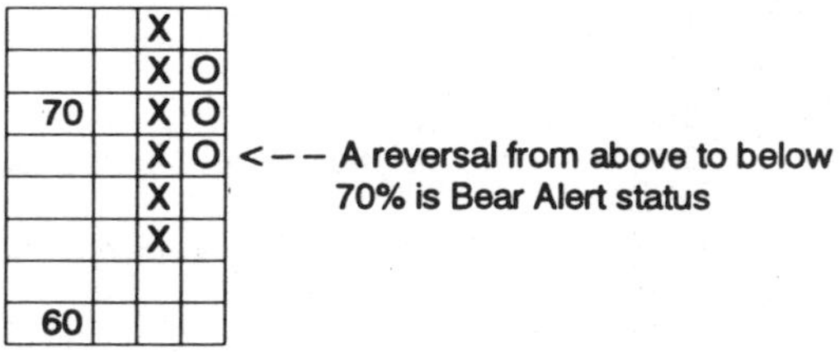

Figure 6.8   Bear Alert status.

Bullish Percent down to the 50 percent level at a minimum. A 6 percent reversal back up in the columns of X's will put the market back in a Bull Confirmed status. In the Bear Alert market, defensive action should be taken using the options market for hedging purposes. Short positions can be established in the S&P or common stocks. A trader's approach should be taken here. Short positions should be liquidated on the next 6 percent reversal to the upside in this index. Investors must be nimble because the market will eventually revert back to Bull Confirmed or slip into Bear Confirmed status. If the market slips into Bear Confirmed status, the short positions should be held and should prove extremely profitable. If the Bullish Percent reverts back to Bull Confirmed status, the short positions should be liquidated. The traffic light in this risk level changes from green to red.

Bear Correction Market

This indicates a pause in a bear market in which stocks will retrace some of their decline. This phase is characterized by a 6 percent reversal into a column of X's from above the 30 percent level from a Bear Confirmed status. Let's think about field position for a moment. If the NYSE Bullish Percent Index was at 32 percent and reversed up, the risk level would change to Bear Correction. If the index instead was at 30 percent and reversed up, the risk level would change to Bull Alert. Note the importance of the 30 percent level. Remember that reversals from 30 percent or below change the risk level to Bull Alert. The same thing would happen on the upside. A reversal at 68 percent from Bull Confirmed status would change the risk level to Bull Correction. A reversal from Bull Confirmed status at the 70 percent level would be Bear Alert status. The Bear Correction risk level is like a red light changing to flashing red. It may be OK to proceed through the intersection, but be sure to stop, look both ways for Mack trucks, and be fully aware

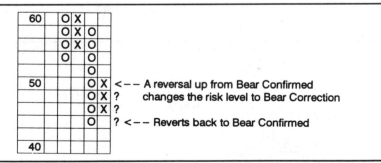

Figure 6.9 Bear Correction status.

that the opposing traffic have the right of way. Good stop-loss points must be established on any new long stock commitments here. Bear Confirmed status is likely to return soon. A reversal back down into a column of O's reverts the risk level back to Bear Confirmed. In Figure 6.9, this is depicted by the question marks (?).

SIGNIFICANT FACTS ABOUT THE BULLISH PERCENT

You should keep the following points in mind:

- Pre- and post-1987 crash signals were given in September 1987 (sell) and November 1987 (buy).

- In the past 20 years, the index has created just 66 columns across on the chart—about 2¾ changes per year. Signals are infrequent, but when they are given, they should be heeded.

- Up moves reach overbought levels when the Bullish Percent rises above the 70 percent level. The strength of the bull market will dictate whether the index stays above that level. The highest level seen in the past 20 years is 86 percent in 1982.

- Down moves reach oversold levels when the index moves below the 30 percent level. Again, the strength of the bear market will dictate the bottom. In 1974 and 1987, it dropped as low as 6 percent.

The following excerpt comes from our *Daily Equity Market Analysis Report* dated October 7, 1994. It gives a taste of what we say in our daily report. The Bullish Percent was close to reversing into Bear Confirmed Status, and we felt that it was important to discuss a potential game plan in the event the reversal did in fact happen. We try to think ahead a few moves as we go along.

GAME PLAN I

10:23 A.M. "Iraq Mobilized Some Troops on Kuwait's Border State Department says:"

It's time to discuss a potential game plan in the event the NYSE Bullish Percent reverses down. We have no sign that it will happen, but now that we are within 3 percent of doing so it helps to get the game plan firmly in mind. Once again, the reversal has not happened yet so don't jump out of your skin.

Anytime the NYSE Bullish Percent Index moves into Bear Confirmed status it warrants serious consideration. The picture in this market is exactly the same as July 1990 with only one change, the Dow is not at a new high. The Dow almost went to one on August 29th, I guess close is almost as good. Hell, this isn't a science anyway. The point is the Bullish Percent is at 50 percent, just about exactly where we were in July 1990. The risk level is the same, Bear Correction Status. The international event that coincided with the reversal to Bear Confirmed in the first week of August 1990 was the invasion of Kuwait by Iraq. Today at 10:23 A.M. on Bloomberg the headline read "Iraq Mobilized Some Troops on Kuwait's Border, State Department says." Wouldn't it be ironic if the same catalyst causes a reversal this time. This time we might not have the resolve to do anything, if you know what I mean. Okay, at this time take a look at the chart below [Figure 6.10] to get your perspective for a second. Compare both periods August 1990 and October 1994.

In the event the index does reverse down the game plan is to bring the Defensive Team on the field. Actually, they should have been on the field when the short term went to sell but most don't take that precaution. A reversal down in the NYSE Bullish Percent Index would suggest the 30 percent level was in the cards. If the reversal down occurs, you should prepare your portfolios for damage control. At a minimum you should curtail any further buying and devote your time to making sure you give as little money back to the market as possible. Don't worry about missing opportunity. You can always make up opportunity. It's hard to make up lost money. If you must buy stocks, be sure you place orders in below the market and make them come to you. Short sales are a viable tool in this type of market and have a high probability of success. Select short sales from sectors which are above the 50 percent level, in one of the three sell modes, trading below the Bearish Resistance line and the relative strength is negative. When you have this stock, play the trend. Take all sell signals and stop on all buy signals as long as the stock remains below the Bearish Resistance line. Do not go long below this trend line. Only go short on sell signals and stop shorts out on the first buy signal after the short goes on. Play the trend and keep your losses small by stopping on all buy signals.

Options are great defensive tools. If you have a portfolio approximately representative of the S&P consider buying one put on the S&P 100 index on the CBOE. If you buy one S&P 100 puts struck at 420, it represents $42,000 worth of stock. One put would provide protection for that portfolio in a general market decline. A portfolio worth $420,000 might consider 10 contracts. These puts are the same as insurance policies. Another way to hedge on a specific basis is to buy puts on the individual stocks in the portfolio or on those stocks you perceive as vulnerable. Selling calls is another way of hedging but the premium received is very minimal in relation to the downside potential.

The long and short of this dissertation is if the NYSE Bullish Percent reverses, take some action. The cause of the reversal IF IT COMES is not important. The only thing that is important is it did reverse. Be ready.

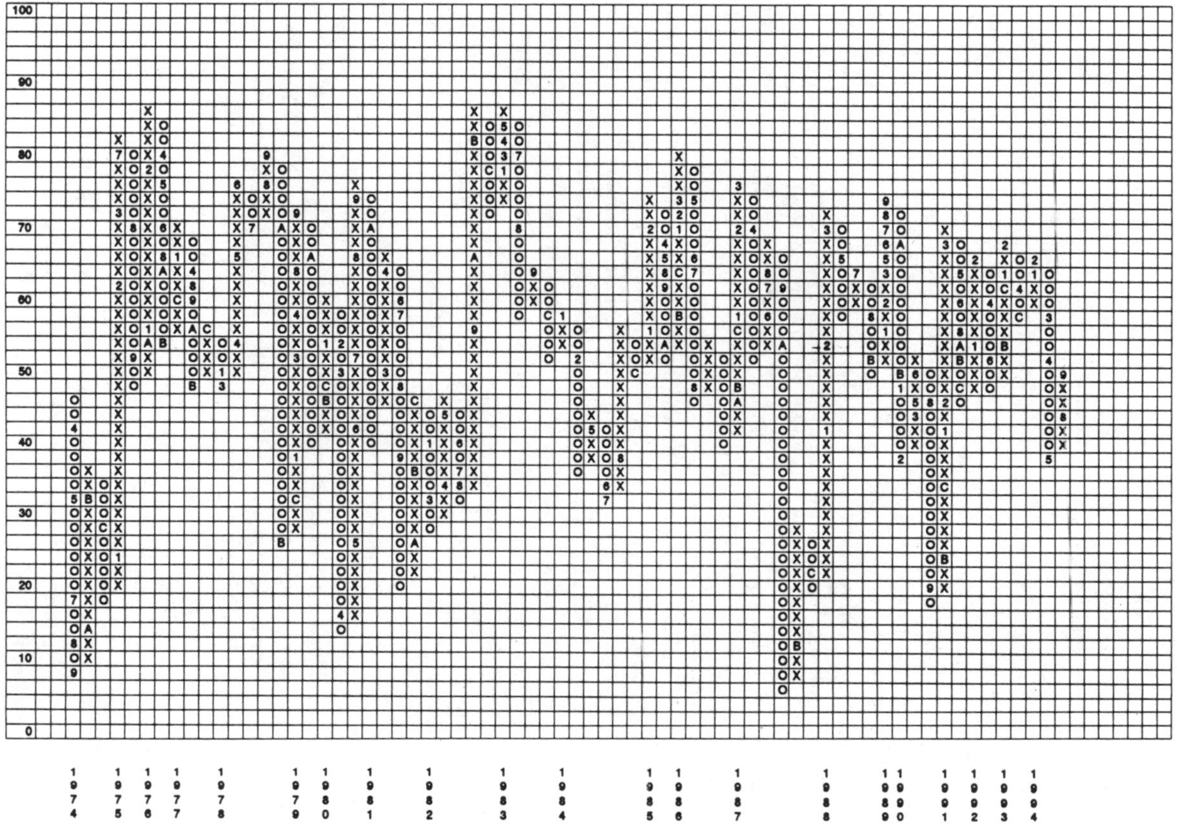

Figure 6.10 NYSE Bullish Percent.

TOMORROW GAME PLAN II: THE SOFT LANDING

"U.S. Carrier Reaches Red Sea as U.S. Troop Buildup Continues"

The beat goes on. Where this ends is anyone's guess. The worst thing we can do is begin to put our gut feel into the equation and avoid heeding the indicators which have brought us through bull, bear and neutral markets unscathed, including 1987. The NYSE Bullish Percent Index has seen us through. In fact, all you hear about is how Elaine Garzarelli called the crash. We got our clients out on September 4, 1987 with the reversal in the NYSE Bullish Percent. One thing you don't hear about is when Wall Street had strength in their conviction to go back in and buy. We got our clients back in the first week in November 1987. Not bad. We take no credit for it. The credit does to Chartcraft for creating the NYSE Bullish Percent in 1955 and in particular A. W. Cohen. Credit also goes to Mike Burke for so thoroughly indoctrinating me in the importance of this one indicator. The beauty of the index is it represents all there is to be known about the market. Everything there is to know about each and every stock on the NYSE is represented in the Point and Figure chart for in the end it is the irrefutable law of supply and demand which drives the world. When the aggregate of what is known about each stock underlying the NYSE is transformed into an index, you have the best window on the market that can be found anywhere. However, the whole can only be as good as the sum of its parts. It is the evaluation of the parts which makes the Bullish Percent so different from the rest of the market indicators. When changes take place in the index, there is no fanfare, no articles in *The Wall Street Journal* or *Investor's Daily*, no discussion of it on CNBC. The change is loud and clear to those who know, but silent to those who do not. Another positive is that relative to the number of investors in the market, only a very, very, small fraction of them have any idea the index exists. Those of you who do understand the Bullish Percent concept are truly in a minority. A select minority I must say.

The short-term indicators of the market are the Percent of Stocks above Their Own 10-Week Moving Average Index and the NYSE High-Low Index. These two indexes move like sports cars and can move from overbought to oversold and vice versa without changing the NYSE Bullish Percent Index. The reason for this is stocks can easily move above and below their 10 Wk Moving Average without ever giving a buy or sell signal. In the case of the High-Low Index, the ratio of new highs versus new lows has nothing to do with a stock giving a buy signal or sell signal. This year we have seen the Percent of 10 give 3 buy signals and 3 sell signals, almost moving coast to coast on each of them. The only change in the Percent of 10 and High-Low which spilled over into the Bullish Percent Index was the change in February of this year. It led to a reversal down and subsequent Bear Confirmed reading in the Bullish Percent. The short-term indicators have been on sells for 4 weeks now and have moved from 66 percent in the Percent of 10 and 70 percent in the High-Low to below 30 percent in each of them. At this writing, the High-Low is

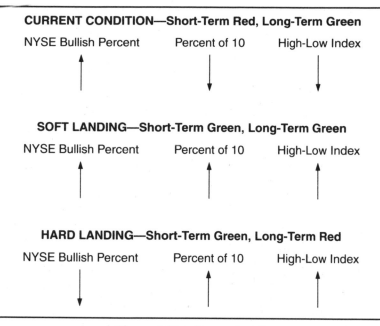

CURRENT CONDITION—Short-Term Red, Long-Term Green

NYSE Bullish Percent   Percent of 10   High-Low Index

SOFT LANDING—Short-Term Green, Long-Term Green

NYSE Bullish Percent   Percent of 10   High-Low Index

HARD LANDING—Short-Term Green, Long-Term Red

NYSE Bullish Percent   Percent of 10   High-Low Index

Figure 6.11   Game plans.

around 25 percent and the Percent of 10 is around 30 percent, levels we consider washed out. The NYSE Bullish Percent has held tough and is within 3 percent of a reversal.

If we get a reversal back up in the short-term indicators from this oversold level without the Bullish Percent changing risk levels, then we would look for an acceleration in stock prices on the upside. Wednesday's numbers will tell the story. As long as the NYSE Bullish Percent holds up and if the Percent of 10 and the High-Low Index reverse up, we will have a soft landing and an extended rally. If the Bullish Percent instead reverses and at the same time the short-term indicators reverse up, we will expect a short-term rally within the confines of a Bear Confirmed market.

7

OTHER MARKET
INDICATORS

OTHER TECHNICAL INDICATORS

When I was thinking about what indicators to use in this book, it
dawned on me simply to include the indicators we rely on the most on a
daily basis. We keep a book of indicators we use each day. It contains all
the Sector Bullish Percent charts, the NYSE Bullish Percent Index, Point
and Figure charts on the indexes, and other indicators that are essential
to our operation. Many investors make the mistake of trying to follow
too many indicators. The more you follow, the more confused you will
become. Our most important indicator is the NYSE Bullish Percent
Index discussed in Chapter 6. The Bullish Percent is our long-term
coach. We also follow an OTC Bullish Percent Index because of the
plethora of high-tech, over-the-counter stocks we deal with each day.
Chartcraft developed this index a few years ago because the over-the-
counter market is becoming more important as more technology stocks
come to market (the largest capitalization stock that trades in the U.S.
Markets is an OTC stock, Microsoft). We now have our own computers
do the calculations, but the methodology has not changed. The two
most important short-term indicators we use are the Percent of Stocks
above Their Own 10-Week Moving Average Index and the NYSE High-
Low Index. If I had to choose three indicators to use exclusively I would
choose the NYSE Bullish Percent Index, the Percent of 10, and the High-
Low Index. The following sections evaluate each of the indicators.

The OTC Bullish Percent Index

The OTC Bullish Percent Index is a compilation of the percentage of over-the-counter stocks that are on Point and Figure buy signals (see Figure 7.1). This OTC Bullish Percent Index can give you a great deal of insight into what the small stocks are doing. In 1982, the small stocks bottomed out much earlier than the large cap stocks. By the time the big cap stocks were ready to go in August 1982, the small stocks were already up 70 percent. The chart is read the same way as the NYSE Bullish Percent Index. When the index is rising in a column of X's, you have the football. Conversely, when it is in a column of O's, the OTC market has the ball. The best sell signals come from above the 70 percent level and the best buy signals come from below 30 percent. Much of the time, the truth lies somewhere in the middle.

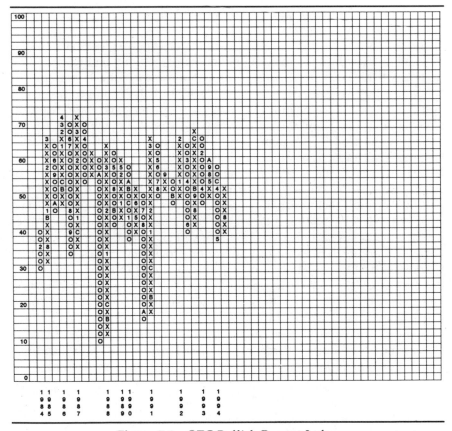

Figure 7.1 OTC Bullish Percent Index.

The AMEX Bullish Percent Index

The stocks that trade on the American Stock Exchange are typically small cap stocks. They are also very heavily weighted in the tertiary stocks like oil and mining issues. We don't place a lot of emphasis on this index, but if you follow small AMEX type stocks, this might be the indicator for you. This index is evaluated the same as the other Bullish Percent indexes (see Figure 7.2).

The Percent of Stocks above Their Own Ten-Week Moving Average Index

This index has become our most important short-term market indicator. It should be used in conjunction with the NYSE Bullish Percent Index. As its name implies, the Percent of 10 is simply made up of the

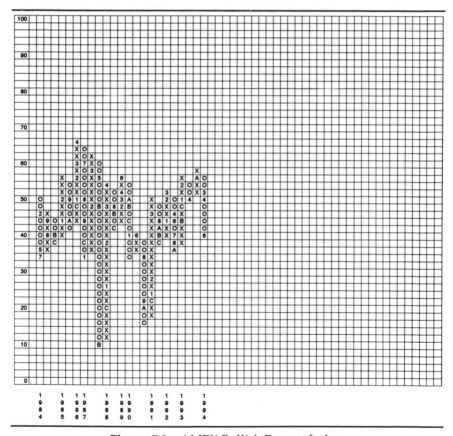

Figure 7.2   AMEX Bullish Percent Index.

percentage of stocks on the NYSE that are trading above their own 10-week moving average (see Figure 7.3). It is as important to keep abreast of the short-term trend of the overall market as it is to keep abreast of the long-term trend. We use the same grid with this index that we use with the Bullish Percent Index. The vertical axis has a value of 2 percent per box and runs from 0 to 100 percent. The best sell signals come when the index rises above the 70 percent level then reverses down below that critical level. In cases like this there is a very high probability that the broad averages have begun a short-term correction. This is significant because the short term often spills over into the long term. Conversely, the best buy signals come when the index declines below the 30 percent level then reverses back up. In the case of the buy signals below 30 percent, the index does not have to cross that level on the upside to be valid. Reversals in the index from below 70 percent or above 30 percent are considered short-term changes within the confines of an

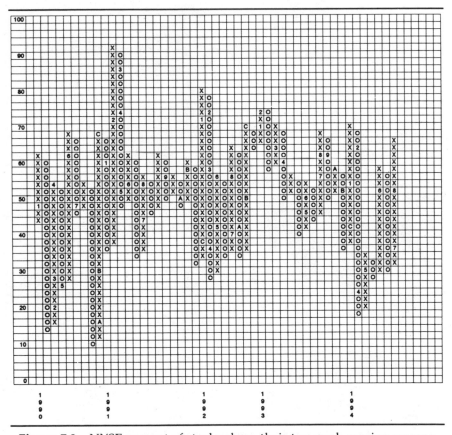

Figure 7.3 NYSE percent of stocks above their ten-week moving average.

existing long-term trend. To change market posture the index must exceed a previous top or bottom, or reverse down from above 70 percent to below 70 percent or simply reverse up from below 30 percent.

For example, say the Percent of 10 reverses up from below 30 percent changing the prevailing risk level to a short-term buy signal. The index then rises to 58 percent where it encounters supply and reverses into a column of O's. This reversal would only suggest that the short-term rally that was in effect is now on hold. It would not be a sell signal. I must add however that since this index is short term it moves like a sports car. An interruption in the trend such as the one we are discussing could easily find the index back below 30 percent, where the whole process would start over. Let's say the index subsequently reverses back up and carries the index to the 74 percent level. It has now crossed that critical 70 percent line where any reversals that carry down below 70 percent will change the signal from short-term buy to short-term sell. The same thing happens when the index moves below 30 percent and reverses up; only at this end of the field, the signal turns to a buy.

This index is of great benefit when you are planning your trade. Investors, however, should never use the Percent of Stocks above Their Own 10-Week Moving Average Index as their sole indicator in making new stock commitments. Traders can effectively use it as a market timing indicator for short-term trades. If the main trend in the market is up as dictated by the New York Bullish Percent Index and the Percent of 10 is on a short-term sell signal, then expect the market to move lower near term. If the main trend is up and the Percent of 10 is on a buy signal, then you are in a market that is bull configured both short and long term. In the latter case, an investor would want to be fully invested. In the former case, an investor looking to make new commitments in the market might postpone buying stock, expecting to take advantage of near-term weakness in the market before making any commitments. I will discuss this index again when we put it all together in later chapters.

The NYSE High-Low Index

This index is another short-term indicator that we use in conjunction with the Percent of 10. You can calculate this one yourself. Just take the daily NYSE Highs divided by the Highs plus the Lows. Then take a 10-day moving average of this number and plot that figure on a grid exactly like the Percent of 10 (see Figure 7.4). The vertical axes will extend from 0 to 100 percent. We evaluate it the same way as the Percent of 10. The two critical levels are 30 percent and 70 percent. Buy signals come from reversals from below 30 percent. Sell signals come from

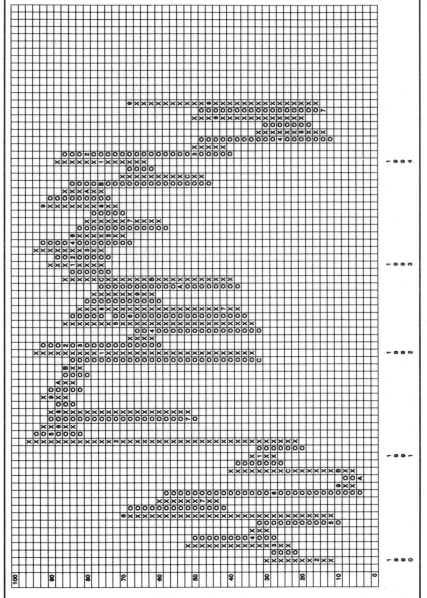

Figure 7.4 NYSE High-Low Index.

114

reversals from above to below 70 percent. Buy and sell signals can also come by exceeding a previous top or bottom respectively. Reversals from above 70 percent suggest that there is a trend change from more stocks making new highs to more stocks making new lows.

One way we have used this indicator is to assist us in timing index option trades. When the index reversed down from above 70 percent, we would buy market index puts. Conversely when the index reversed up from 30 percent, we would buy market index calls. This worked so well that we named the strategy "The Real Deal." We thought we really had something here, like a secret weapon or something. It was like shooting fish in a barrel. It worked so well that we featured the trade, named it the Real Deal, and got all our clients in on the next put trade on a reversal from above 70 percent. The reversal came and we all went in. Well, you know what happens when you begin to think this business is easy and you have found the Holy Grail. You are right, we took the pipe on the trade as we bet lower prices in the market and the market decided to go up like a homesick angel. Some of our customers are the largest trading operations in the world. When they do size, they do real size. Our capital melted on that trade like an ice cream cone on Coney Island in July. After we all tanked on the Real Deal the traders at Morgan Stanley renamed it the "Raw Deal." We haven't gone back to the well on that one yet. As usual, most subsequent trades would have worked well. Those of you who trade index options might want to work this index into your decision-making process. Index traders should also keep close track of the Percent of 10. At any rate, this index does give you a good handle on the short-term picture of the market.

The Percent of 10 and the High-Low typically go in tandem but not always. Sometimes one lags the other. Nothing is ever exact in the markets. These two indicators are our main short-term guides.

The OTC High-Low Index

Because of the increasing number of OTC stocks now traded, I decided to include the OTC High-Low Index in the book (see Figure 7.5). It is evaluated in the same way as the NYSE High-Low Index discussed previously. You can keep this chart yourself with the numbers derived from financial newspapers like *Investor's Daily* or *The Wall Street Journal*.

The Percent of Stocks above Their Own
Thirty-Week Moving Average Index

The Percent of 30 is a longer term index that we follow religiously on a weekly basis. It is constructed by calculating the percentage of stocks

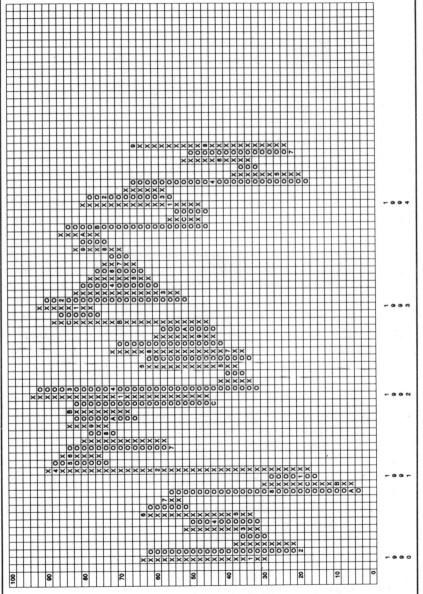

Figure 7.5 OTC High-Low Index.

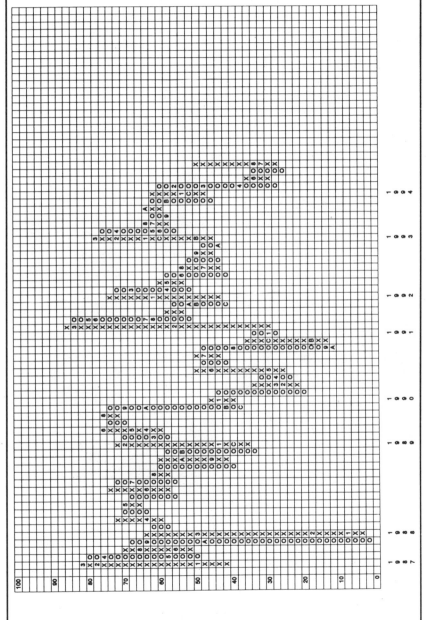

Figure 7.6 NYSE percent of stocks above their thirty-week moving average.

on the NYSE that are trading above their own 30-week moving average (see Figure 7.6). This long-term index does not give many signals; we use it in conjunction with the Percent of 10 and the High-Low Index. We also follow the Percent of 30 on the American Stock Exchange equities as well as the OTC market.

The Daily Range Index

This is a simple index that we set to a Point and Figure chart (see Figure 7.7). The calculation is done on the Bridge Data System, and we transfer that number to a Point and Figure chart. The concept is simple. The Daily Range simply shows where stocks are closing in relation to their quote range each day. Let's look at it on an individual stock basis. If XYZ stock had a high today of $22 and a low of $20 and closed the day's trading at $21, we would say the stock closed at a daily range of

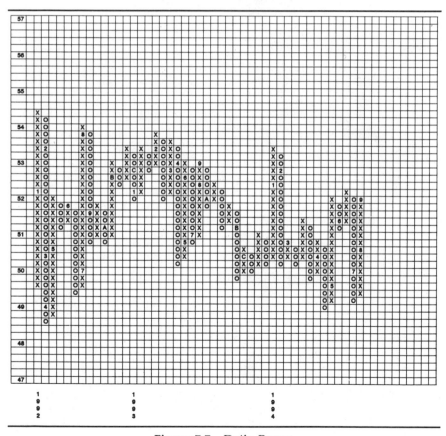

Figure 7.7   Daily Range.

50 percent because $21 is midway between the high and the low for the day. If a stock is consistently closing in the upper quadrant of its quote range each day, it is bullish. Conversely, if a stock is consistently closing in the lower quadrant of its quote range each day, it is bearish. If the stock is closing at 50 percent each day, it is neutral. The Daily Range Index calculates this number on all listed stocks and produces an average range. This gives us a handle on whether the market in general is closing in the upper or lower reaches of its aggregate quote range. We watch for Point and Figure buy and sell signals to suggest whether the Quote Range is about to change direction.

The calculation for the daily range, which is based on each stock's high and low price of the day, is:

$$(Last-Low)/(High-Low) \times 100 = Daily\ Range$$

We keep this indicator daily, and we use a 26-day moving average to smooth it out. Strong buy signals are given when the indicator falls below the 46 percent area. This means that more stocks have been trading below their midrange (50 percent reading). When the 26-day moving average gets below the 46 percent mark, this is generally a low-risk buying opportunity in the market. Previous buy signals have come in June 1982, February 1984, and October 1987. We have not had any buy signals in this index since 1987. As you can see there are few signals, but when they come they require action.

Strong sell signals are given when the indicator rises above the 54 percent area. On a 26-day moving average, a reading above 54 percent shows that a great deal of buying pressure has been occurring. The risk in the market has increased significantly at this point. Sell signals that we have seen in the past were given in November 1982, May 1983, February 1985, December 1985, March 1986, February 1987, January 1992, and August 1992.

Bullish Sentiment Index

Mike Burke of Chartcraft/Investors Intelligence created this index (see Figure 7.8) long ago. He receives hundreds of newsletters each week. He reads them all and categorizes them in either the bullish, bearish, or correction camp. His theory is that when everyone is on one side of the ship, it is best to go to the other side. Most money managers never outperform the broad averages—they have, in essence, become contrary indicators. When the majority of investment advisors are bullish, the market has a high probability of going in the opposite direction, and the opposite is true when there is a high level of bearish

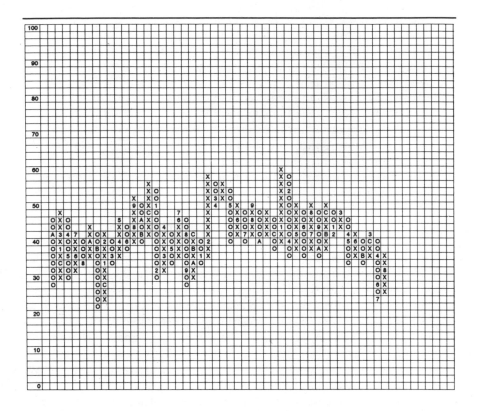

Figure 7.8   Bullish Sentiment Index.

advisors. When the majority are looking for a correction, the current trend will probably continue. Chartcraft/Investors Intelligence puts these numbers out each week along with many other indicators we are covering in this book. I highly recommend you get some samples from this company, which is the biggest and best purveyor of Point and Figure chart information in the world. You will find everything you need to follow this program.

Bearish Sentiment Index

This index is the exact opposite as the Bullish Sentiment Index. It just gauges the percentage of investment advisors that are bearish (see Figure 7.9). When the majority are bearish, expect the market to turn.

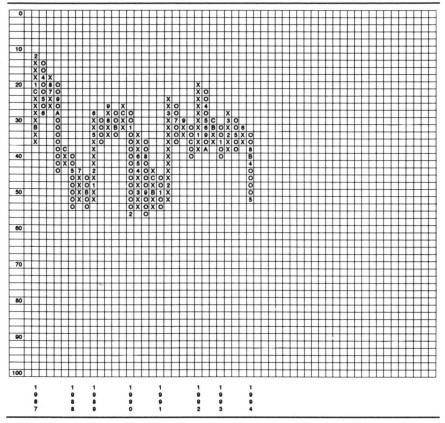

Figure 7.9   Bearish Sentiment Index (inverted).

The Advance-Decline Line

This index is a nonprice measure of the trend of the market. It is based on the number of issues advancing and declining and not on the price of these issues. Every day, the difference between the issues advancing and the issues declining is calculated. If more issues advanced than declined, the difference is added to the preceding day's total; if more issues declined than advanced, the difference is subtracted from the previous day's total. The direction taken by the Advance-Decline line is always compared with an index, such as the Dow Jones Industrial Average. Like the High-Low Index and the Percent of 10, we like to see them both go in the same direction. A divergence typically suggests a change is in the wind. When both these indicators are falling, the market is considered bearish; and conversely when both are rising, the market is considered bullish. This index does not have the weight we place on the Bullish Percent Index.

The Advance-Decline indicator is kept on the New York Stock Exchange as well as on the American Stock Exchange. These charts are interpreted in the same way as the preceding indexes.

Mike Burke has a nifty way of gauging the short-term direction of the market by comparing the cumulative total with the total of 10 days earlier. This can really help in short-term trading conducive to trading in the options market. A total above that of 10 days earlier is positive while a total below that of 10 days earlier suggests lower prices. The levels at which they change are the optimum action points. You can keep this indicator with the numbers found in any reputable business news paper, such as *Investors Business Daily*. By the way, *Investors Business Daily* is probably the best research report you can get on Wall Street for the price. They have some great earnings and relative strength numbers that can help you make stock selection decisions.

The Block Discount

The Block Discount (Figure 7.10) measures the percentage of block trades, 5,000 shares or more, that trade at a discount from the previous trade. Typically a discount from the prior trade means a block of stock was sold as it hit the bid side of the market. The more block selling that occurs, the higher this indicator will go. Remember that institutions can have a major effect on swings in the market. In the case of the chart shown in Figure 7.10, the more blocks that sell, the lower the index will go, because we inverted the chart to more closely correspond with advances and declines in the actual market. We just tend to think in terms of more equals up, and less equals down. The higher the index goes, the more wholesale selling is taking place. We keep this indicator daily and then keep a 26-day moving average of the daily figures to smooth out the chart. We then plot this number on a Point and Figure chart to derive buy and sell signals for this indicator. This indicator was not designed to be Point and Figure driven, but we have found that you can take almost any indicator and set it to a Point and Figure formation. For us, it makes things much more clear and orderly. This has been a good intermediate-term indicator. The following table outlines the buy and sell signals from August 1982 to present. As you can see, we are only going from buy signal to sell signal. It has been a better buy indicator than a sell indicator. But when you get a sell signal in this indicator, it means there is risk in the market and you should closely check the stocks you own for potential problems.

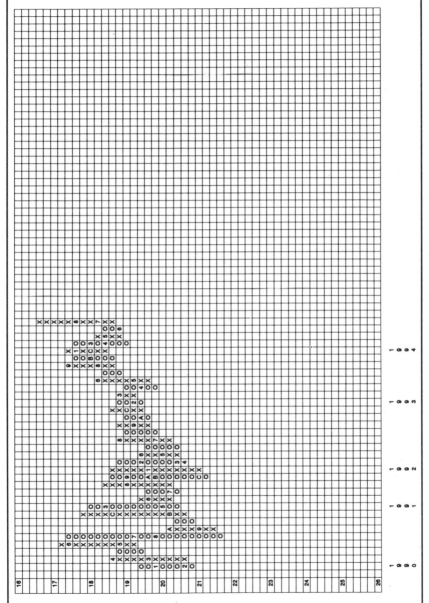

Figure 7.10 Block Discount (inverted).

123

Signal	Date	Dow Level	Percent Gain
Buy	8-31-82	901.31	
Sell	11-12-82	1039.92	+15.38%
Buy	1-20-83	1070.82	
Sell	6-6-83	1214.24	+13.39
Buy	12-13-83	1255.89	
Sell	2-13-84	1150.13	−8.42
Buy	7-2-84	1130.08	
Sell	3-14-85	1260.05	+11.50
Buy	10-23-85	1367.16	
Sell	4-7-86	1735.51	+26.94
Buy	10-27-86	1841.82	
Sell	3-16-87	2248.44	+22.08
Buy	7-9-87	2451.21	
Sell	9-1-87	2610.97	+6.52
Buy	12-30-87	1950.10	
Sell	5-18-88	1951.09	+0.01
Buy	5-31-88	2031.12	
Sell	6-28-89	2504.74	+23.32
Buy	3-9-90	2696.17	
Sell	7-27-90	2898.51	+7.50
Buy	11-5-90	2502.43	
Sell	11-25-91	2902.06	+15.97
Buy	7-29-92	3379.19	
Sell	4-8-93	3396.48	+0.51
Buy	5-21-93	3492.80	
Sell	4-20-94	3598.71	+3.03

The U.S. Dollar Index (J. P. Morgan Index vs. 19 Currencies)

It is always helpful to follow the dollar. We generally don't see strong market rallies last long without the dollar accompanying it. The J. P. Morgan Index is a long-term picture of the dollar (see Figure 7.11). We follow dollar futures each day that move like sports cars compared with this index. For the purposes of stock market investing, we find the J. P. Morgan Index the best. Signals in this index come few and far between but typically are long-lasting. I have also gone back and compared past performance with this index and the NYSE Bullish Percent and found that their signals are usually within a couple of months of each other. Sometimes the dollar leads and sometimes the NYSE Bullish Percent leads. This index was compared with 15 currencies until January 1994. That change is an indication of how global we are becoming. My guess is that in a couple of years the number will increase again.

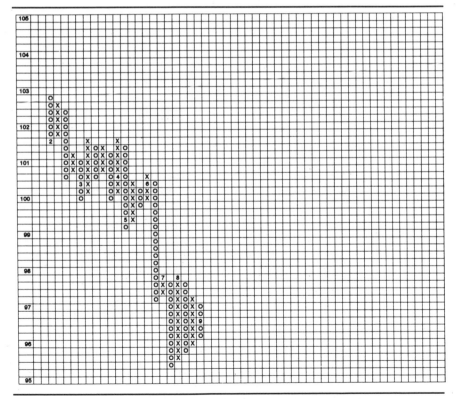

Figure 7.11 U.S. Dollar Index (J.P. Morgan Index vs. 19 Currencies).

TREND CHARTS OF MARKET INDEXES

I want to present the charts of a few indexes we keep on a daily basis to help you see how we use trend charts of sectors along with the Bullish Percent sector indices. I must say though, we defer to the Bullish Percents as our guides for investments. They are the charts that put us in at the bottom and out at the top.

The following charts are trend charts and are evaluated just as you would a stock Point and Figure chart. Keep in mind that a handful of stocks within each average can easily affect the chart, which is why we find the Bullish Percents more useful. Take for instance the Dow Jones Industrial 30. If Coca-Cola, IBM, and General Motors were moving up while the rest were virtually neutral, the average would rise. This is why the NYSE Bullish Percent Index can go through a major decline while the Dow Jones holds up very well. For example in October 1989. The NYSE Bullish Percent reversed down from the 76 percent level, then proceeded to decline all the way to 38 percent. The Dow Jones held up very well during that time because a handful of stocks did well. If your portfolio was made up of those few stocks that did well, then your portfolio was profitable. On the other hand, if you did not have those stocks, you suffered losses. This is why we find the Bullish Percent Indexes more reliable than trend charts of the averages. Despite their weaknesses, however, the trend charts can be helpful.

Dow Jones Industrial Average 10 × 30 (DJIA)

The Dow Jones is the index most widely used to represent the broad market. The 10 × 30 simply means that each box in the chart represents 10 points and a three-box reversal is 30 points (see Figure 7.12). It's an intermediate-term picture. When I was a broker, the first thing my clients would say when they called me was "What's the market doing?" They mean, "What is the Dow Jones Industrial 30 stocks doing." The Dow rarely had anything to do with their portfolio. Although the average can be skewed by a few stocks, we find the guide is useful, especially for the short-term picture. Our market decisions however come from the Bullish Percent Indexes and not the Dow chart.

Dow Jones Industrial Average 20 × 60 (DJIA)

This chart is a very long-term picture of the Dow Jones. The box size is 20 points, and it takes 60 points to reverse three boxes. In Figure 7.13, you can see the large box size reduced the number of signals given. The chart is very orderly. The only problem is that the stops are very painful for anyone wishing to trade using this chart as a guide. We just

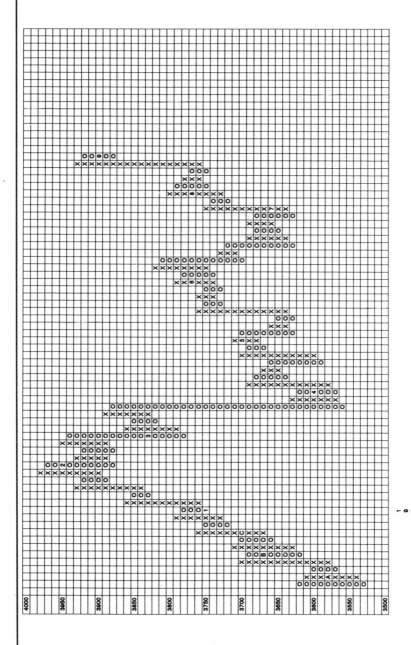

Figure 7.12 Dow Jones Industrial (10 × 30).

127

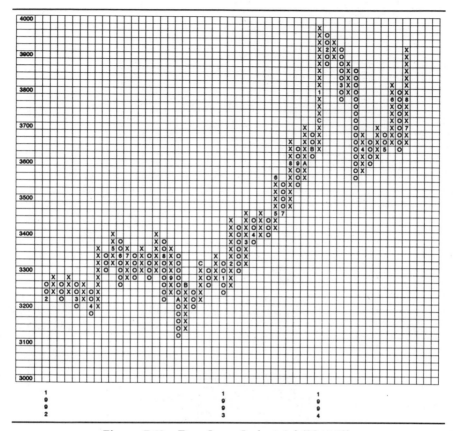

Figure 7.13   Dow Jones Industrial (20 × 60).

keep it for the long-term guidance it provides.

Dow Jones Transportation Index 5 × 15

To confirm a trend, this index should be going in the same direction as the Dow Jones. It's been a tough year for the transports. Figure 7.14 shows a drop in transports from 1850 to 1500.

Dow Jones Utility Average

This index is a good leading indicator for the overall market. It usually changes trend about 3 months before the general stock market. In Figure 7.15, notice the sell signal given in November 1993. Three months

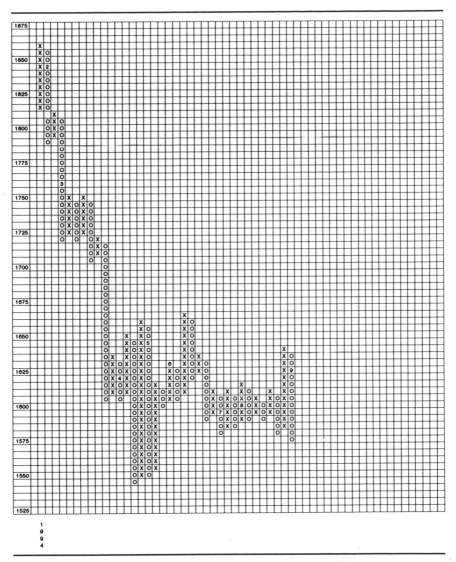

Figure 7.14 Dow Transportation (5 × 15).

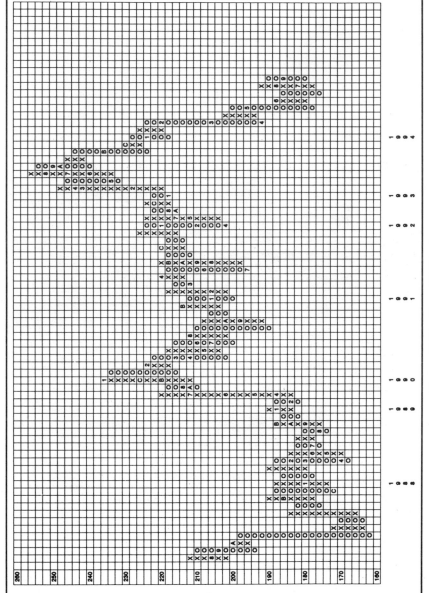

Figure 7.15   Dow Utility Average.

later, the Percent of Stocks above Their Own 10-Week Moving Average Index gave a major sell signal by reversing from above to below 70 percent. This is a good leading indicator. Keep track of it.

AMEX Index (Close Only)

This one is self-explanatory. Once again, this index is heavy in small metals and oil stocks. The rise in August 1994 was helped tremendously by the rise in gold (see Figure 7.16). We don't find much use for this chart; however, we keep it up each day. I guess we are hoping that some major revelation will be revealed by this chart some day.

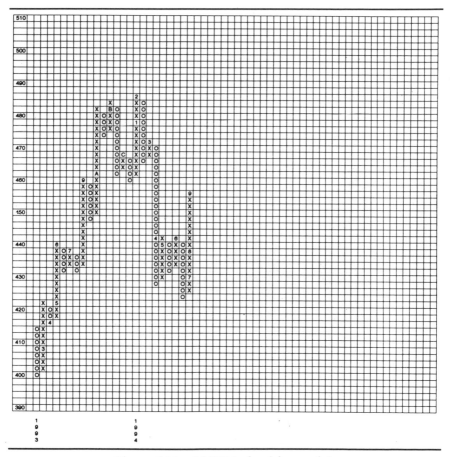

Figure 7.16 AMEX index (close only).

NASDAQ Composite

As shown in Figure 7.17, this chart is somewhat volatile. Our main coach for the OTC stocks is the OTC Bullish Percent. This one helps in timing general advances and declines in the OTC stocks. Always compare this index with the OTC Bullish Percent Index. It is best to have both going in the same direction.

Standard & Poors 500 (SPX)

This is the big Kahuna that most institutions watch. In Figure 7.18, notice the great buy signals this chart shows during 1993. Look at the Triple Top buy signal in August 1993 at 452. The next signal was a

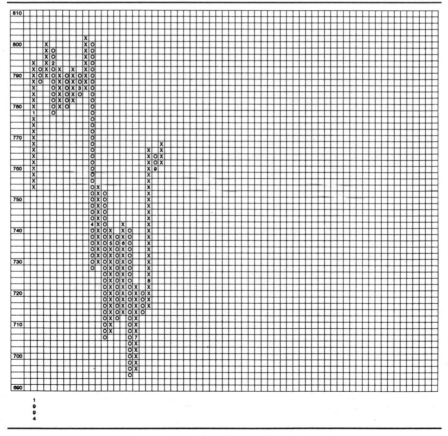

Figure 7.17 NASDAQ Composite.

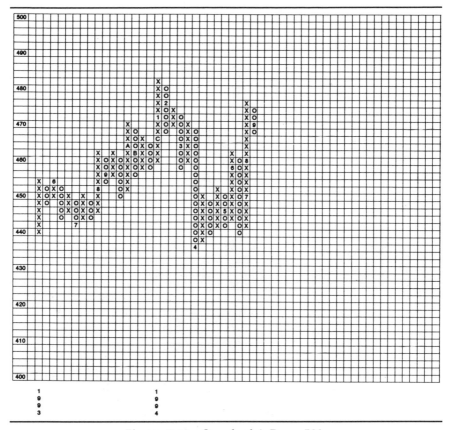

Figure 7.18   Standard & Poors 500.

Shakeout formation at 452 in September 1993. The Shakeout turned into another Triple Top buy signal at 464 in October. The next signal was the breakout from a Triangle formation at 466 in December 1993. What incredible signals! It's interesting to note that the first sell signal off the top came in March 1994 which coincided with a Bear Confirmed reading in the NYSE Bullish Percent Index. Markets in strong uptrends should produce higher bottoms as the chart rises.

New York Stock Exchange Composite Index (NYA)

There are about 2,000 stocks in this index. Just feast your eyes on most of these chart patterns going back to 1990 (Figure 7.19). They'll make your eyes roll like the tape on a cash register. The long-term trend line remains intact during the whole trend. The Point and Figure signals

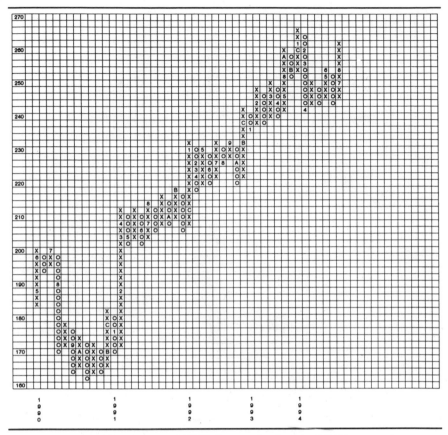

Figure 7.19   NYSE Composite Index (NYA).

were impeccable. All investors had to do was buy the index futures on the buy signals and stop out on the sell signals. The net result would have been a tremendous profit. Most market participants do not watch this index as closely as the Dow Jones and the Standard & Poors 500, but we think it is worthy of comparison with the other broad averages. It is a large index and not easily swayed by a few stocks.

Value Line Index (VLE)

This index (see Figure 7.20) is the king of the little guys. Although this is looked at primarily as a small cap index, it does have the S&P 500 stocks in it. There are about 2,500 stocks underlying the index. Options trade on the Philadelphia Stock Exchange.

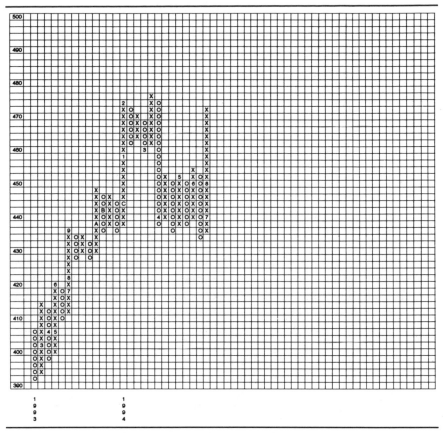

Figure 7.20 Value Line Index (VLE).

BOND MARKET INDICATORS

For years now the stock and bond markets have been closely linked. For this reason, I feel it is important to show you a couple of the bond indicators that we use on a daily basis. Interest rates are a critical ingredient in investors' decision making. They weigh the advantages of holding interest rate-bearing securities against holding equities. As rates rise, investors typically move out of stocks and into interest-rate-bearing securities. This disintermediation causes excess supply in the equity markets driving prices lower. This is a very simplistic explanation of how interest rates affect the stock markets. There have been books written on the subject. For our purposes, we simply want to get a handle on whether we expect rates to rise or fall. Again, we will endeavor to keep things simple. There are only a few indicators we use daily. What we really do is simply update the charts each day by hand and that forces us to keep track of what is going on in the bond market. These indicators were all created by Chartcraft many years ago.

The NYSE Bond High-Low Index

This Bond High-Low Index is exactly like the NYSE Stock High-Low Index. It too is short term in nature. It is simply calculated by taking the NYSE daily bond highs divided by the daily bond highs plus the lows. Then you take a 10-day moving average of that calculation and plot the result on the graph with the vertical axis going from 0 to 100 percent. When the Bond High-Low Index is above the 70 percent level, we say it's high, or overbought. Conversely, when the Index is below the 30 percent level, we say it's low or oversold. In most cases, the truth lies somewhere in between. Reversals from above to below 70 percent are sell signals suggesting lower prices in bonds and thus higher interest rates. Reversals from below 30 percent are short-term buy signals and suggest lower rates. When the index is rising in a column of X's, traders should be long bonds. As the index rises, your enthusiasm for bonds should diminish correspondingly. At the 30 percent level, X's convey a very different meaning than at the 70 percent level. Conversely, O's at the 70 percent level carry far more risk than O's at the 30 percent level. There are only two ways a buy signal can be reversed: (1.) By the index exceeding a previous bottom thus giving a simple bearish signal; (2.) by rising above 70 percent and then reversing to below that critical 70 percent level. Sell signals cannot be reversed unless a buy signal is given or the index declines below the 30 percent level then reverses up. In Figure 7.21, notice how a reversal from below 30 percent is all that is required to put the index on a buy signal. From that level, the index does not have to cross that critical 30 percent level. When the index is above 70 percent, it must cross that level to actually give a sell signal. These are the rules governing this index. We have a tendency to be a little more flexible with the rules in our daily operation.

Investing is not and never will be a science. It is an art that requires the human thought process. Investors who buy into computer programs that are supposed to do all the thinking for them, will be unhappily surprised when they find out there is no substitute for a thorough education in how the market works.

The Dow Jones 20 Bond Average

This is one of our long-term bond indicators. The Dow Jones 20 Bond Average is simply placed on a Point and Figure chart. The box size is .20 per box. The average moves slowly and does not often give signals, but

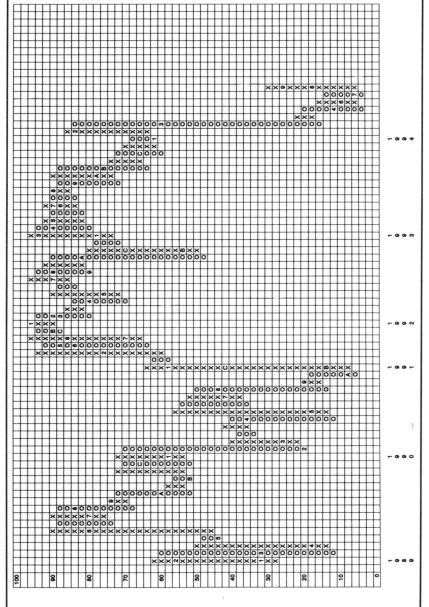

Figure 7.21 NYSE Bond High-Low Index.

when they occur, you must pay close attention. Figure 7.22 shows the infrequency of signals. In our daily *Equity Market Report* back in October 1993, I said that if this bond index gives a sell signal it will suggest that rates are about to rise and anyone who has an adjustable mortgage, lock in the current rate. I watched the sell signal given in November 1993, and the index was dead on the money. Did I lock in my adjustable mortgage? No. Here I sit praying for lower rates. The moral to the story is, trust the indicators. At this writing (September 1994), the chart (Figure 7.22) is in a column of O's, at the 97.20 box. A move to 98.40 would give a Double Top buy signal and be very positive for bonds. Right now, we sit and wait. At this point, we do not know if the bond average will take another move south and break the Double Bottom already made at 96.60 or break the top at 98.40. You can get the data to

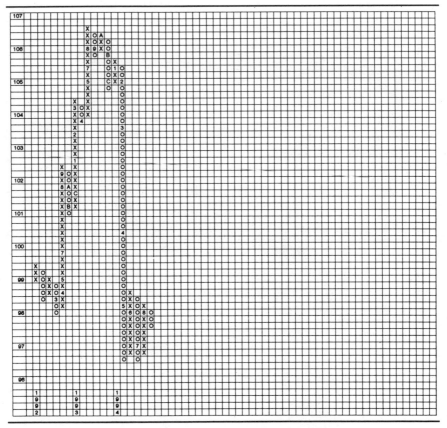

Figure 7.22　Dow Jones 20-Bond Average.

keep this bond chart from *The Wall Street Journal* or any reputable daily business paper that contains bond quotes.

NYSE Bond Cumulative Advance-Decline Line

This indicator is the cumulative sum of the daily advancing bonds minus the number declining. Like the advance-decline stock indicators, this is a nonprice measure of bond market performance. The direction taken by the advance-decline line is compared to that of the

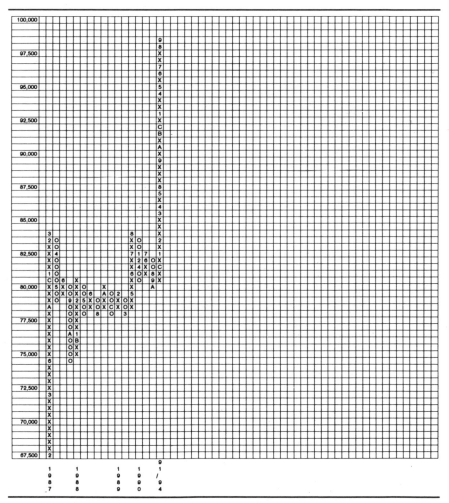

Figure 7.23 NYSE Bond Advance-Decline Line.

Dow Jones 20 Bond Average. When both are advancing, the bond market is bullish. Conversely, the bond market is bearish if both are declining. A divergence in direction between the two usually indicates a coming change in trend. Chartcraft compares the most recent cumulative total to the total 10 days ago to check the short-term momentum in the bond market. A total higher than 10 days ago is positive, while a lower total is negative. We have found this to be very helpful in short-term moves in bonds.

8

SECTOR ANALYSIS

SECTOR ANALYSIS WITH BULLISH PERCENT INDEXES

Chartcraft developed this way of thinking many years ago. Sector analysis is one of the most important yet least analyzed parts of the market. We place tremendous emphasis on sector rotation in our daily work. I have said in previous chapters that probably 75 percent of the risk in a stock is the market and sector. Stocks don't just jump about with no rhyme or reason. Moves tend to be orchestrated.

When I think of Sector Rotation one analogy keeps coming to mind. I picture a herd of wildebeest romping across the African plains. They move in unison, first in one direction, then another. A few of the herd get out of sync, but the majority go together. Sectors operate the same way. Wall Street tends to follow the herd. First one analyst raises the earnings expectation, then the rest follow and before you know it the sector is in play.

As the sector moves up, other institutions see the move and climb on board. Eventually the mainstream financial periodicals catch wind of a major move underway and begin to write articles about how the industry has made a turnaround and should have clear sailing ahead. This draws in the individual investor just in time to catch the top. By the time the articles appear in magazines about how great the industry is, almost everyone is in that wants to be in. The last group is the unsuspecting public, who use newspapers and magazines as their primary source of stock market research.

Once the public is in, virtually no one is left to do the buying. Remember that prices move as a direct result of supply-and-demand imbalances. If there are no more buyers left to cast their vote, supply by definition must take the upper hand. The sector then begins to lose sponsorship, and the whole process begins again only in reverse this time.

Watch magazine covers carefully. The next time you are in the airport look at the magazine rack and see if you can find a widely read magazine that makes a major statement on its cover about some sector of the market—something like "The Banking Industry Is Dead." If you find one, buy the magazine and keep it. Normally, the trend in that sector will continue to move for a couple of months in the direction the cover describes. Give that sector 8 months, and you will find its behavior is the exact opposite of that suggested on the magazine cover. The reason for this is that the cover stirs Mr. Jones and Ms. Smith into action and while all the Jones and Smiths are busy reacting, the sector moves in the forecasted direction. Once these investors are in and the door slams behind them, there is no more buying or selling pressure (whichever the cover suggests) left to sponsor the sector. The forces of supply and demand slowly begin to change, and the sector takes the opposite track. Try it—you will be amazed. It's simply human nature.

Magazines are in business to write about what is happening today, not in the future. Think of the magazine covers that forewarned the demise of the automobile industry in 1992. They would have had the American public believe that the auto industry was dead on arrival: cause of death, Japanese competition. Well that was right at the bottom of the auto cycle, and the opportunities for those willing to step up to the plate and buy were tremendous; I mean prices like Chrysler in January 1992 around $15 per share on its way to a high of $63½. Very few Wall Street companies were willing to take that step in early 1992, but by January 1994 everyone wanted this new efficient, profitable sector.

It's absolutely amazing how you can use many magazines as contrary indicators. Mike Burke, the editor of Chartcraft/Investors Intelligence, instilled in me a long time ago that everything written about stocks in the media is designed to make you do the wrong thing. If you keep that in mind, you will never get caught up in the story of the moment. You must remember, to be successful in the stock market you must look ahead: What is happening in the market today has already been discounted many months ago.

When evaluating sectors, you must be a contrarian. You must find the courage to buy stocks in sectors that are out of favor. You must avoid the crowd, go the opposite direction. This is extremely difficult as it goes against human nature. When I was a stockbroker, I went with the crowd. It was easier to do business that way. Although I was at a major wirehouse with highly paid fundamental analysts, my primary source of research was *The Wall Street Journal* and *Barron's* weekly financial newspaper. When those didn't yield enough ideas, I listened to the broker next to me pitching a stock. All of us got ideas the same way, and as you have already guessed, the process was hit or miss at best. Our training back then was basically sales training and not much else. It really hasn't changed much since then. Now the emphasis is on packaged products, and good stockbrokers are a rare breed indeed. When you find one, stick with that broker. Real money is still made in the stock market, not the package products.

Our method of evaluating sectors is the Chartcraft method developed back in 1955. Mike Burke adapted the method developed by A. W. Cohen to sector analysis. Sector rotation is one of the most important parts of our daily operation. We have made some of the most tremendous calls on sectors an analyst could make. All the credit goes to Mike Burke, not us. He had the foresight to create a way to buy sectors when they are out of favor and sell sectors when they are in favor. Our success has come simply from following his lead and having the strength in our conviction to go out on a limb, way out, when need be. We also have a great computer programmer, who understands us. He has written us some tremendous programs that do numerous sector calculations for us.

Like Chartcraft, we run Bullish Percent calculations on *Investor's Daily* sectors. In Chapter 6, we discussed the NYSE Bullish Percent Index in detail. The same principles apply here. Years ago, Mike Burke decided that since the Bullish Percent philosophy worked so well with the New York Stock Exchange, it should be adaptable to broad industry sectors. He was right on the money. I have found no better way to evaluate sectors. The Bullish Percent Indexes provide a soulless barometer of sector valuation.

In the 1940s, Earnest Staby first began to think of developing a contrary indicator for the market. He was concerned because trend charts of broad averages were always bullish at the top and always bearish at the bottom. There was a need for an indicator or coach that would put the players in at bargain prices and take players out at inflated prices. It took until 1955 for A. W. Cohen to develop the first Bullish Percent Index. The Bullish Percent Indexes are simply a compilation of the percentage of stocks underlying the index that are on Point and Figure buy signals. I really don't think he realized how accurate and important this indicator would become.

This method of analysis is also relatively unheard of on Wall Street. You would be hard-pressed to find a broker, outside our clients or Chartcraft's, that understand this philosophy. The reason is simple, it takes some education to understand it, and most investors and professionals are interested in the computer program that will supply the Holy Grail. Those of you who are reading this book are a rare breed indeed. You are learning a lost art. Just as in the NYSE Bullish Percent, the Sector Bullish Percents are simply a compilation of the percentage of stocks underlying the sector that are on Point and Figure buy signals.

In a recent daily *Equity Market Report* I wrote an article about how it's OK to be wrong in the market but staying wrong is the real killer. The discussion revolves around how the Bullish Percent Indexes, by definition, will prevent you from staying wrong in your evaluation of the prevailing risk in any particular sector.

It's OK to Be Wrong But Not OK to Stay Wrong

Equity Market Report October 27, 1994

There is no crystal ball in this business although most investors continue to search high and wide for it. What totally changes my life is coming to the realization that supply and demand drives the stock market as it does every other thing in our lives, bar none. This simple concept is such a major revelation to clients when I hold customer seminars. It's a relief to them to see the same forces they understand when shopping in the supermarket are the same forces which drive their portfolios. The average person in America has a very good handle on why winter squash is expensive in July and summer squash is expensive in January. When they find out stocks and sectors come in and out of season just like produce they become much more comfortable about investing. When they have a broker or money manager who has a good solid approach to assisting them in managing their money, using both fundamental analysis and technical analysis side by side, they need look no further.

No one expects their broker or money manager to be perfect. There will be mistakes made and detours taken but it's the broker or manager who can find his way back to his original route after a detour is taken that shines like a diamond. The NYSE Bullish Percent is your guiding light. It won't always be perfect but the very few times it is not a leading indicator it, by definition, must get back in stride in short order. Let's say over the next few weeks we do see the NYSE Bullish Percent Index hit the 44 percent level where the risk level changes to Bear Confirmed. Let's further say instead of moving lower the market begins to rally leaving you bewildered, especially those who are new clients. If the rally is more than a flash in the pan, more stocks will go on buy signals than sell signals and within a couple of weeks will reverse up again going back into a column of X's and force you to change back to bullish. This type of action prevents you from being one of these analysts (investors) who becomes bearish and never changes, not believing the market can go against them. The net result is they run their clients into a pack of wolves like many I could name. This index takes the subjective feelings out of it. In the case above, the worst thing that happened is you missed an opportunity but got back in stride in short order. The example is not likely to happen and has only happened once since we have been using this index as our guiding light for over a decade. Our fine-tuning mechanisms are the two short term indicators, the Percent of Stocks above Their 10-Week Moving Average and the NYSE High-Low Index. With the three we won't be off base for long. Don't worry about being wrong, just don't stay wrong.

This same philosophy applies to sectors. Being in the wrong sector can happen. Staying in the wrong sector is a mistake that need not be made if one simply uses the Sector Bullish Percent Indexes to guide their investment decisions.

A REVIEW OF THE SIX RISK LEVELS

As discussed in Chapter 6, there are six degrees of risk. We will go over them once again before we evaluate Sector Bullish Percent Indexes:

1. *Bull Alert.* A reversal up to a column of X's from below the 30 percent level. Strategy: Buy stocks with positive chart patterns and positive relative strength in that sector. The tide has come in, and all stocks underlying the sector should rise. If you have held on through the last decline, don't sell now. The news will still be negative in this sector. Disregard it. Offensive team comes on the field.

2. *Bull Confirmed.* The index simply exceeds a previous column of X's by one or more boxes. Strategy: Continue to buy stocks as the rally is broadening out.

3. *Bull Correction.* A reversal down to a column of O's from Bull Confirmed status when the index is below the 70 percent level. Strategy: Hold off making any more stock commitments while the underlying sector remains in this risk level. You will probably get better prices if you hold off and allow the stock to come to you. Stocks should correct in the near term but the Bull Market is still on long term. Declines in the broad averages are likely to be limited while rallies will be more extended.

4. *Bear Alert.* A reversal into a column of O's from above to below 70 percent. Strategy: Evaluate all stocks in your portfolio in this sector. Sell any stock giving sell signals. Go into a heightened state of awareness with respect to this sector. The probability is lower prices for all stocks underlying the sector. The news will still be very positive in this sector; disregard it. OK to sell short. Defensive team comes on the field.

5. *Bear Confirmed.* The index simply exceeds a previous column of O's by one or more boxes. Strategy: Continue to sell bad stocks; you can continue to sell short as long as this risk level takes place above 50 percent. We want good field position when initiating short sales. Good field position for a short is when the sector is above 50 percent.

6. *Bear Correction.* A reversal up to a column of X's from Bear Confirmed status when the index is above the 30 percent level. Strategy: Discontinue selling short for now. Stocks should rise and the
Dow Jones will likely move higher but the percentage of stocks that
go on buy signals from that level will be limited. The next reversal
down reverts back to Bear Confirmed. Rallies will be limited while
declines will be extended.

Keep firmly in mind that field position is as important as the risk
level. Think of the vertical axes on the Bullish Percent Index as a football field—0–100 yards. The 30 percent level and below is the green
zone and 70 percent and higher is the red zone. When I stress the importance of field position, I mean that your relative location on the
playing field is critical in determining what play to run. It is possible
for a sector to change risk levels to Bull Confirmed status at the 68 percent level. Although Bull Confirmed means the rally is broadening out,
70 percent also begins the red zone. Field position in this case would
override the risk level. By the same token, Bull Confirmed at 30 percent
is a very powerful signal and should be played heavily. In football ver-
nacular, Bull Confirmed at 30 percent means you can throw the long
passes, take the most chances, go for the most yards. Bull Confirmed at
68 percent means that you still have the ball but your plays should be
conservative. Give the ball to the biggest back and let him try to inch
his way up the field. Run conservative plays. When the index is rising
in a column of X's you have the football. When the index is declining in
a column of O's, the sector has the ball. I can't emphasize this concept
enough. Be constantly aware of your field position. Investing can be so
much fun and so rewarding when you have a game plan to go by. Here
are some guidelines we use when investing in stocks. We have a money
management arm of Dorsey, Wright & Associates in Beverly Hills, California, that adheres to the following principles:

1. Buy stocks when the NYSE Bullish Percent is in one of the three
   buy modes.
2. Buy stocks in sectors that are on one of the three buy modes.
3. The underlying sector being considered for purchase should be
   below the 50 percent level. This ensures adequate field position.
4. Look for potential short sales when the NYSE Bullish Percent is in
   one of the three sell modes.
5. Sell weak stocks with negative relative strength in sectors that are
   on one of the three sell modes.
6. The underlying sector being considered for short sales should be
   above the 50 percent level. This ensures good field position for a
   short sale.

THE MAJORITY OF RISK IN A STOCK— THE SECTOR AND THE MARKET

Another word for risk is volatility. A dictionary definition of volatile would be "likely to shift quickly and unpredictably; unstable; explosive; not lasting long; vaporizing or evaporating quickly . . ." The way we judge the risk in a stock, sector, or the market is to gauge their respective volatilities. We use computer systems to do these volatility calculations. The one we find to be most accurate is the Bloomberg Financial Markets. At this writing, the Standard & Poors 500 has a volatility of approximately 14.43 percent. Amgen (AMGN) has a volatility of approximately 21.87 percent. The American Stock Exchange Biotechnology Index (BTK) has a volatility of approximately 19.62 percent. OK, now let's calculate the implied risk in each component of the underlying stock. If we divide the S&P 500 volatility of 14.43 by AMGN's volatility of 21.87 we get a percentage of 65.98 or market risk equals 65.98 percent of the stock price. To calculate the Sector risk level, we divide the volatility for the Biotech sector which is 19.62 by the volatility of the stock which is 21.87 and we get 89.71. This calculation gives us both sector risk and market risk. To separate out the percentage of risk the sector has on the stock, we would substract 65.98 (market risk) from 89.71 (sector risk + market risk) to get 23.73 percent. The net result of all this is:

Market risk	= 65.98%
Sector risk	= 23.73
Amgen risk	= 10.29
Market and sector risk	= 89.71

This suggests that investors should spend more time evaluating the overall market and sector than evaluating the fundamentals of the individual stock. The components of risk will change as volatility changes, but this example points up why we are spending so much time on this chapter. I want you to become very familiar with the Sector Bullish Percent Indexes.

Aerospace—Airlines

The first thing your eye can readily discern in Figure 8.1 is how this sector typically tops out in the 70 percent to 80 percent level and typically bottoms out between 10 percent and 30 percent. Remember the red zone is above 70 percent and the green zone is below 30 percent. In many cases, the truth lies somewhere in between. Remember that if the index is rising in a column of X's you have the ball and a column of O's suggests the sector has the ball. Notice in the chart the letters A, B, and

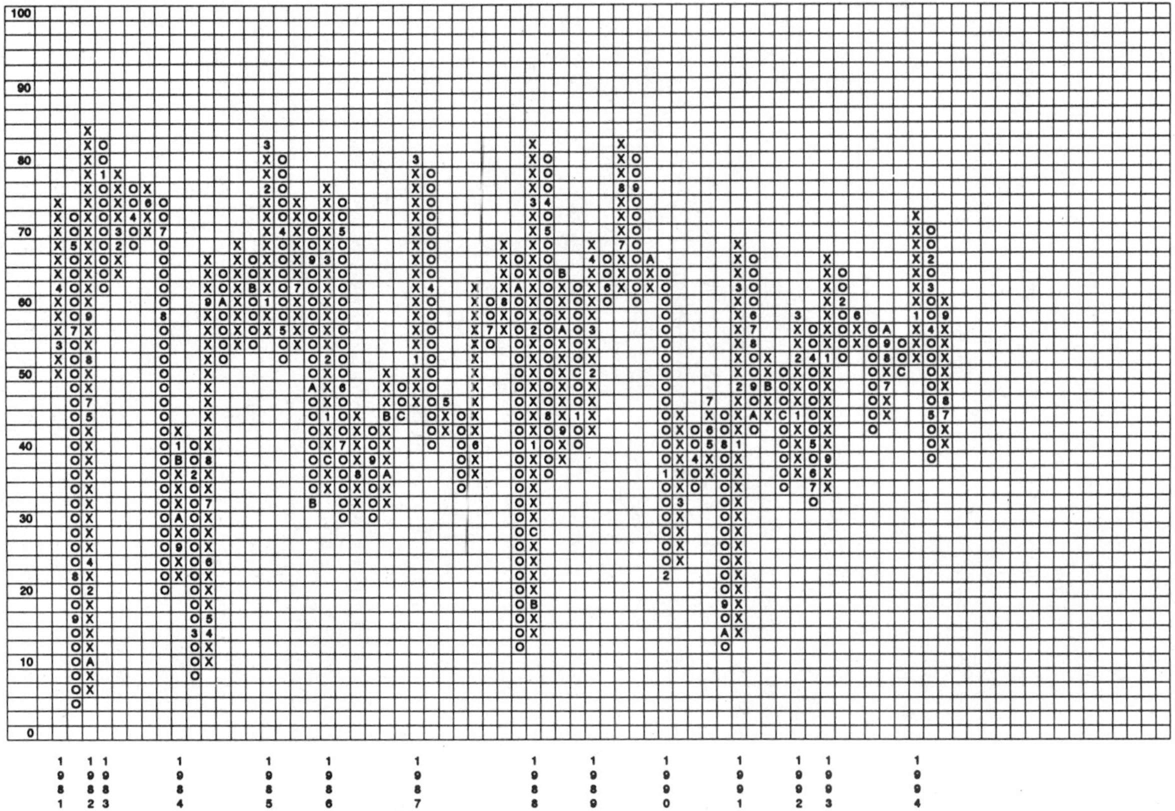

Figure 8.1 Aerospace—Airlines.

C. They represent the months October, November, and December. The other numbers in the chart represent the months of the year. If you were looking for January 1994, go over to the 1994 column and up to the number 1 for January. The months in the chart represent the first entry on the chart that month. Look over to the 1981 column and the letter "A" at the 10 percent level. Notice how this index reversed up in October 1981 giving you possession of the ball at the 10 percent level. What field position! The index then moves up over the next year to a level of 84 percent before trouble set in. Another thing interesting to note in this sector is that after the first reversal in January 1983, the index produced lower tops each subsequent time it reversed up until the plug was pulled in July 1983. Now go over to the right in the chart to 1994. Notice how the sector took possession of the ball in February 1994 placing your defensive team on the field. I say the sector took possession of the football because the index reversed into a column of O's in February 1994 (notice the 2 in the column of O's. The risk level changed in April at 48 percent by exceeding a previous bottom. In July, the index reversed back up into a column of X's again, changing the risk level to Bear Correction.

Autos and Auto Parts

September 1987 is one of the most interesting dates to evaluate in the chart shown in Figure 8.2. Go to the 1987 column and over 5 columns to the right. The column is O's declining from 70 percent to a low of 14 percent. Now look up to the "9" in that column. It shows that in September 1987 the autos and auto parts sector went to defense, or in this case Bear Alert status, suggesting lower price. Anyone willing to follow this index was able to get out before the October crash. In February 1994, the sector gave the exact same signal, and it was right on the money. Let's look for a moment at the other side of the coin. How was it at major turning points from low levels? Look at the bottom of the 1987 crash. The subsequent reversal into a column of X's happened in November 1987. Notice the "B" in the column of X's following the crash. "B" represents November. We use the letters *A*, *B*, and *C* for October, November, and December, as mentioned earlier, because those months have two digits and cannot fit in the small box. Notice the reversal in November 1990 off the bottom. Remember, you take possession of the football when the index reverts to a column of X's. At this writing, the reversal into a column of X's in August 1994 simply changes the risk level to Bear Correction status. This is similar to a traffic light changing from red to flashing red.

The following excerpts are from news releases issued when the auto sector was at the bottom. The news releases on Chrysler appeared

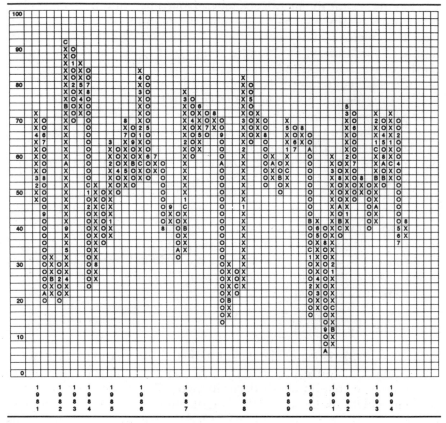

Figure 8.2   Autos and auto parts.

when the stock had already bottomed and was in a strong uptrend and the relative strength chart had turned positive. See if this news would give you confidence to invest in the auto stocks close to the bottom:

1992 AUTOMOBILE NEWS

Detroit, March 12 (Bloomberg Financial Markets) Chrysler Corp. said today it will close three of its eight U.S. vehicle assembly plants for between one and three weeks because of slow sales.

Earlier today, General Motors Corp. said it would idle its Pontiac West truck plant in Pontiac, Mich., and car plant in Doraville, Ga., because of slow sales.

New York, March 13 (Bloomberg Financial Markets) Chrysler Corp.'s sales of U.S. built cars fell 12.6% in early March to 13,550. Year to date, Chryslers domestic car sales were estimated to have fallen 20.0%.

New York, Sep. 8 (Bloomberg Financial Markets) Paine Webber widened the estimated loss per share of General Motors Corp.

New York, Sept. 9 (Bloomberg Financial Markets) General Motors was cut to "Neutral" from "Attractive" by a Wertheim Schroder analyst on concern that the auto manufacturer will have trouble pushing through its cost-cutting plan, brokers at the firm said. GM $33⅝.

New York, Sep. 9 (Bloomberg Financial Markets) Goldman Sachs lowered the estimated earnings per share of General Motors Corp.

New York, Sept. 10 (Bloomberg Financial Markets) A Merrill Lynch analyst reduced his 1993 earnings estimates for General Motors Corp., Ford Motor Co., and Chrysler Corp., based on continued softness in the economy.

New York, Sept. 10 (Bloomberg Financial Markets) General Motors, Ford Motor, Gentex Corp., and Superior Industries were changed to "Hold" from "Buy" this morning by a Prudential Securities analyst. The rating changes were predicated on the economy. "Basically the economy is dead in its tracks and the recovery in the auto industry has stalled" the analyst said. GM $33⅝, Ford $40⅜.

New York, Sep. 11 (Bloomberg Financial Markets) Salomon Brothers lowered the estimated earnings per share of General Motors Corp. for the fiscal year ending December 1993 to $2.75 from $3.50.

New York, Sep. 11 (Bloomberg Financial Markets) Smith Barney lowered the estimated earnings per share of General Motors Corp. for the fiscal year ending December 1992 to a loss of 17 cents from a profit of 33 cents.

New York, Sept. 17 (Bloomberg Financial Markets) General Motors and Volvo AB were lowered to "Hold" from "Buy" this morning by a Bear Stearns analyst, brokers at the firm say. GM $33¼.

New York, Sept. 22 (Bloomberg Financial Markets) Chrysler Corp. was lowered to "Neutral" from "Attractive" this morning by a Wertheim Schroder analyst, brokers at the firm said. Chrysler $23½.

Chrysler was now up $6 from our recommendation based on the Point and Figure chart, and in addition, the relative strength Point and Figure chart turned positive for the first time in 4 years in March 1992.

New York, Sept. 23 (Bloomberg Financial Markets) General Motors Corp. was lowered to "Neutral" from "Outperform" by a Lehman Brothers analyst, research officials at the firm said. GM $32¾.

New York, Sept. 23 (Bloomberg Financial Markets) General Motors slump continues; Merrill drops rating. The slump in General Motors Corp. is gaining momentum as analysts turn increasingly pessimistic about the earnings outlook for the automobile manufacturer.

News like this will have a tendency to hold investors back. They typically want to wait until they read favorable stories about what is happening fundamentally with an industry before they jump in. The good news they are waiting for usually comes at the top.

I can tell you that if I had these charts to use when I was a broker, I would have avoided a lot of heartache. When we get to the precious metals sector, I'll tell you a story that will make your hair stand on end.

Banks

Here's an interesting group. This sector isn't quite as easy to analyze as possibly the autos. They don't produce durable goods. Lots of economic factors can affect banks and many investors have just thrown

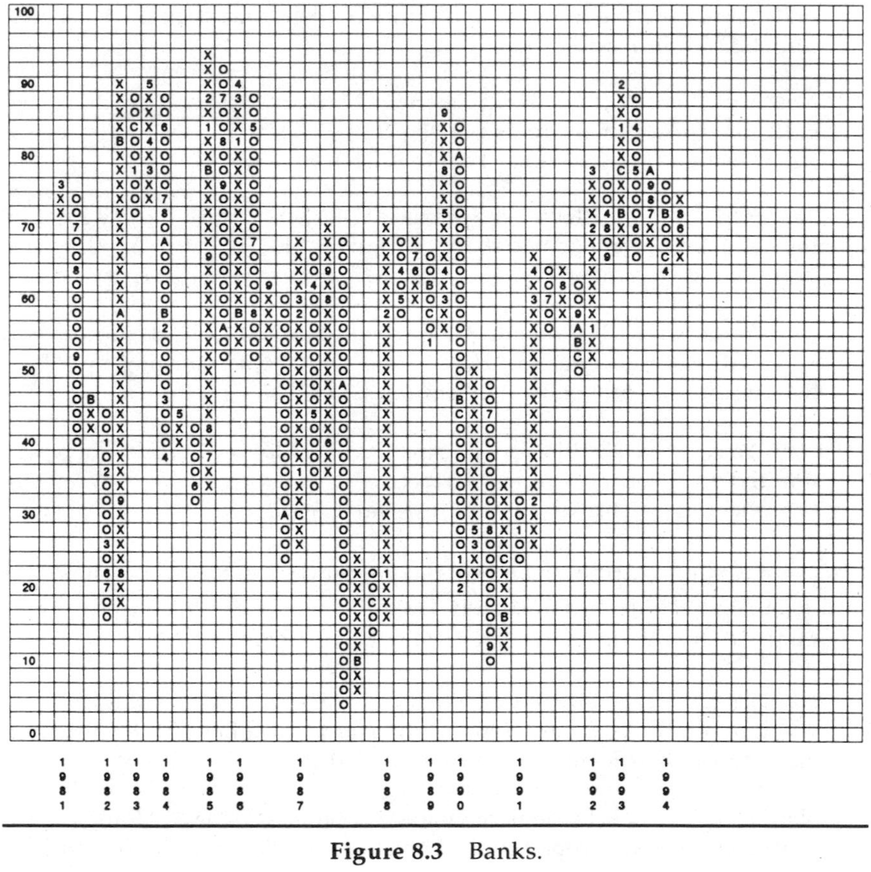

Figure 8.3 Banks.

their hands up in confusion and have chosen to avoid these stocks. It does not have to be that difficult. The idea with the Bullish Percent Indexes is that those who really do understand a particular sector operate early on. As they begin to operate in the group, they buy or sell stocks that cause the Point and Figure charts to give buy or sell signals. By compiling these charts into one index, investors can see what the insiders are doing. As shown in Figure 8.3, the index declined to 10 percent in October 1990. The magazine articles of that time suggested that the banking industry would go the way of the savings and loans. Bankruptcies would abound; it was definitely a group to avoid. I remember this so vividly I get goose bumps as I'm writing this because of the unbelievable opportunity the sector Bullish Percent presented us at that time. Well, in November 1990, the index reversed up from 10 percent (notice the "B" in the column of X's right after the bottom at 10 percent in 1990). That reversal suggested that investors now had possession of the football and they had better start running plays. In February 1991, the index exceeded a previous column of X's and the risk level changed to Bull Confirmed status at the 36 percent level. That's like riding into Dodge City on your horse, planning to rob a bank, and finding out the sheriff is on vacation. Anyone who bought bank stocks in November 1990 did exceedingly well. Of course, the business periodicals led most investors down the wrong path. In August 1994, the index was at 72 percent and in a column of X's.

Biomedics/Genetics

Here is a wild sector. This is not one to invest in haphazardly. These stocks can really move about and tend to go in unison. Figure 8.4 shows that the index reversed down from a high of 74 percent in December 1992. Notice how the column of O's declines down to 24 percent without a reversal. Premier companies such as Amgen were virtually cut in half without the benefit of a split. There was nothing wrong with the company itself. Their outlook was still just as bright. The management was the same but the stock still got cut in half. Could this have been avoided? Yes. Simply by taking action when the sector went to defense. Let's evaluate the sequence of events beginning at the bottom of the crash we just discussed. In February 1993 the index bottomed at 24 percent. The subsequent reversal into X's in March 1993 changed the risk level to Bull Alert status. This is the same as the traffic light changing from red to green. This risk level was very short lived as the index again reversed down in April to a low of 26 percent. Notice how that low was higher than the previous low in March of 24 percent. This is a sign that things are getting better. The reversal back down in April is not important because it took place in the green zone below 30 percent. It does

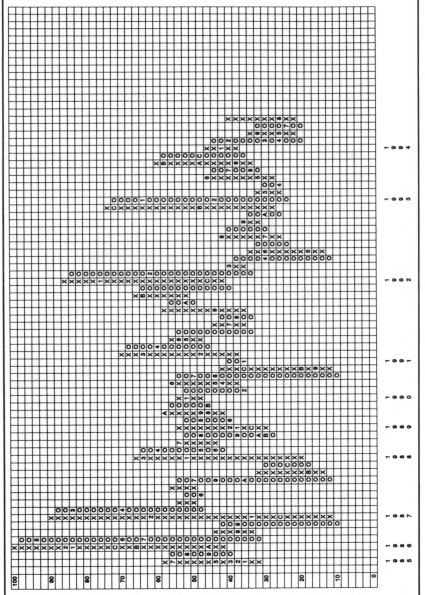

Figure 8.4　Biomedics/Genetics.

however suggest that no further buying be done in this sector. Any stocks you bought on the reversal up should be held. In May ("5"), the index reversed up into a column of X's and also exceeded the previous column of X's. The risk level now changed to Bull Confirmed status.

Over the next month, the index rose to 46 percent where it once again lost sponsorship. In July ("7"), the index reversed down changing the risk level to Bull Correction status. This means that the bull market was still intact but you have experienced an interception and your opponent now has the ball temporarily. No further buying but hold the stocks you have. In September ("9") the index reverses up into a column of X's changing the risk level back to Bull Confirmed status. OK to begin buying stocks again. This run takes the index up to 60 percent in November ("B"). This example helps illustrate how the risk levels change. The most important clue the Bullish Percent Indexes provide is the knowledge of who has the ball.

Biomedics News—January 1993

I went back into THE BLOOMBERG to get some comments on Biomedics stocks around January 1993. The Biomedics Bullish Percent chart had already reversed down from above 70 percent placing the sector in Bear Alert status. This means that the probability is the sector has lost sponsorship and you have lost the football. The defensive team must come on the field. The following comment was made about Biogen on January 8, 1993. "Biogen Rebounds after Bear Stearns Analyst rates it 'Strong Buy'." On January 11, 1993, Oppenheimer repeated Biogen as a 'Buy' based on optimism about the company's treatment for multiple sclerosis. The stock was at $43⅝. The stock proceeded to decline to $29 in less than 90 days. I am here to say that there is absolutely nothing wrong with the analyst's fundamental work. Biogen's problem was one of supply and demand, not fundamentals.

"Biogen Inc. shares rebounded slightly after yesterday's 10 percent decline, when a Bear Stearns analyst changed his recommendation from 'Buy' to 'Strong Buy.'"

"Analysts blame yesterday's decline on speculation about the effectiveness of the company's potential heart drug, Hirulog, which is in the final phase of government-required human studies."

There is always an excuse why things happen on Wall Street. The only explanation for the stock's decline is that there were more sellers than buyers willing to buy. That's it.

In the same month, January 1993, Kidder Peabody put the stock on "Hold." This is almost as bad as buy because it gives the investor the false hope that everything is alright. Holding a stock through a major decline is as bad as buying the stock and holding it through the decline. If you haven't already learned, "Hold" really means "Hedge."

April 1994—At the Bottom

Biogen was now at the bottom having lost 10 points since it was recommended in January. The price was now $29½ and here is the comment: "New York, April 15 (Bloomberg Financial Markets) Biogen Inc. was lowered to 'Underperform' from 'Hold' by a Hambrecht & Quist analyst, a research official said." (The analyst was unavailable for comment. As usual.) OK, what has just happened? The stock was on "Hold," meaning you should keep it in your portfolio. The Sector Bullish Percent Index was now at 26 percent having gone coast to coast. As you know, 26 percent is in the green zone. The analyst has now decided that the stock will underperform the market. I ask you, what has the stock been doing coming down from $39 to $29? It's already been underperforming. Comments like these scare investors out at the bottom. What would the average investor think if he has already held the stock on the way down as he was told to do, only to find a prominent Wall Street firm saying the stock will now underperform.

The point of all this is had the analyst understood how to use the Bullish Percent Indexes and was willing to meld technical with fundamental research, he might have tempered his enthusiasm for a stock when the sector was in or close to the red zone. This is not likely to happen which is why it is necessary for you to be able to take control yourself.

Buildings

This chart only goes back to 1990. It's pretty self-explanatory. What is interesting is that the building and related industry has never yet been able to get above 70 percent. You can see in Figure 8.5 that a great opportunity is about to present itself if the index can just go one more box lower to 30 percent. A reversal up from 30 percent or lower changes the risk level to Bull Alert (red light to green light). If the index reverses from above 30 percent from its Bear Confirmed status, the risk level will only be changed to Bear Correction status (red light to flashing red).

Chemicals

For about the past 4 years, this sector has held above the 40 percent level. Most sectors have visited the 30 percent level since then. This index provides a good example of how the risk levels change on the bearish side of the equation. In Figure 8.6, look at the September 1989 column where the O's begin at 76 percent. That is three columns to the right of 1989. The top of the market in chemicals came at 78 percent in

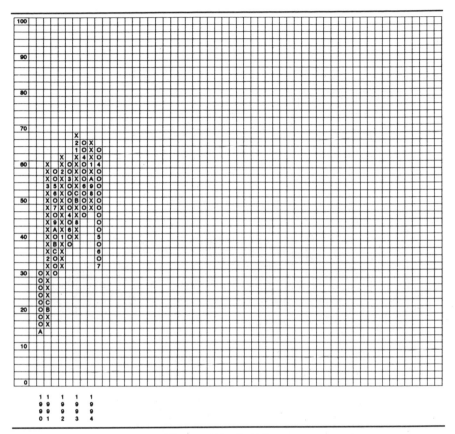

Figure 8.5   Buildings.

August. The subsequent reversal in September suggested the investor lost the ball to the sector. The sector's job now is to take as much money away from those investing in chemicals as possible. Your job at this juncture is to prevent the sector from taking your money. One way is to get out. Another way is to hedge with derivatives. At any rate, the index clearly showed trouble ahead. The newspapers at this time were probably extolling the virtues of the chemical industry because at the 78 percent level everyone is happy with their investments. All the fundamentals are now coming to fruition and are clearly visible. At such times, it is the invisible factors that can kill you. By October (A), the index exceeds the previous bottom in May (5). This changed the risk level to Bear Confirmed status. The decline is broadening out.

Most investors can't see what is happening at this point because there is no fanfare in the papers when a stock gives a Point and Figure sell signal. The sector in general is still doing well. Remember a reading

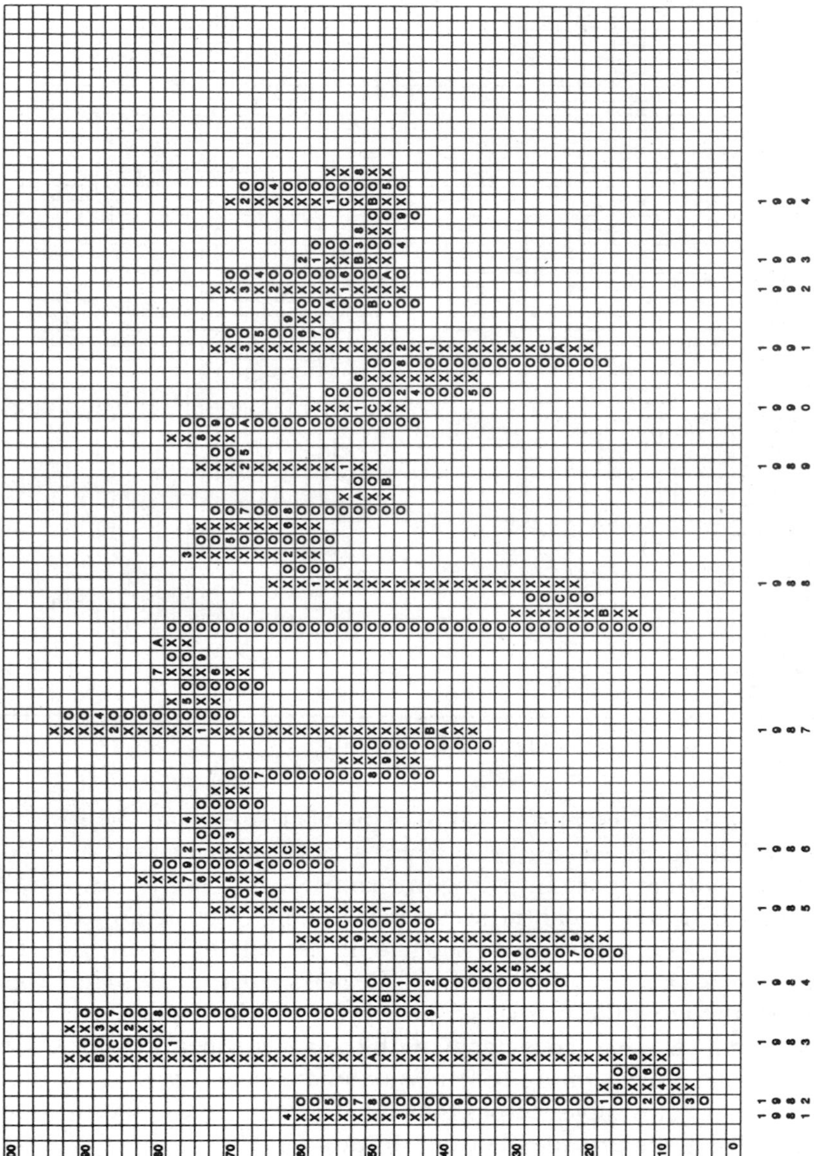

Figure 8.6 Chemicals.

of 66 percent means 66 percent of the stocks underlying the sector are bullish. How about at the level where the signal is first given, 72 percent? This means that only 28 percent of the stocks underlying the index are negative and 72 percent are positive. As *Mad Magazine*'s Alfred E. Neuman says, "What, Me Worry?" Well, to the astute Point and Figure trained investor, there is something to worry about.

The index declines to a low of 44 percent in October (there is no entry suggesting November in that column because there was no movement during the month). In December (C) the index reverses up at 50 percent. The risk level changes to Bear Correction. By January, the index reverses again to a column of O's at 56 percent reverting the risk level back to Bear Confirmed. That move carries the index down to a low of 34 percent. It's getting tense for those investors still in these stocks. A reprieve comes in May with a reversal back up to X's at 40 percent. The risk level reverts to Bear Correction. The chemical stocks float back up to 52 percent in June (6). By August, the index reverses down again (8) at 46 percent changing the risk level back to Bear Confirmed status. This move carries the index below 30 percent (green zone) to a low of 18 percent. In October 1990, the index reverses up changing the risk level to Bull Alert status (red light to green). That buy signal carries chemicals up to 74 percent without a reversal, where the whole process begins over again.

Computers

This sector has basically been in a trading range between 30 percent and 60 percent for the past 4 years. There was a major buy signal in July 1994 with a reversal up from 30 percent. The real good news was that we were able to remain defensive in the sector from 60 percent in March 1994 to the buy signal in July 1994. Avoiding severe losses is one major key to success in investing. This sector is constantly in flux with new products and innovations (see Figure 8.7).

Drugs

Probably the most important signal this Bullish Percent Index has given was in February 1992. Just one month after Clinton took office, the index said "Get Out." You can see this in Figure 8.8 by looking at the column of O's one column to the right of 1992. The Clintons, after taking office, promptly bashed the drug industry. The net result was billions upon billions were lost by pension funds. The good news is that anyone willing to follow the drug coach (Bullish Percent Index) and put the defensive team on the field avoided the calamity and possibly profited from it. Well, 2½ years later we received a major buy

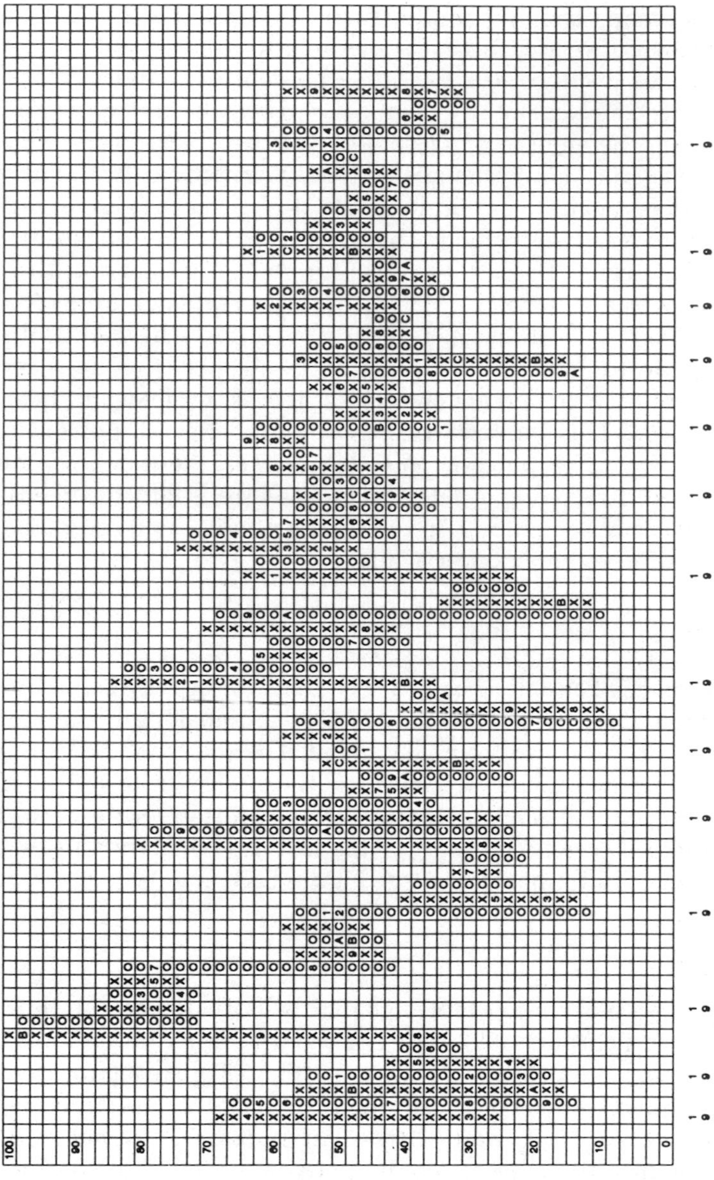

Figure 8.7 Computers.

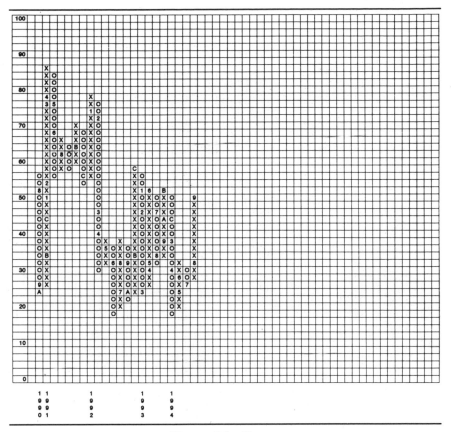

Figure 8.8   Drugs.

signal off the bottom in May and again in August 1994. Eventually the drug group will exceed 70 percent (the red zone) and everyone will become a believer.

Electronics

The electronics sector has the semiconductor group in it as well. This might account for the wide swings the index has in each direction. A quick glance at Figure 8.9 shows that this index had a tendency to move coast to coast during the 1980s. From 1990 on, the index has had a tendency to stay above the 40 percent level. There really hasn't been a great opportunity to buy this group since October 1990. At this writing, the index is in a column of X's at the 54 percent level with the last entry in August (8) 1994. The risk level is Bear Correction, which suggests that the index should have limited upside potential but there is no point anticipating anticipators. As long as the index is in a column

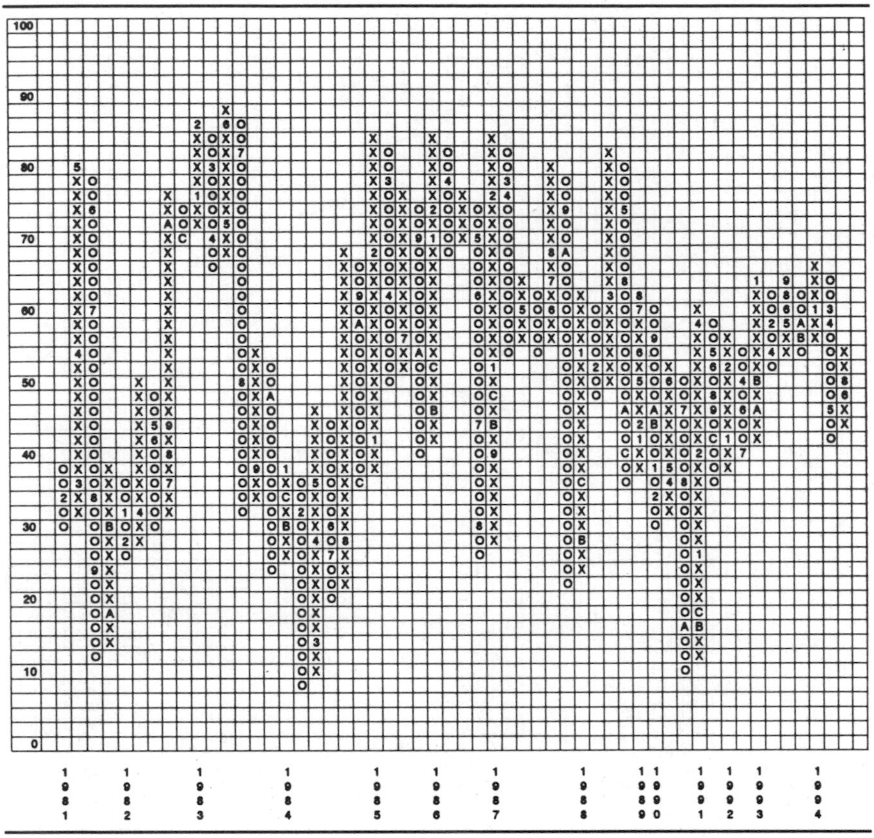

Figure 8.9 Electronics.

of X's and rising, we have the ball. In Bear Correction status though, we will keep a short-term outlook until the risk level can revert to one of the three bull modes. The traffic light is flashing red at this point. It's OK to proceed through the intersection, but be very cautious and be aware the opposing traffic has the right of way. Good buying opportunities (declines below 30 percent) have come about every 2 to 2½ years. We are overdue. One more thing that can be gleaned by a quick glance is that this index has a tendency to top out in the 80 percent level.

Food, Beverages, and Soap

This whole sector seems to have lost sponsorship in the 1990s. Times have really changed from the roaring 1980s. Notice how Figure 8.10 shows that in the 1980s the sector had a tendency to hang in the upper reaches of the chart. Now in the 1990s, the index is hanging in the lower half. Interestingly, the Bullish Percent chart for this

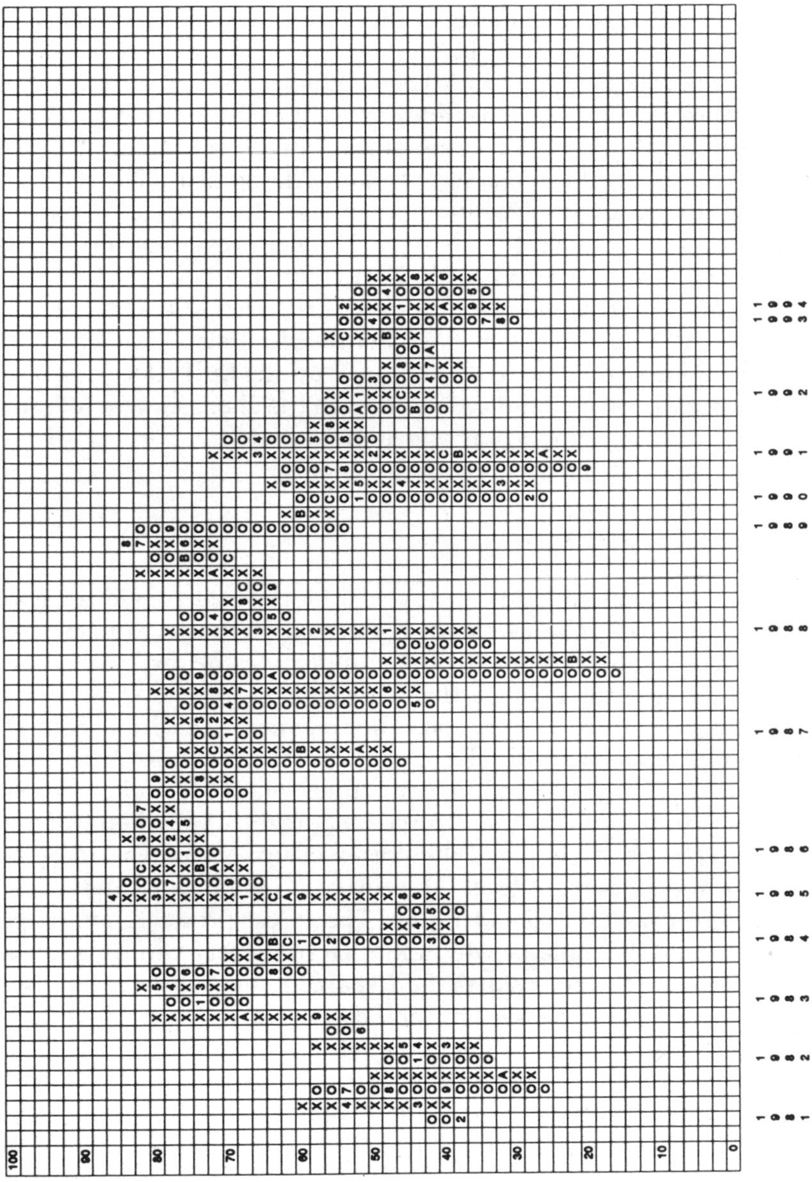

Figure 8.10 Foods, beverages, and soap.

163

industry went to defense September 1987, just in time to avoid the crash in October.

This chart provides a good illustration of how reversals in columns pick up the previous signal. Look at the Bear Confirmed reading that takes place at the 40 percent level in the column 1993. Remember, Bear Confirmed status is obtained by the index exceeding a previous bottom. Notice how that happens at 40 percent where the previous column of O's ends in October (A). The index subsequently declines to 30 percent. The reversal up into a column of X's where September (9) closes the third box changed the risk level to Bull Alert status. The red light effectively turned green. The index then rises to a top at 54 percent with February (2) closing the last box. The next reversal into O's, in April, changed the risk level back to Bear Confirmed. *Reversals between 30 percent and 70 percent pick up the previous risk level of the "X" or "O"*. In this case, the risk level was Bear Confirmed status. Therefore the next reversal into a column of X's will pick up the Bull Alert risk level. Review this progression, and go over it with the chart shown in Figure 8.10. It is extremely important you understand this concept. If you didn't catch on, go back and reread this section.

Forest Products and Paper

This index goes back to 1990 on the chart. Figure 8.11 provides a good example of why the risk level does not actually change to Bear Alert until it reverses into a column of O's and declines below 70 percent. I have always taken the posture that a reversal from above 70 percent was serious enough to take action. This is where we differ from the original guidelines. We will take action on a reversal anywhere above 70 percent. We have just seen too many times where the index reverses from a very high level, declines to the 68 percent level where the risk level changes to Bear Alert, and then reverses up. Too much can be lost waiting for the 70 percent level. This situation is not a normal occurrence but does warrant consideration. The forest products and paper sector is a good example of why taking action early can save lots of pain. Sometimes the index skirts the 70 percent level without breaking it, reverses up leaving those that took defensive action prior to a decline below 70 percent, whistling in the wind. This is exactly what happened in 1991 with the reversal into a column of O's that hits 70 percent but doesn't actually exceed it. It really isn't until August that the index reverses back into a column of O's and does exceed 70 percent. In this case, it exceeds 70 percent and simultaneously exceeds a previous bottom changing the risk level to Bear Confirmed status. That's when the real decline begins. Those who took action early waited on the sidelines for a couple of months but that's OK, never cry

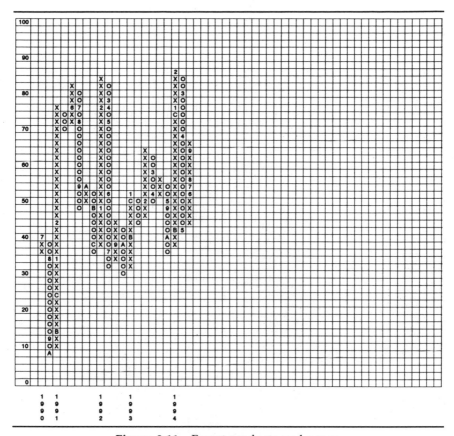

Figure 8.11 Forest products and paper.

over missed opportunity. You can always make up opportunity, it's lost money that is hard to make up. Now go over to the long column of O's in 1992, a reversal that started in March 1992 at 78 percent. That reversal was dead on the money, and you would have been better off to hedge or take defensive action prior to the decline below 70 percent in May. The best thing to do in cases like this is to play it safe. Go to defense, and if you are wrong, you will simply miss opportunity not money. The reversal in March 1994 started down at 80 percent, and defense was the right action to take. Since this is not a science and never will be, always take the most prudent action.

Healthcare

As shown in Figure 8.12, the healthcare sector gave great long-lasting signals for most of the 1980s. Since the Presidential election in 1992, the

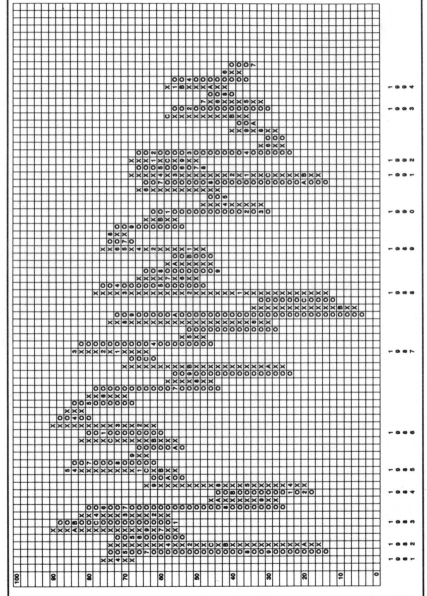

Figure 8.12 Healthcare.

index has been under a cloud. The only thing you can say about it now is let's see how the health care plan comes out. This industry will be under pressure until this whole situation is resolved. It may very well be decided by the time you read this book. As of July 1994, it remained in Bear Confirmed status at the 34 percent level. The good news is the field position is very good. All we need is the ball. My guess is the health care plan languishes and this index gets in gear. If the plan goes down, these stocks will rise nicely.

Household Goods

This index is only 4 years old. You can see from an examination of Figure 8.13 the real trouble came with the reversal from 72 percent down to 66 percent in April 1993. The index has never recovered since. Notice how the tops are lower on each reversal up. A clear sign that demand is

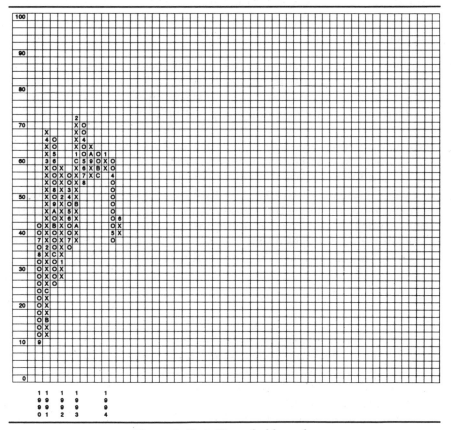

Figure 8.13 † Household goods.

losing its steam. At this writing, the index is in Bear Correction status at 44 percent. The traffic light is flashing red—OK to proceed after you stop and look both ways.

Insurance

In Figure 8.14, you can clearly see the influence a President can have on an industry if he chooses to bash it. The red flag goes up in January 1993 with a rise above the critical 70 percent level. The reversal comes in April and the decline is underway. The risk level does not change until May with a Bear Alert reading as the index sinks below 70 percent. Before the Clinton administration got hold of the sector it had a propensity to give some great long-lasting signals. Just look at some of those signals in the decade of the 1980s. They'll make your eyes roll like the tape on a cash register—coast to coast moves in a few months. What a life. Once the health care situation is resolved, we assume this one will get back to normal. Things are always changing in the market.

International Funds

This has been a fun sector to work in. It is made up of foreign sector funds that trade primarily on the New York Stock Exchange. These funds have added a new dimension to stock investing and have gotten a tremendous amount of sponsorship in the United States. Figure 8.15 shows that this group has a tendency to move to extremes. We have been able to time investment in these sectors very well using this index. I just can't emphasize how easy evaluating sectors will be once you get used to using the Bullish Percent Indexes. In August 1994, the index was in Bull Confirmed status at 42 percent. Once you have the directional move in the sector, you must then evaluate the charts of the stocks (funds in this case) to determine exactly what you will buy. Some countries' funds will not do well while others will. In general, the group should get a lift once the sector finds sponsorship.

Leisure

The leisure group has become the gambling capital of the world. All the gaming stocks are contained in the leisure sector. Since 1990, it's almost been a "deal's on" "deal's off" kind of sector. In Figure 8.16, you can see the sponsorship it had on the way up beginning in November 1990 with the reversal up from below the 30 percent level. That rise was primarily due to the gaming stocks. Likewise, the decline beginning in November 1993 was a result of the gaming stocks' demise. They will have their day again when you least expect it. The beauty of the

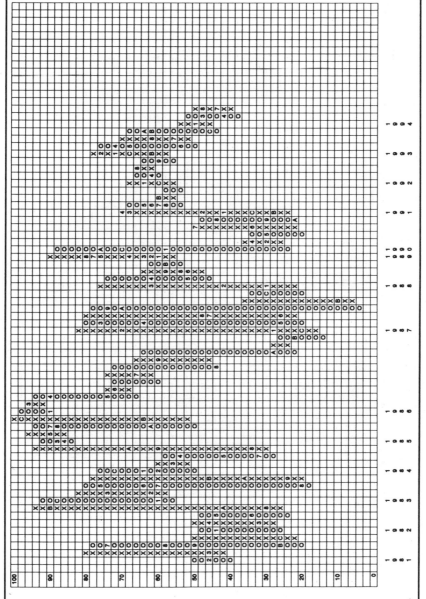

Figure 8.14 Insurance.

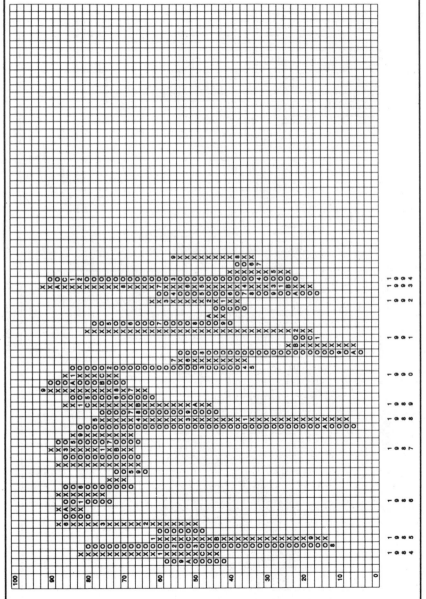

Figure 8.15　International funds.

170

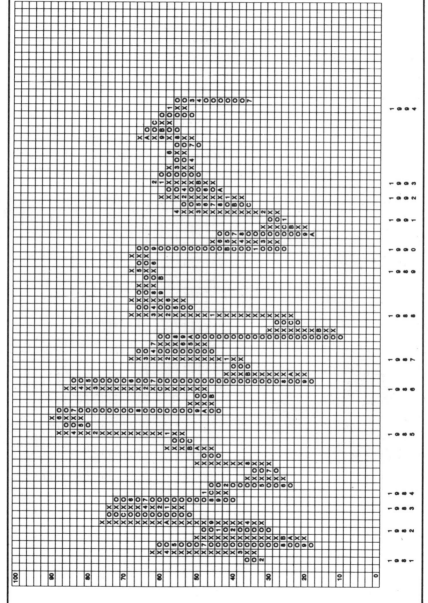

Figure 8.16 Leisure.

171

Bullish Percent Indexes is that they will signal when it is time to take action. A reversal from the 36 percent level will simply change the risk level to Bear Correction—a breath of fresh air, but only for traders. A move to 30 percent or below will set up a potential change in the risk level to Bull Alert on the next reversal up into a column of X's. There is no point in anticipating an anticipator, however, so we'll just go with the flow. When the reversal comes, we'll be ready to go with the best stocks in the group.

Machinery and Tools

This sector has been a good one for the last few years. Notice on the chart shown in Figure 8.17 how the only sell signal came in May 1994 by exceeding a previous bottom. Prior to that, the sector did place the defensive team on the field a number of times but gave no outright sell

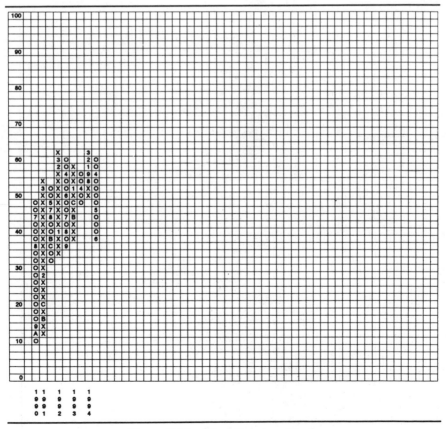

Figure 8.17   Machinery and tools.

signals because it never went over 70 percent or exceeded a bottom. Following the major buy signal in November 1990, each column of O's began in April, with the exception of the one that began in May. For some reason, this sector loses sponsorship around the spring each year. This is a piece of information to keep in the back of your mind. Remember, a reversal back up the chart from Bear Confirmed status is called Bear Correction as long as the index is above 30 percent. Going over this in this depth will help you remember the six risk levels. Also notice the box with the 5 in it in 1994 that exceeds a previous bottom by moving to 46 percent. That changed the risk level to Bear Confirmed. Look at Figure 8.17 carefully and get it straight in your mind before you move on to the next sector.

Media

Let's take a little quiz on the media sector. Look at the chart shown in Figure 8.18 and locate January 1994 (box at 68 percent with a 1 filling the box); next, tell me what risk level the index changed to with the subsequent O in the box just below the 70 percent level. Think about it for a moment. Meanwhile, let's discuss the risk level when the index reversed from its high at 86 percent. Since the reversal came from above 70 percent, it was a Bull Correction. Keep in mind however, we always take defensive action on any reversal above 70 percent. We prefer to be extra cautious at this altitude. Remember, it takes a move below 70 percent to be called Bear Alert. The answer to the preceding quiz is Bear Confirmed. Bear Confirmed happens when the index exceeds a previous bottom. You might have said Bear Alert because of the decline below 70 percent, but the index also exceeded a previous bottom, which is always Bear Confirmed. At the same time, keep your field position in mind. This Bear Confirmed reading comes at 68 percent, which is significant and warrants immediate action. If the Bear Confirmed reading came at 30 percent, we would ignore it as 30 percent is at the oversold side of the field.

Metals, Nonferrous

Notice the series of rising bottoms each time this index went into a column of O's beginning at the bottom November 1990. From March 1991 to January 1994 this index has either been in Bull Confirmed or Bull Correction. Notice in January 1994 it rises above 70 percent. The subsequent reversal in March changes the risk level to Bear Alert status. What this suggests is the long run of bullish risk levels just might be over. I look for Metals, Nonferrous to work its way down to the 30 percent level over the next year completing the cycle. Notice it's almost

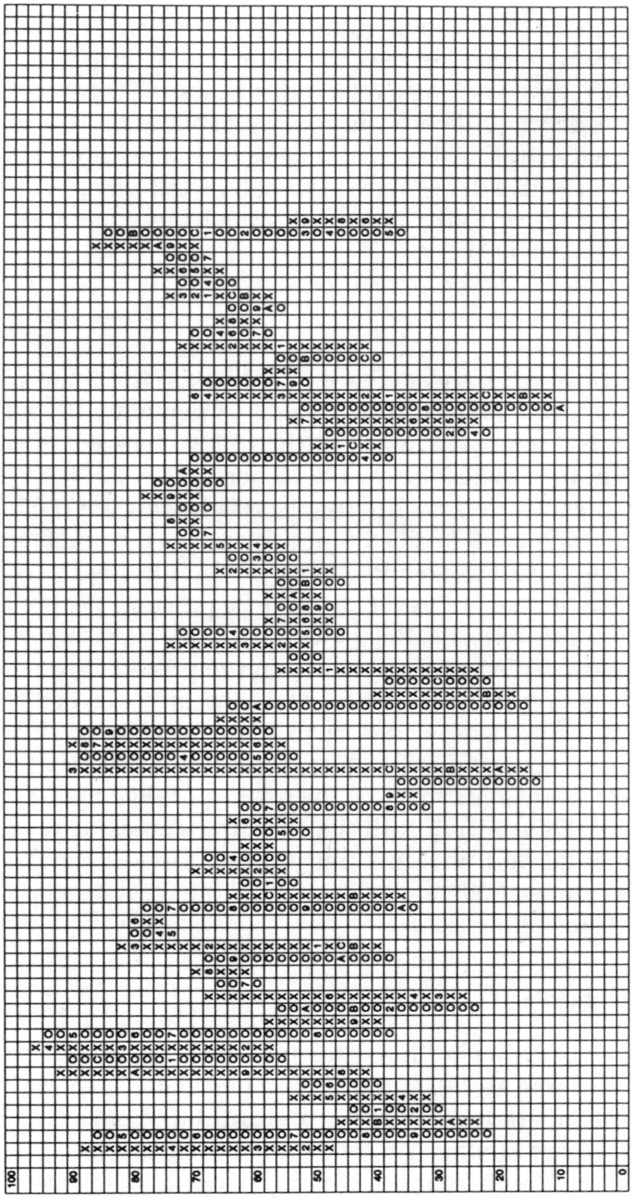

Figure 8.18 Media.

174

like clockwork that you have great buying opportunity below 30 percent every few years in this index. All you need is patience.

Oil

Oil has a tendency to have extended moves. Notice the signals that were given in 1987 (see Figure 8.20). They were very good. A great signal was given in January 1990, which resulted in a move from a high of 88 percent to a low of 22 percent.

Oil Service

This is another good one for a quiz. In Figure 8.21, look at the column of X's two columns to the right of 1992. It has the numbers 5 (May) and 6 (June) in it. What risk level change takes place with the reversal down into a column of O's right next to that column? It is the column with only 4 boxes filled and the last one has a 7 (July) in it. Look at the chart and tell me what the risk level changed to. Go ahead, say it out loud. The answer is Bear Bottom. The first reversal up into a column of X's is Bull Alert. Reversals back to 30 percent or lower from Bull Alert are called Bear Bottom. The action to be taken is, Hold on to the stocks you have bought in the sector, don't buy any more, and light a candle.

Precious Metals

From a glance at Figure 8.22, you can see that this sector has a tendency to go to extremes. Notice how it is one of the few that have ever hit the 100 percent level and the 0 percent level. There is a time in my career that the Precious Metals Bullish Percent Index would have saved me from a major mistake.

I had just come to my new firm to develop the Options Strategy Department when one of my long-term clients called me inquiring about someone to manage her family accounts. This woman was the daughter of the founder of a Fortune 500 company located in the Southeast. I acted as stockbroker for her accounts for a few years. One day out of the blue, she asked me if I would manage the accounts on a discretionary basis. Following about one second's thought, I accepted. This was the first time I was able to operate as a true money manager, not an order taker. I thought long and hard, formulating a game plan for the accounts. After a week of deliberation I decided to take a very conservative approach in this new management endeavor. The accounts were overweighed in precious metals stocks that paid very low or no dividends. The prices of these stocks had been depressed for a good while

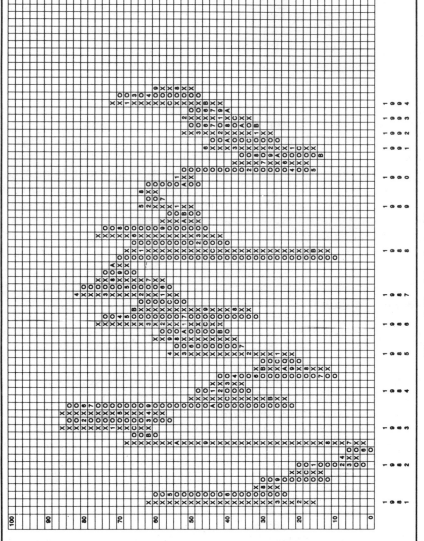

Figure 8.19 Metals, nonferrous.

176

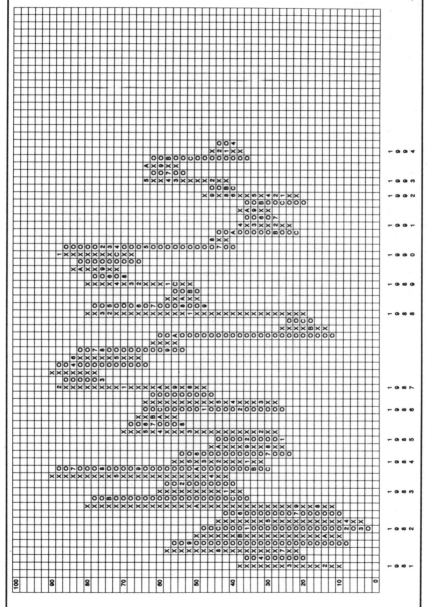

Figure 8.20 Oil.

177

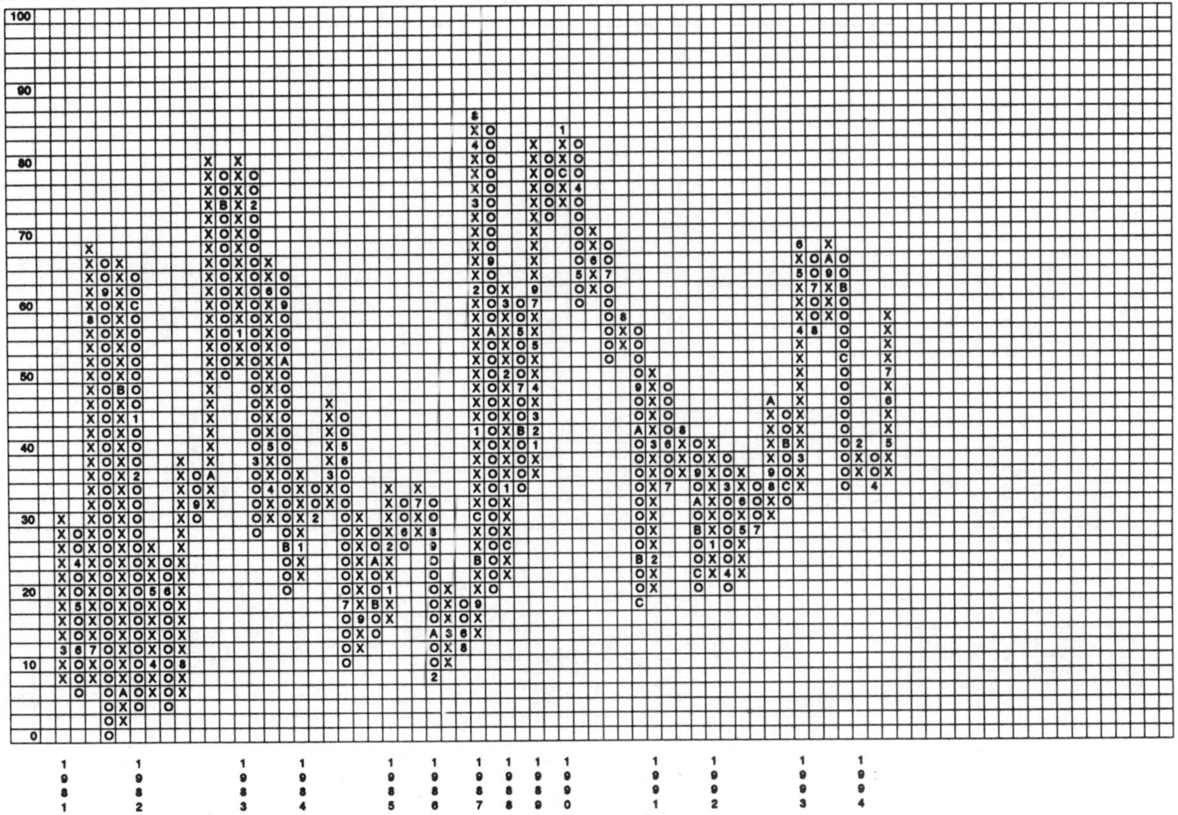

Figure 8.21 Oil service.

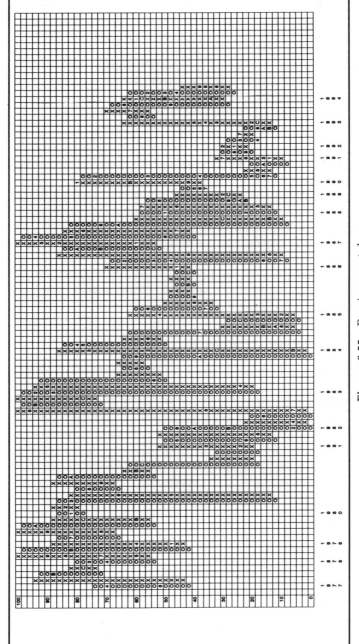

Figure 8.22 Precious metals.

and I assumed that they would continue to remain depressed. My grand plan was to sell those mining shares and reinvest the money in big cap, conservative stocks that had listed options. I would further reduce the risk and increase the income by selling call options against the position, a strategy known as covered writing.

What happened after implementing the plan remains a nightmare to this day. I effectively called the exact bottom in the mining stocks. The mining stocks I sold out went straight up without ever looking back. The big cap stocks began their cycle of underperformance. I remember a stock named Hecla Mining rising from $5 to $47 before the run was over.

The point of this discussion is that the mistake I made selling the mining stocks out at the bottom would not have happened had I been educated in the Point and Figure way of thinking. Not only was my sector evaluation faulty but my selection of the strategy covered writing was equally as bad. This strategy, although appearing conservative, can often be the riskiest strategy you can employ in the equity markets. It effectively caps off any strong gains your stocks might experience and on the downside offers limited protection. Man, what a difference this Bullish Percent chart would have made. You will never make that same mistake if you allow the Bullish Percent Index to guide your sector commitments.

Protection—Safety Equipment

This index only goes back 4 years. Let's take another quiz on this sector. As shown in Figure 8.23, what risk level is the index in, having reversed up into a column of X's from a low of 32 percent. Don't jump at the answer. Look at the chart carefully. OK, say it out loud. The answer is Bear Correction. The reversal missed Bull Alert by one box. Had this index declined to 30 percent or lower, the reversal would have been Bull Alert status. Instead, since the index stopped at 32 percent, the reversal up is considered Bear Correction.

Real Estate

Although we don't watch for patterns in Bullish Percent Indexes, it is interesting to note that this index shown in Figure 8.24 rose three times to 42 percent before it finally was penetrated on the third attempt. I can't think of any logical reason why 42 percent was the resistance level. Also notice how each time the index went into a column of O's beginning in September of 1991, they produced higher bottoms.

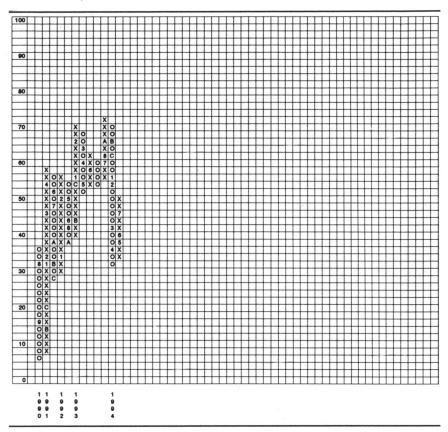

Figure 8.23   Protection—safety equipment.

Restaurants

There have been only two major swings in this index (see Figure 8.25). In 1987, it reached the 12 percent level, and in 1990 it hit the 12 percent level. With the exception of those two years, the lows are usually confined to 30 percent.

Retailing

In Figure 8.26, notice how from the high at 80 percent in 1988, the retailing sector has produced lower tops on almost every reversal up into columns of X's. It's almost as if the United States is in a retailing slump. What's going on here? By looking at this chart, you might

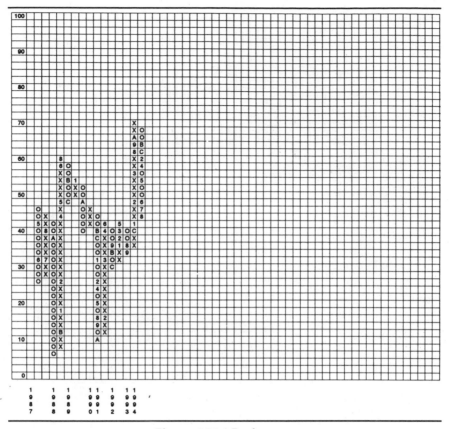

Figure 8.24   Real estate.

surmise that there is less and less retail buying going on in the United States. Whatever the cause, it's alarming. The good news is, one day the index will make some sort of bottom and will produce higher highs as it moves up over the years. My guess is it will take a fiscally responsible government to produce this result, and that's not on the horizon. The red light will turn green on the next reversal up. Buy these stocks on the first reversal up into a column of X's.

Savings and Loans

This was the sector that was never coming back from the dead. In October 1990, the business periodicals were saying the S&L's were finished as we knew them. They would never recover. Well they did recover as usual and now reside at the 76 percent level (see Figure 8.27). With the index at a high level, we would avoid the group. These stocks

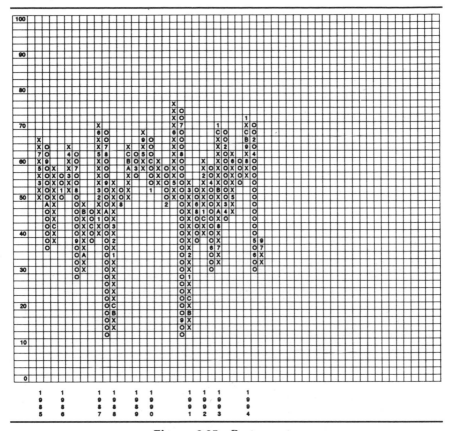

Figure 8.25 Restaurants.

could still move up; however, the real play was in October 1990 when no one wanted them at 8 percent. It is interesting to note each reversal in this index since March 1993 has produced a lower top and a lower bottom. Sponsorship is evaporating.

Software

This sector has a tendency to become oversold but not very over-bought. In Figure 8.28, notice how a number of times the sector has declined below 30 percent but never once since the chart has been kept has it risen above the 70 percent level. (Up to August 1994, this sector has not seen to date is Bear Alert.) Remember Bear Alert happens when a Bullish Percent Index rises above 70 percent then reverses into a column of O's and crosses that 70 percent level on the downside. It hasn't happened yet. Sixty percent has been that area where the index

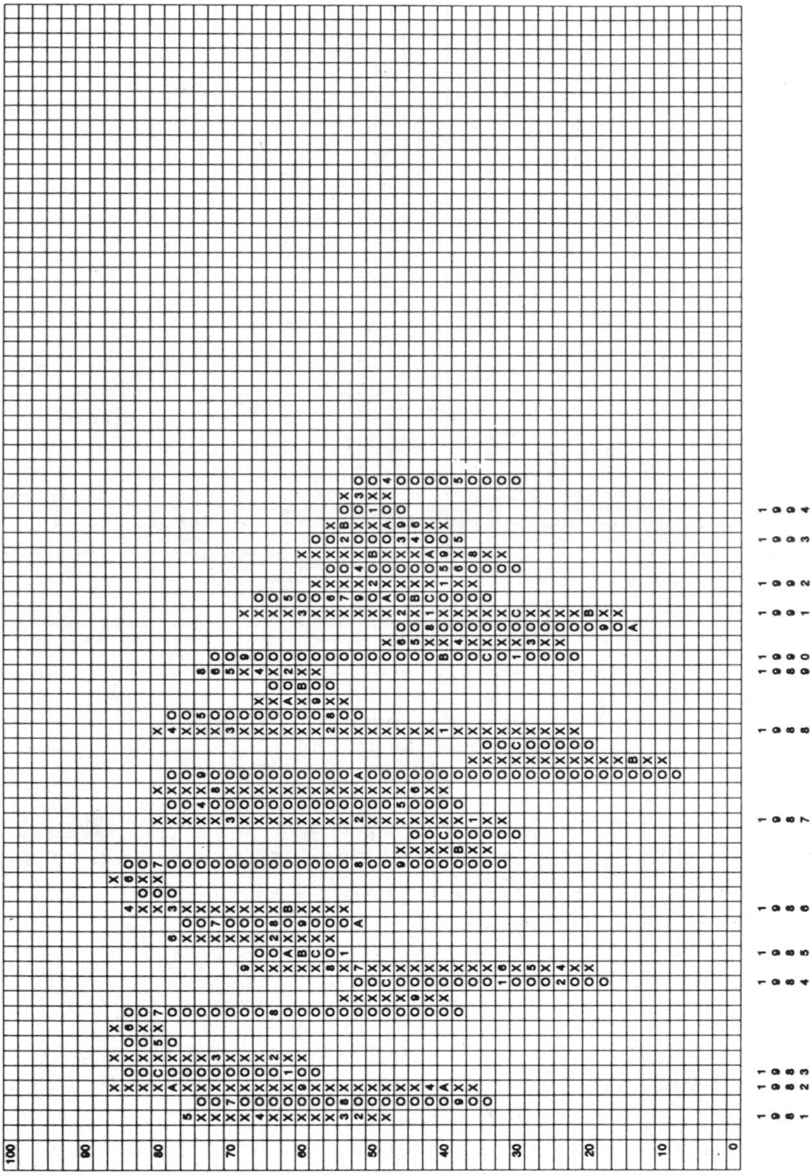

Figure 8.26 Retailing.

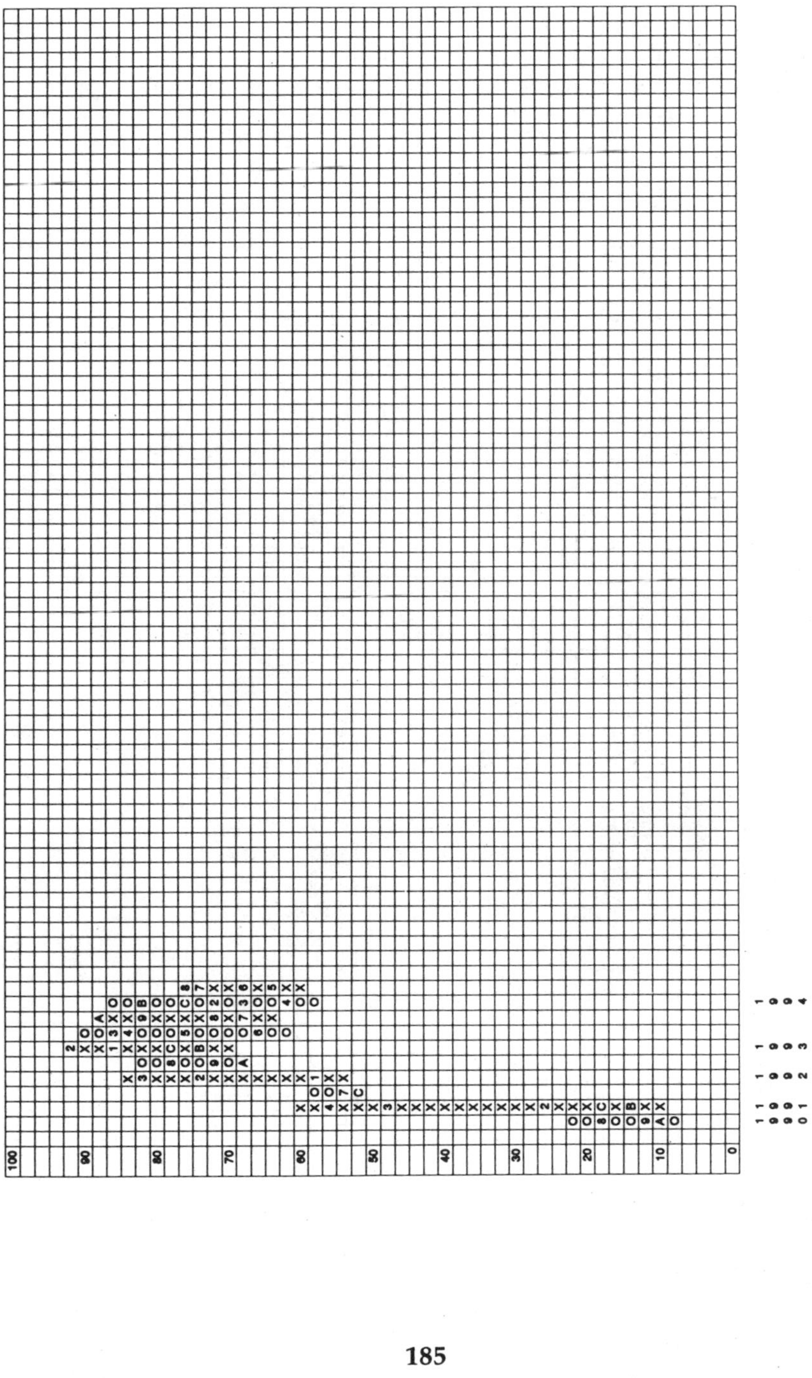

Figure 8.27 Savings and loans.

becomes overbought. We are currently in Bull Confirmed status at the 54 percent level. It's been a great play since the reversal from below 30 percent. These Sector Bullish Percent Indexes can make you feel like a kid in a candy shop. Think of times like October 1990 when all the sectors are below 30 percent. All you have to do is just wait for them to reverse one at a time. To use another analogy, it's like picking apples in an orchard. All you have to do is reach up and pick the low apples. No need for a ladder.

Steel and Iron

Like the software sector, up to August 1994, this one has not visited the 70 percent level. It's crossed 30 percent twice. This index, as shown in Figure 8.29, presents a good example of why field position is

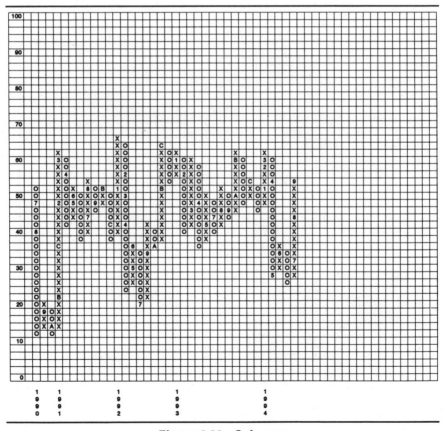

Figure 8.28   Software.

so important. Notice how it goes into Bear Confirmed status by exceeding a previous column of O's at the 38 percent level. That takes place one column to the right of 1994. The risk level goes to Bear Confirmed status, but with a reading of 38 percent, there is no point becoming too bearish. Keep the field position clearly in your mind when evaluating the risk level.

Telephones

We had a great ride on this sector in 1994 after it reversed up from 30 percent in May 1994. This was one of the first to reverse up from 30 percent after the NYSE Bullish Percent went to Bear Confirmed status in March 1994. The reversal up from 30 percent in May 1994 is a good example of how an index can get to Bull Confirmed status at a low level

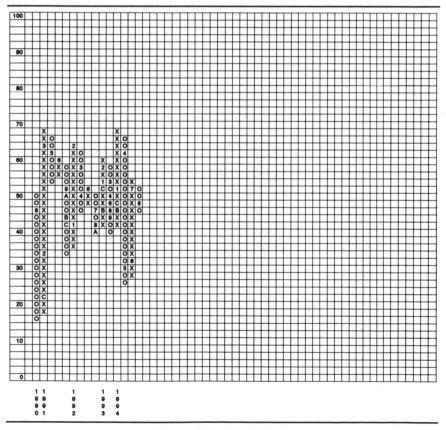

Figure 8.29   Steel/Iron.

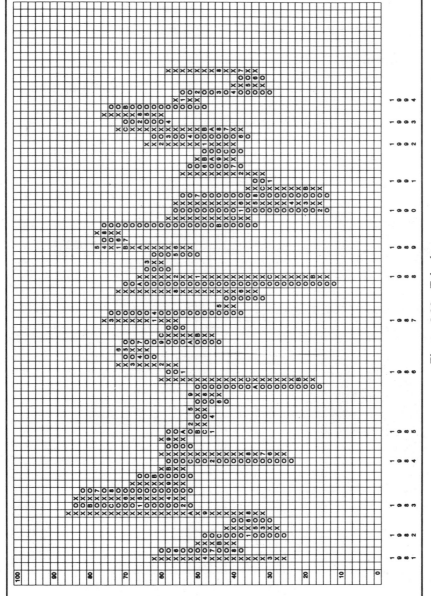

Figure 8.30   Telephones.

(see Figure 8.30). The reversal only carried up five boxes to 40 percent before it lost sponsorship and reversed down in June. The reversal was not really actionable because of its proximity to the 30 percent level. The reversal did, however, suggest you do no further buying in the sector while the Bullish Percent remained in a column of O's. The next reversal up in July suggested that the green light was back on. It then exceeded the previous top at 40 percent, which changed the risk level to Bull Confirmed status at 42 percent. Net result: Bull Confirmed with great field position. Start throwing passes.

Textiles and Apparel

In Figure 8.31, notice the reversal in 1987 from above 70 percent came in September. Another great out. Let's take another quiz. After 1993, what month and percent produces the first Bear Confirmed reading? Look at the chart now. The answer is May at 50 percent. The index exceeds a previous bottom there.

Transports, Non-Air

There isn't much to discuss with this one so let's take another quiz. What month does the index go to Bear Alert status in 1994? Look at Figure 8.32. We discussed this earlier. If you remember it, great; it won't hurt to go over it again. The answer is April. The reversal actually comes in March but the index does not cross the 70 percent level until April. Remember, we take action on the first reversal above 70 percent, but the risk level will not change until the index declines below 70 percent.

Utilities, Electric

You can see by Figure 8.33, that this index does not speak often. This small chart goes back to 1981. I find it interesting to examine 1987 using this index. The real trouble in 1987 was signaled by a reversal in this chart at the 70 percent level in March of that year. The culmination of the move ended in October 1987 at 10 percent. The index reversed up in August briefly, then bottomed with the crash in October. The correction in the utilities had almost run its course by August 1987. The current reading is 26 percent. We are just waiting for the reversal. We have recommended taking half positions at this level with the intent of adding the other half on the reversal up whenever that comes. We are not likely to see a low level like this for years to come.

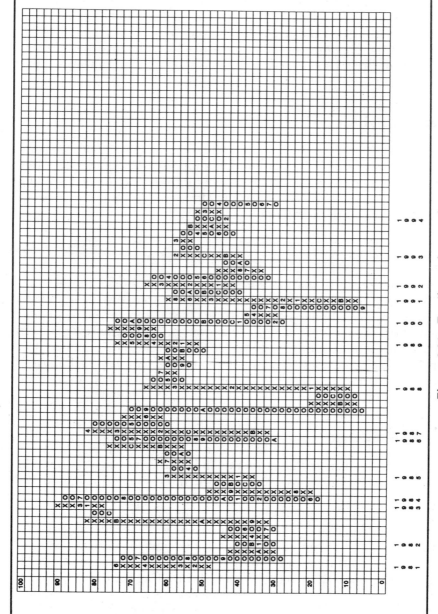

Figure 8.31   Textiles and apparel.

190

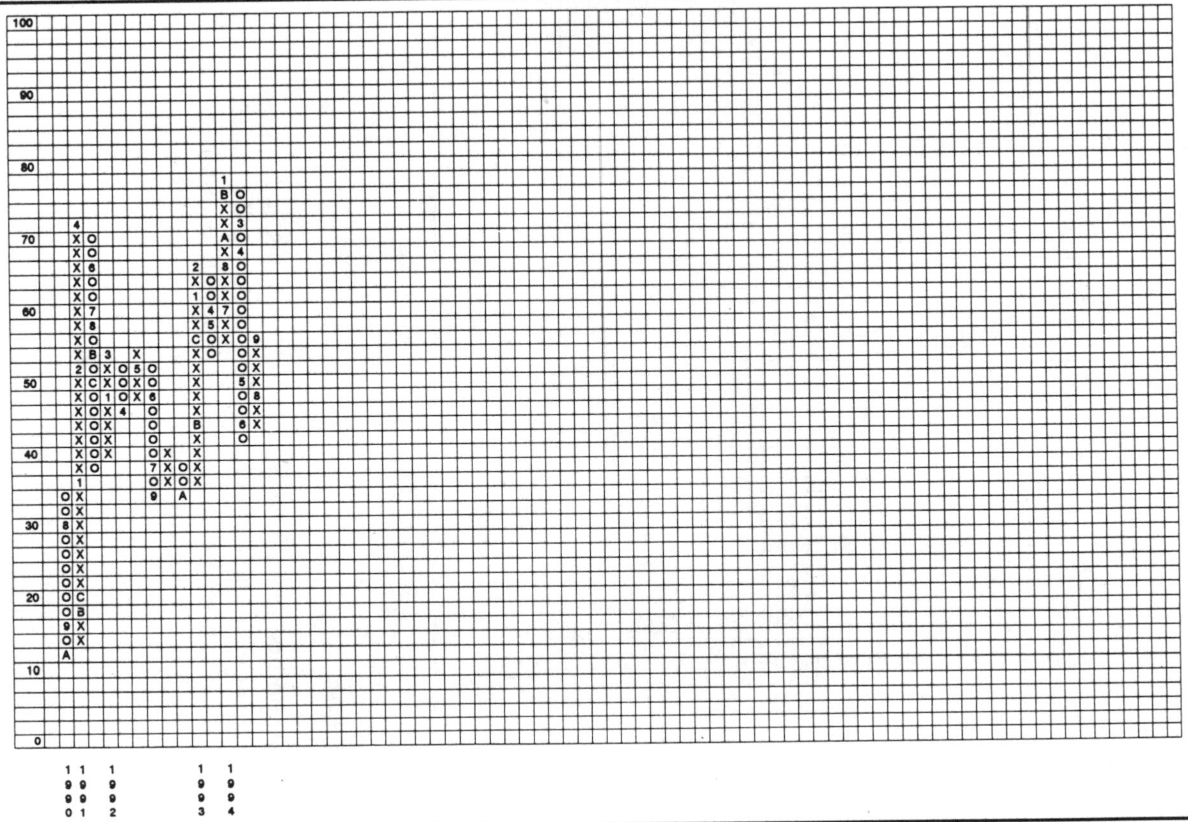

Figure 8.32 Transports, non-air.

191

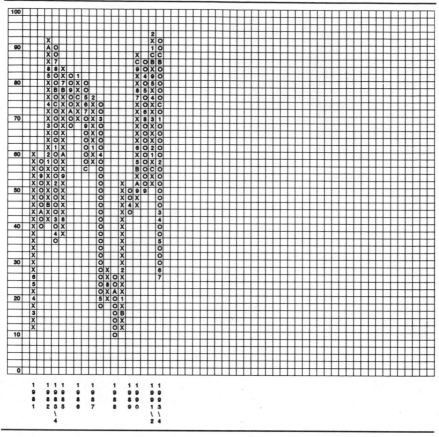

Figure 8.33 Utilities, electric.

Utilities, Gas

Figure 8.34 points up another opportunity waiting to happen. At this writing, the index is at 26 percent. The last opportunity like this was in October 1987. Prior to that it was 1982. We simply wait for the reversal and then buy the best-looking chart patterns in the sector.

Wall Street

We got the reversal up in this sector the third week of August 1994. We went long the brokerage stocks. The index reversed up from the 24 percent level. The last great opportunity was October 1990. Look at the major sell signal in January 1994. It not only reversed from above

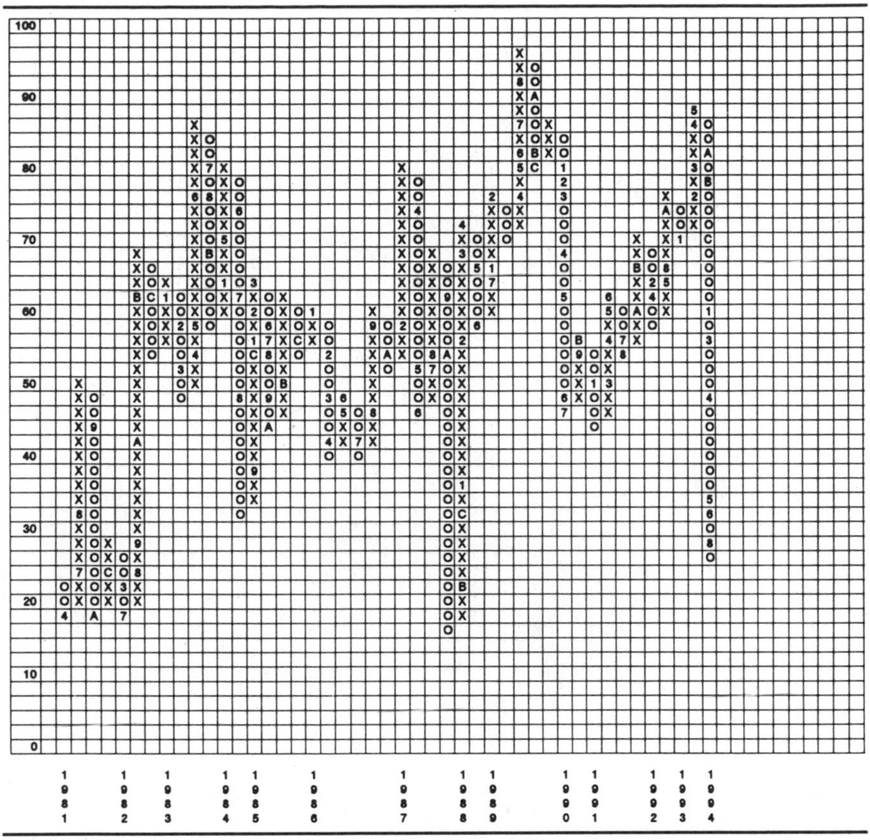

Figure 8.34 Utilities, gas.

to below 70 percent, but it exceeded a previous bottom putting the risk level in Bear Confirmed status. Those who followed that signal avoided getting hit by a freight train. It feels so good to wait for your opportunity and then pull the trigger. The beauty of the Bullish Percent Indexes is they are contrary indicators that give clear action points. Another good thing about them is very few investors use them because it takes some education in this way of thinking before the charts can be useful. Most investors are not willing to take the time to learn.

Waste Management

This sector had its heyday in the 1970s and 1980s. Look at January 1992. Many people thought when Clinton and Gore got in office, they

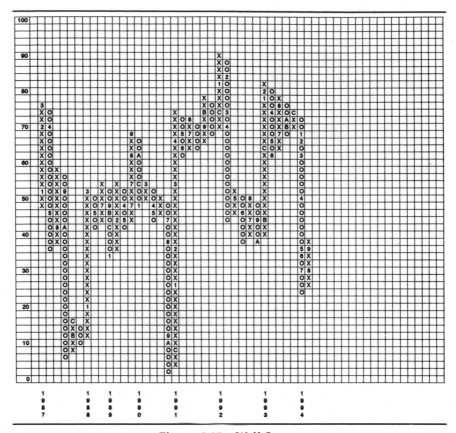

Figure 8.35   Wall Street.

would clean up the world. The index reversed up December 1991, ran up to 90 percent with everyone clamoring to catch the cleanup train. By February, the show was over. The index has been working its way down since then.

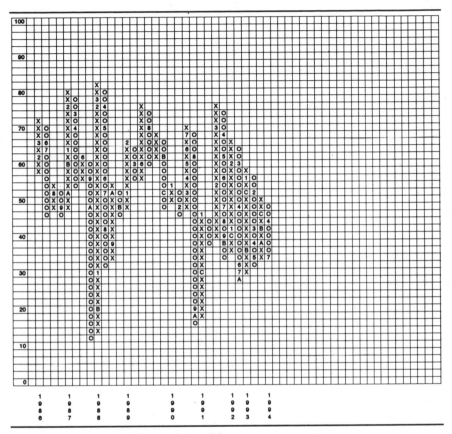

Figure 8.36   Waste management.

9

TRADING OPTIONS USING POINT AND FIGURE

The option business can be as complicated or simple as you want to make it. I developed and managed an options department for a broker dealer for the better part of a decade. I've seen it all. I found out one thing for sure during that period—the more complicated the option strategy, the lower the probability of success. There are basically two strategies that make sense for the individual investor: One is buying calls or puts as stock substitutes; the other is using puts as an insurance product to protect portfolios against disastrous declines in the overall markets. Using options as a vehicle to speculate wildly in the market will surely result in losses in the long run. In the short run, anything is possible.

I have taught many classes on options to both stockbrokers and individual investors and have written numerous articles on the subject. The key to understanding options is understanding the definitions of a put and call. All option strategies hinge on these definitions. No matter how difficult the strategy, if you break it down into its pieces and evaluate each piece separately, you will find options are no more difficult than basic arithmetic.

Let's start with the definitions. Learn these well enough to write them down from memory. If you ever get confused with any particular option strategy, stop, write the definition down, and evaluate each piece of the strategy separately. This is exactly how I learned options. I took a legal pad home on weekends and practiced breaking strategies up into pieces. I would then evaluate the pieces at expiration when there was no time premium left in the option and before I knew it, options became second nature. It can be just as easy for you. Just remember, keep it simple.

CALL DEFINITIONS

Call Option (Buyer) This is a contract that gives the buyer the right to call (buy) 100 shares of the underlying stock covered by the contract, at a stipulated price (exercise price) and at a stipulated time in the future (expiration date), in return for paying a premium to the seller of that call. Numerous exercise prices are attached to each stock. They generally go in 2½-point intervals up to $22½ and 5-point intervals above that level.

Call Option (Seller) The seller of a call option contracts to sell 100 shares of the underlying stock covered by the contract, at a stipulated price (exercise price) and at a stipulated time in the future (expiration date). The seller receives the premium (cost of the option) from the buyer.

The Call Buyer

The buyer of a call has tremendous leverage because of the ability to control a large amount of stock for a very small amount of money. Leverage is what draws investors to this arena. Philip Morris is currently around the $60 level. A call option to buy Philip Morris at $60 for the next 6 months costs $4 per share. Each contract represents 100 shares so the total cost, not including commissions, is $400. One hundred shares of Philip Morris at $60 costs $6,000. To control that dollar amount of Philip Morris for 6 months costs $400. You can see that the leverage can be quite high. Let's say you bought the call option we were just discussing. At expiration, Philip Morris is at $80. What is your call worth? Here is where basic arithmetic comes in handy. Let's go back to the definition. The call buyer has the right to call stock away from the seller at a stipulated price. In this example, it is $60. At expiration, or any time before, you can exercise that right—you paid for it. If Philip Morris at expiration is $80 and you have the right to buy the stock at $60, the value of the call is $20 ($80 − $60 = $20) × 100 shares per contract or $2,000. Since you paid $400 for the call, subtract the cost of $400 from your gross profit and you get a net profit, not including commissions, of $1,600. That is a 400 percent gain on the money you put up.

What if Philip Morris instead went down to $55? If you held the contract until expiration, it would be worthless. Why? It would be worthless because you have the right to pay $60 and the stock is at $55. If you wanted to own the stock, you would be better off just buying it in the market. Leverage is a two double-edged sword. Your loss in this case is 100 percent. Where most option traders go wrong is overleverage. A word to the wise, never buy more contracts than you have an appetite for round lots of the underlying stock. It's a quick way to the poor house. Early on in my career as a stockbroker, I routinely allowed my clients to overleverage themselves. The standard number of option contracts most clients aspire to is 10. It's just a round number and each point of profit equals $1,000 if you buy 10 contracts. Think of the example on Philip Morris just presented. You could just as easily put up $4,000 for 10 contracts as you did $400 for 1 contract. With 10 contracts you are now controlling 1,000 shares of Philip Morris at $60. This is now $60,000 worth of stock. The $4,000 is probably less than investors usually put up to buy stock. The difference here is you are buying calls on 1,000 shares of stock. If your normal appetite for stock is, let's say, 300 shares, you have just overleveraged yourself by 700 shares. Such transactions lead to financial disaster. The net result could be that the stock goes down, the $4,000 is lost, and the customer says the option product is too speculative and is responsible for losing a good percentage of investable capital. It wasn't the option product at all, it was the customer's desire to overleverage. Take my advice, if you are a 300-share buyer of stock, never buy more than three contracts. Manage your leverage.

The Call Writer (Seller)

The seller of that call is generally interested in capturing the premium income and is willing to give up the stock at the exercise price if the buyer of the call chooses to exercise the contract and take the stock. The individual should stick pretty much to the basics. Professionals use numerous exotic strategies that work for them simply because their transactional charges are almost nonexistent. One strategy the small investor often uses very effectively is the covered write. This strategy is simply an income-producing strategy in which the investor selling the call is willing to forgo potential upside appreciation in the stock in return for the premium income generated by selling the call. Let's take the Philip Morris example again. You own Philip Morris at $60 and feel the stock is likely to move sideways for a while. You might choose to sell a 6-month call against your stock. Using the previous example, you would receive $400 in cash (transaction fees are left out for simplicity). The $400 goes in your pocket now. You have received payment for contracting to give your stock up at $60 per share if the buyer of that contract so desires. If Philip Morris rises to $80, you will not get that capital gain. Your sales price will be $60. You knew that going in. If Philip Morris declines, the $400 received may partially or totally offset the loss. Your break-even price is $56 ($60 − $4 = $56). If at anytime during the life of that contract you would like to negate it, you can simply instruct your broker to buy the same contract back. You will be at the mercy of the market and may pay more than you received, but the option to cancel is still open to you.

In our daily research, we regularly recommend covered writes and base our selection on several guidelines. The first rule is the stock must be one that we believe is going up in price. In other words, the stock is trading above the Bullish Support line with positive relative strength. Next, we look at the return for selling the call. For us to recommend a covered write on a stock, the annualized called return should be 20 percent, the annualized static return should be 10 percent, and the downside protection should be 14 percent.

PUT DEFINITIONS

Put Options (Buyer) The buyer of a put has the right to put (sell) stock to the writer of that put, at a stipulated price (exercise price), for a stipulated time in the future (expiration date), and for that right must pay a premium to the seller of that put.

Put Options (Seller) The seller (underwriter) of the put stands ready to buy stock at a stipulated price (exercise price) for a stipulated time in the future (expiration date), and receives the premium from the buyer.

PUT VERSATILITY

The put option is the most versatile option tool available. It is also the most misunderstood. There are primarily two strategies that make sense to the individual investor: buying puts as short sale substitutes and buying puts as insurance against severe declines in his portfolio. Let's look for a second at what a short sale is.

Selling Short

Many investors will not sell short. It is simply contrary to most investors' optimistic outlook on things. A completed trade in the stock market consists of a purchase and sale of the underlying stock. Most investors are familiar with buy first-sell later transactions. The short sale entails selling first and buying later. In the end, both ingredients are present for a completed trade, the purchase and sale. Short sellers simply make a bet the stock will decline rather than rise. They borrow the stock they want to sell short through a brokerage firm promising to replace the stock at a future date. Normally, the replacement comes through an open-market purchase of the stock he sold. It may be at a profit or a loss depending on whether the stock subsequently rose or declined following the sale. Short sellers are also liable for any dividends on the stock they borrow. Short sellers are important in the scheme of things because they provide liquidity to the marketplace, thus helping other market participants facilitate their trades.

Actually, stocks decline faster than they rise. Think back for a moment to the probability study done by Professor Davis at Purdue University. It only takes 3.9 months for bearish chart patterns to work out in a bear market versus 7.2 months for bullish patterns to work out in a bull market. Bearish patterns work in bear markets 86.9 percent of the time, whereas bullish patterns work out in bull markets 83.7 percent of the time. This suggests you are better off selling short in a bear market than you are going long in a bull market. Why then do so few investors take advantage of selling short? Aside from the pessimistic view you must have on the market, there is theoretically unlimited risk in a short sale. If you buy a stock, it can only go to zero, and some do. There is no limit to how high a stock can go. The difference in buying a stock versus selling a stock short is that your risk is defined when you buy a stock and undefined when you sell short. Most investors prefer to stick to the known side of the equation. Short sales must also be done in a margin account. Many investors, like my mother, refuse to go on margin no matter what. She still remembers how her father got wiped out as a result of margin (overleverage) in the 1929 crash. There is a tool, however, that can make the short sale more palatable to the individual investor.

Put Options as Short Sale Substitutes

How about using puts as short sale substitutes? Remember the definition of a put? It gives the buyer the right to sell stock at a certain price until the expiration date of the contract. Let's say you bought a put on Philip Morris with an exercise price of $60 and an expiration date 6 months hence. For that right, you pay a premium of $4 × 100 shares or $400. (We'll use the same numbers as we did in the call example to keep things simple.) At the end of that period, Philip Morris is at $45. If you have the right to sell Philip Morris at $60 and it is currently selling in the market at $45, the put option must have some value. That value is the difference between what you can get by selling the stock versus what you must pay to buy the stock. What you could do is buy 100 shares of Philip Morris at the current market price of $45 and then exercise your put option to sell at $60. Your profit is $15 per share. Although you could go through those paces, very few investors do. If Philip Morris is at $45 at expiration, your put with an exercise price of $60 will be worth $15. All you have to do is instruct your broker to sell your option.

I have purposely left out examples prior to expiration because other variables such as time to expiration, volatility, and the prevailing risk-free interest rate come into play to determine the value of the option above its basic intrinsic value. Since this book is not designed to focus on options, I will leave the nuances of options for you to explore in other books devoted entirely to the subject.

What if Philip Morris did not go down but instead went up 15 points? It's simple—your put option would expire worthless if you held it to expiration. Why? Go back to the definition. The buyer of a put option has the right to sell stock. In this case, it is at a price of $60. If Philip Morris rose to $75, you would have to buy stock at $75 and then exercise your right to sell at $60. No one would do that, so the contract would expire worthless. Your loss as the put buyer would be $400—that's it—no matter how high Philip Morris went.

This is the main difference in risk versus the outright short sale. In a bad situation, your risk is defined by the amount you paid for the option. In a short sale, the pain just gets worse as the stock goes against you. If you want to talk about sleep deprivation, short sales will do it. Remember, any time during the life of the contract you can sell that put at whatever the market price is at that time. You do not have to wait until expiration to sell the contract. You can sell it 15 minutes after you buy it if you choose. In this example, the put provided a way to participate in an expected down move in Philip Morris with a defined risk of the premium paid. In this way, put buying can be much more palatable to the individual investor than selling short.

SELLING PUTS—THE UNDERWRITER

The put sellers are a special breed of investor who in many cases really don't understand what they are getting into. Describing the fast-paced 1980s will add flavor to my explanation of this strategy. During that decade, the option business ran rampant. The market just continued to go up, so the easier it got, the more speculative investors became. Selling put options slowly but surely began to expand in popularity until it reached its height in 1987. Whenever a speculative bubble is produced, a pin is not far away. The pin became evident in October 1987. The decade of the 1980s was an amazing period for the option product. It was like Dodge City with the sheriff on vacation.

I was once a featured speaker at an American Stock Exchange Options Colloquium. The AMEX holds this forum each year to give the so-called options experts in the world the opportunity to share their profound research with other practitioners in the investment business. I was so proud to be accepted as a speaker at such a high-powered conference and gave a presentation on the merits of naked straddle writing on index options. I discussed how conservative the strategy was and how the then margin rules helped augment the returns when Treasury bills were put up as collateral for the strategy. I break out in a cold sweat when I think of this speech, which I gave before the 1987 crash. Prior to 1987, virtually no one expected a decline of that magnitude—not in one day. Anyone following my grand plan found out in short order how painful selling put options on indexes could be. In fact, anyone selling any puts found it distasteful at best. We live and learn, but what a hard lesson this was.

What is the investor's motive for entering into this type of strategy? The put seller is simply the underwriter of the insurance policy the previous investor bought for protection. Concerning your car, an insurance seller might be Aetna Life and Casualty, Allstate, USAA, or any of a hundred other insurance companies. Sellers of a put or insurance are simply stating they are perfectly willing and capable of underwriting the risk outlined in the contract. In the case of the car, the insurance company is willing to buy your car from you if you have an accident. In the case of the put, the insurance underwriter is willing to buy your stock from you at the stipulated price if your stock has an accident. The put writer or underwriter is seeking to capture the premium on the contract just as an auto insurer does. It is the premium income from the sale of the contract that interests the underwriter, not capital gain. The success of an insurance company hinges on diversification, and lots of it. The insurance company knows it will have to pay off a certain amount of policies, but not the majority. Put writers typically can't get the diversification they need to act as an insurance company. Typically, put sellers speculate that the stocks they sell puts on will not have an accident. In 1987, all stocks had an accident on October 19. If all the automobiles in the United States were to have an accident on the same day, the insurance industry would be wiped out. Put sellers in October 1987 were wiped out. Almost all put writers at that time were undercapitalized and totally unprepared for the consequences of contracts they had promised to fulfill. Wall Street was in total disarray, and it was rumored that some brokerage houses would go under. I know of numerous cases where people lost their whole life savings and more. This created a rash of lawsuits on Wall Street from brokers who demanded payment for the losses generated by the crash and from customers who sued the broker for allowing them to engage in an investment that was unsuitable for their investment objectives and temperament. Overnight, the option product went from being the darling of Wall Street to being a product that was to be avoided at all costs. The repercussions are still with us. Some brokerage firms will not allow new brokers to engage in option trading until they have been in the business for 3 years.

Most investors blame the trouble on the option product itself but the real problem was overleverage, not options. I guess you could call it basic greed. Recently, we have had another bubble burst. It had to do with overleverage again. This time, it was primarily confined to bond derivatives (another name for option products). Major losses were taken by so-called conservative bond funds. The losses were mind boggling. Again, the culprit was overleverage, not the option product. I recently saw a cartoon of a homeless man sitting on a sidewalk with a cup begging for change. He had a sign beside him saying "No Derivatives Please." Some tremendous books have been written on options if you really want to get into it. For the purposes of this chapter, I want to present some basic ideas on how you can successfully trade options.

Before the crash of 1987, it seemed everyone wanted to get into the game regardless of expertise. I can remember an elderly couple coming into our brokerage firm and telling their broker they wanted to increase their retirement income by selling uncovered put options. They would collateralize the puts with the fully paid Treasury bills they had in their brokerage account. You see, they had heard of this strategy at their bridge club. Apparently, other members of the club had been employing the strategy very successfully. It would work well as long as the market and the stocks they sold puts on, kept going up. A major decline in the market and stocks in general would spell financial disaster for most of them. Remember the definition of buying and selling puts.

PUTS AS INSURANCE POLICIES

To explain puts from a different angle, the buyer of insurance, let me ask you a question. Do you own a put, Yes or No? OK, let me ask you one more question. Do you own a car? If the answer to the second question is yes, you own a car, then the answer to the first question is also yes, you own a put. If you own a car, you also own some insurance on the car. Puts are simply insurance policies. A put option gives the buyer of the put the right to sell stock at a certain price, for a certain time period by paying a premium (cost of the put) for this right. Your insurance policy on your car effectively says you can do the same thing. Let's say you have an accident that leaves your car a total wreck. Your insurance policy will pay you for that wrecked car. Your policy states in the event of an accident, the insurance company will pay you a stipulated amount of money covering the extent of the damages. The insurance policy stays in effect for a certain period of time, let's say 6 months, at the end of which time you must renew or cancel the policy. For the right to own that insurance policy, you pay a premium to the underwriter or seller of that policy, the insurance company. When I was a teenager, I had an accident in my father's car that bent the frame. The car couldn't be repaired. The insurance company paid us book value for the car minus the deductible. I actually think we made out on that deal. My dad didn't.

The put option is no different. Since put buyers have the right to sell stock (underlying stock) at a certain price (exercise price) for a certain period (expiration date) they are entering into a contract very similar to the one you have on your car. Option contracts always represent 100 shares of stock. Let's say you buy Philip Morris at $60 per share. Let's also say you want to protect against a major decline in the market that will undoubtedly include Philip Morris. You might consider buying a 6-month put option with an exercise price of $60. The put might cost you $3 × 100 shares of stock or $300 (in the previous example, we used $400). Option prices change daily as time to expiration as well as other factors change. If Philip Morris declined to $50 over the next 6 months, you could simply notify your broker you would like to exercise your put contract that stipulates you can sell Philip Morris at $60 per share. You might also decide to hold the stock and simply sell the option for the gain. In our example, Philip Morris had an accident and declined to $50 per share. By exercising your put contract, you would be able to sell 100 shares of Philip Morris at $60. With the stock now at $50, you could protect yourself by $1,000. Now what did it cost you to get that protection? The cost was $300 so your net protection was $1,000 − $300 = $700. If Philip Morris didn't have an accident and remained at $60 or higher, the put policy would simply lapse. When we buy insurance policies, we always hope we don't have to use them. So to recap, the put buyer can also be interested in insuring his portfolio rather than making a bet the stock will decline.

The key to successful option trading is successful stock trading. You must be right on the stock before you can be right on the option. Before you select an option to buy, you must first go through the steps I have outlined for stock selection in the previous chapters of this book. You cannot even consider an option until you have done your homework on the underlying stock.

I have tried to avoid confusing terminology thus far but the following definitions will help you to understand options more thoroughly:

Delta The amount an option will move in relation to a one-dollar move in the underlying stock.

Exercise Price The stated price to buy the underlying stock in a contract, generally fixed at 2½ point intervals below $22½ and 5-point intervals above $22½.

Expiration Date Date on which the option contract expires. The owner of an option can sell the contract at any time before expiration at prevailing market prices. The seller of an option may repurchase the option he sold at prevailing market prices.

Option Premium Value of the option determined by market forces, including underlying stocks volatility, risk-free interest rate, time to expiration, and underlying stocks dividend.

In-the-Money In the case of a call, an exercise price below current market prices of the underlying stock; in the case of a put, an exercise price above current market prices of the underlying stock. If it sounds confusing, go back to the definitions of puts and calls earlier in this chapter.

Out-of-the-Money In the case of a call, an exercise price above the current market price of the underlying stock; in the case of a put, an exercise price below the current market price of the underlying stock.

At-the-Money In the case of both put and call, an exercise price and underlying stock price that are the same.

Intrinsic Value With reference to the premium of an option, the amount the option is in-the-money. If IBM was at 65 and an October 60 call was trading at $6, we would say that $5 of that $6 represents intrinsic value (amount in-the-money) and $1 of that $6 represents time to expiration. If the stock just sat there until expiration, the call option would eventually be worth the exact amount it was in-the-money—in this case, $5.

Time Premium The value of an option above its intrinsic value. If there is no intrinsic value the total cost of the option represents time to expiration.

The key to successful option trading is successful stock trading. If you are wrong on the stock, you will be wrong on the option. All we want the option to do is replicate the stock as much as possible. Once you have selected the underlying stock, then and only then can you consider the option. This is where the term *delta* comes into play. The deeper the put or call is in-the-money, the higher the correlation to a point-for-point move with the underlying stock.

RULE OF THUMB FOR DELTAS

A general guideline for deltas is as follows: An option that is 5 points in-the-money will have an option delta approximately 75 percent. In other words, you can expect about a 3/4-point move in the option for each 1-point move in the stock. An option that is at-the-money will approximate a delta of 50 percent, and an option that is 5 points out-of-the-money will have a delta approximating 25 percent. Computers can fine-tune the delta down to $\frac{1}{10}$ of a percent, but who needs to know exactly what the delta is when market forces keep that figure in constant flux? Just try to stay in the ballpark and you'll be fine.

When I was a broker, we usually bought options by price. What I mean is our selection typically had nothing to do with how the option would move in relation to the underlying stock. If a client had $1,000 available to buy options, we bought the exercise price that fit that client's pocketbook. Keep in mind that back in the 1970s and early 1980s we didn't know much about options. We flew by the seat of our pants. Let me give you an example. In the previously stated rule of thumb, I said that a strike price 5 points out-of-the-money would carry a delta (amount the option will move in relation to a 1-point move in the stock) of approximately .25. Let's say IBM is at $60 per share and I choose to buy a 3-month call with an exercise price of 65. The exercise price is 5 points above the current price of the stock. We say it is 5 points out-of-the-money since "the money" is the current price of IBM. The delta of this call option will be around .25. If IBM moves up $1, my option will move up .25. At expiration, IBM must be trading at $65 for this 3-month call to be worth nothing. Think back to the definition. The buyer of a call has the right to call stock away from someone at a stipulated price. If the price is, in this case, $65 and the stock is currently at $65 there is no advantage to holding the call at expiration. Thus its value is zero. This is a situation where the investor was dead right on the stock and dead wrong on the exercise price selection. Here are some of my rules of the road:

1. **Always Buy In-the-Money Calls or Puts Because the Delta Is Relatively High.** Remember you want the option to look as much like the stock as possible. Some strategists recommend you buy two at-the-money calls instead of one in-the-money call to replicate the move in the stock. Think about that statement for a moment. We said in the rule of thumb that an at-the-money call had an approximate delta of .50. If you bought two options with a delta of .50 you would have a delta of .50 + .50 = 1. This would give you a move in the combined options of 1. As the stock rose, moving further in the money, the deltas would increase thus giving you a greater than 1 move in the calls versus the stock. The only problem with this is that if the stock sits still during the life of the contract (which can often happen), the total premium paid will be lost. Since a deep in-the-money call is almost all intrinsic value, the time premium will be minimal. Thus if a stock stays neutral during the life of the contract, the majority of the option's price will remain intact. In my estimation, this aspect of an in-the-money call is more important than gaining any added delta from the purchase of two at-the-money calls.

2. **Never Overleverage.** Only buy as many contracts as you would otherwise buy round lots of the underlying stock. Keep the remaining

money you would have invested in the stock in the money market fund. Overleverage is a very common mistake made by options traders.

3. **Buy Time.** Time is the silent killer of options, the Grim Reaper. Always go out longer than 6 weeks because time premium decays most rapidly beginning around 6 weeks to expiration. Since you are keying off a move in the underlying stock, be sure your option does not expire before the average time for the pattern to work out for the stock. For instance, the average time for a Triple Top buy signal to work out in a bull market is 6.8 months. A 6-month option would be required when you are using a Triple Top buy signal in the stock. The best pattern to use is the Bearish Signal Reversal as its average time to work out is 2.5 months. The most conducive patterns for call option trading are the Bullish Triangle at 5.4 months, Triple Top at 6.8 months, and the Bearish Signal Reversed at 2.4 months. Any pattern is fine for puts because the longest time for a pattern to work out in a bear market is 4.7 months. Remember that the option must work out within the time frame of expiration.

4. **Stop Losses.** There are two ways to look at an option trade. The simplest is to look at the premium you pay for the put or call as your stop. Had you bought the underlying stock, you would have been willing to take a certain loss up to your stop point. You can consider that loss you would have taken in the stock as the premium you pay for the option. If the stock does not move in your favor, you simply hold until expiration. This gives you second and third chances to succeed. Lots can happen to a stock over a 6-month period. Another possible loss-limiting strategy would be to sell the option at the point you would normally stop the loss in the stock. Since you are attempting to create a position in the option that is similar to the stock, treat the option as if it were the stock. This might save you 50 percent of the premium, but you also give up the chance to make it back later on. I have a tendency to play it both ways depending on the situation.

5. **Keep It Simple.** The more sophisticated, the lower the probability of success. Remember, you cannot consider an option before you have done all the work on the stock first.

In evaluating which option to buy, the market is your first consideration. Who has the ball? Buying calls in a bear-configured market will be difficult at best. On the other hand, bear-configured markets are conducive to put buying. Be sure you know who has the ball before you jump into the game. Check the short-term picture. It might be best to hold off the purchase of calls when the short-term indicators are bearish. Remember, time is the silent killer of options. Timing is everything here. The long-term trend might be bullish while the short-term trend is bearish. Have both the long and short term going in the same direction before you buy an option. Evaluate the Sector Bullish Percent Indexes before you select the stock. In the case of a call, the sector should be on one of the three buy signals and below the 50 percent level for optimum conditions. In the case of a put, the sector should be on one of the three sell signals and residing above the 50 percent level.

Once the sector is selected, find a stock within the sector that is fundamentally sound. Simply check to see if a Wall Street firm is recommending the purchase of this stock. The best place to start is with your broker. Most have numerous correspondent firms' research and can answer this question in a moment. This goes a long way in ensuring the stock is fundamentally sound. Along with the fundamentals, it's nice to see some insider buying in the stock (like the president buying his own stock). This is not essential, but it's nice to have.

After you have selected the list of fundamentally sound stocks, check the Point and Figure chart patterns and select the best and strongest looking stock. Be sure the stock is on a buy signal and is

Market	NYSE Bullish Percent in Bull Alert status—you have the ball.
Short Term	Percent of 10 & High-Low Index on buy signals
Sector	Health care—Bull Confirmed at 40 percent and rising
Stock	U.S. Surgical (USS), $25
Stock Fundamentals	Ranked "Buy" by three major Wall Street firms.
Stock Technicals	Strong uptrend, above Bullish Support line, relative strength chart positive.
Stock Price Objective	Vertical count off the bottom suggests a price objective of $33 for potential 32 percent gain. Stock's Triangle formation suggests 30.9 percent gain in 5.4 months. Both exceed the average gain for bull market patterns.
Option Expiration Date	Must be long enough for chart pattern to work out.
Option Exercise Price	20—5 points in-the-money
Option Delta	.80 option should initially move 80 percent for each point in USS.
Number of Contracts	Only as many as you would otherwise have an appetite for round lots of the underlying stocks.
Stop Loss	Trend line break along with Triple Bottom Sell signal at $22. Alternative stop is to simply hold until expiration.

(Use this outline to evaluate your selection the next time you are going to trade options.)

Figure 9.1   Steps to option selection.

trading above the Bullish Support line. Be sure the relative strength is positive and preferably within the past year.

When you have selected the stock, do a vertical count or a horizontal count to determine its price objective. Also check the last pattern you are working from and be sure its average gain exceeds the total average gain of 29.5 percent of all bull market patterns. In the case of a put, be sure it exceeds 24.8 percent which is the average for bear market patterns.

Next, select the expiration date allowing enough time for your pattern to work out. In selecting the exercise price, be sure you go deep enough in the money so the delta equals or exceeds 75 percent. Normally 5 points in-the-money is sufficient. Only buy as many contracts as you would usually buy lots of 100 shares. If you normally buy 300 shares, then only buy 3 contracts of options. Never overleverage. Last, set your stops. Either stop the option out where you would have stopped the stock out had you owned the underlying stock instead of the option, or consider the option premium as your stop and hold on until expiration.

If you follow these simple steps, you will increase your probability of success trading options. In many cases, it makes more sense to buy the options than the stock. Take a look at the steps shown in Figure 9.1 (on page 209). After you go through this exercise, try it yourself using a sample stock.

10

TRADING COMMODITIES USING POINT AND FIGURE

I have been asked a number of times to teach a class on Point and Figure technical analysis for commodity traders at the futures magazine conventions. I have accepted each time and have found the experience to be an eye opener. Our company, Dorsey, Wright & Associates, does not provide any commodity research to professionals. We do, however, trade a proprietary commodity account for our own money as a diversification from other investments we are involved in. We also manage a hedge fund. Each time I attend these seminars I am amazed at how little commodity traders understand about supply and demand. Most of them could discuss the merits of Fibonacci retracement numbers, fractals, and the like; but supply and demand—not a chance.

The responses to my seminars on commodity trading have been absolutely overwhelmingly positive, not because I have any special talent, but because attendees feel they have had a revelation when they become reacquainted with the nuances of supply and demand. I am the only instructor I know of who teaches at these seminars with no products to sell the attendees. Not only that, I have to pay to go. Am I nuts? I often wonder. I go because I have a plan that will help people become more successful in their commodity trading and I sincerely desire to impart this knowledge to them. That is the basis of our whole company, to help others.

Trading commodity futures is a little different from trading equities. Equities are relatively slow compared with the moves in futures. For this reason, patterns we normally associate with equities don't have time to materialize in futures—at least not often. The primary signal we go with in futures trading is the Double Top Buy Signal and the Double Bottom Sell Signal. Trend lines take on major importance in futures trading. I think the best commentary on futures trading was done by A. W. Cohen, the first editor of Chartcraft. John Grey now heads up the futures division of Chartcraft and he is super. I highly recommend you subscribe to their commodity service as it has all the charts plus commentary on the futures that trade and you don't have to worry about having the right box size for the contract. They take care of that.

I have studied A. W. Cohen's methods in detail and wholeheartedly concur with his approach. We use this method in the proprietary commodity account we trade for our own funds and find the approach suits us perfectly. The key to success in commodity trading is to let your profits run and cut your losses short. Brilliant statement, you say. I thought the same thing at first glance. Think about it for a second. What is the reason most commodity traders lose? Taking small profits and large losses. Things happen so fast in commodity trading that a trader who has a profit feels obligated to take it. Another killer in commodity trading is overleverage. Earl Blumenthal has a good way to overcome that problem.

The Point and Figure method offers you clear buy and sell signals that other methods of analysis do not. The crucial part of trading is clear action points. The way you keep your losses low is by taking every sell signal the Point and Figure chart gives you, don't second-guess them. You allow your profits to run by going long on any buy signal and holding on to the position, no matter what, until a sell signal develops. Trend lines are extremely important. If a future is trading above the Bullish Support line, always trade long. If the future is trading below the Bearish Resistance line, always trade short. Earl Blumenthal suggested that you begin with one contract and add one contract on each buy or sell signal depending on whether you are long or short. Stop all contracts out on the first sell signal. A. W. Cohen never suggested pyramiding and only discussed trading one unit at a time. Figure 10.1 shows the chart from A. W. Cohen's book, *The Three-Point Reversal Method of Point and Figure Stock Market Trading*, which illustrates the process.

This chart comes in on a short sale and ends on a buy signal. The key to the success of the trades made on this chart is the trades were allowed to run. You can easily see how all trades were made with the trend, never against the trend. Trend lines can be adjusted when the chart, in the case of a downtrend, gives a buy signal and then resumes the trend and gives another sell signal. The trend line can be moved down to the new top. In the case of an uptrend, the trend line can be adjusted when the chart gives a sell signal followed by a buy signal. In this case, the trend line can be moved up. A good example of moving a trend line down is shown in Figure 10.1. Let's look at the cotton chart

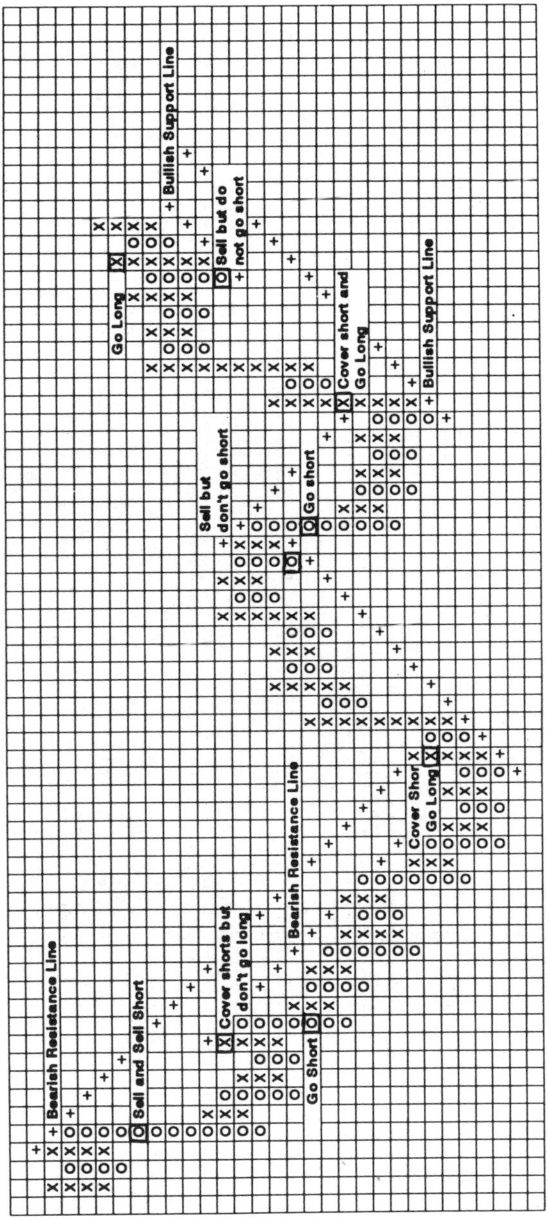

Figure 10.1 Commodity trading chart from A. W. Cohen.

Figure 10.2 Cotton, December 1994 (QQCTZ).

214

(Figure 10.2) and apply these principles. At first glance, you might have thought this trend was untradable. It actually panned out to be a great play.

It is also important to diversify and trade a few commodity futures at the same time, both long and short. Stay with the future as long as it continues to trend. For example, if the underlying future is above the Bullish Support line and your position gets stopped out, go right back in on the next buy signal and continue on with the program. It's the kiss of death to jump around to different contracts each time you get stopped out. Stay with the trend.

We go short on the first sell signal off the top at 75.80. The contract drops to a low of 68.20 but we don't get stopped out until a Double Top buy signal is given at 70.40 + 5.40. Do not go long as the contract is still below the Bearish Resistance line. The contract subsequently rises to the trend line at 74.20 and reverses. A Double Bottom sell signal is given at 72.40 that you take and go short. The next buy signal that stops you out is at 67.80 + 4.6. You are stopped out but do not go long as the contract is below the Bearish Resistance line. The next sell signal comes at 69.60 and the stopping buy signal comes at 68 on a Triple Top + 1.60. Do not go long. Cotton then rises and breaks the Bearish Resistance line at 69 on a buy signal (go long). The stopping Double Bottom happens at 68.40–.60. You now place a buy stop order to buy one contract at 70.20 on the next buy signal. If another buy signal develops lower than the GTC buy at 70.20, cancel the order at 70.20 and go with the buy signal at the lower price. The net result of trades on cotton from June 1994 would have been 11 points or $5,500 on a one-contract basis. Let's subtract 15 percent for slippage and commissions and the net would be around $4,675.

Let's recap the rules for trading:

- Only trade long when the commodity is above the Bullish Support line.

- Only trade short when the commodity is below the Bearish Resistance line.

- If you are long, remain so until you receive the first sell signal, then stop the position out. If the commodity is still above the Bullish Support line, repurchase a contract on the next buy signal and stop out on the first sell signal. You will never catch a trend unless you are relentless in your pursuit of a trend.

- If you are short, remain so until you receive the first buy signal, then stop the position out. If the commodity is still below the bearish resistance line, sell short another contract on the next sell signal. The same applies here to the pursuit of a trend.

- Never trade against the trend under any circumstances.
- Raise or lower the Bullish Support line or Bearish Resistance line whenever possible. To raise the Bullish Support line you must first receive a sell signal followed by another buy signal. To lower the Bearish Resistance line you must first receive a buy signal followed by another sell signal.
- If the underlying commodity breaks the Bullish Support line, begin to trade short as the trend is now down.
- If the underlying commodity breaks the Bearish Resistance line, begin to trade long as the trend is now up.
- When you are long a contract continue to raise your stop point each time a new sell signal is created. Never, never sell the contract until you receive a sell signal.
- When you are short a contract continue to lower your stop point each time a new buy signal is created. Never, never cover the short until you receive a buy signal.
- Diversify whenever possible. It is good to be both long and short. Don't put all your money in one contract. Develop some money management techniques.

11

PUTTING IT ALL TOGETHER

So far, we have been examining the pieces of the puzzle. It's time to put the puzzle together. The successful dinner is generally the product of a cook who religiously followed the recipe. The same goes for successful investing. Truly successful investors have some guidelines they adhere to religiously. I have never seen a successful investor who over time haphazardly went about this business. The following seven steps will help you develop an effective game plan:

Guidelines for Stock Selection

1. Evaluate the NYSE Bullish Percent Index.
2. Evaluate the two main short-term indicators: The Percent of Stocks above Their Own 10-Week Moving Average Index and the High-Low Index.
3. Evaluate the Sector Bullish Percent Indexes and select a sector for investment.
4. From the sector, select a group of fundamentally sound stocks.
5. Examine the Point and Figure charts of the stocks underlying the sector you choose to invest in and make an inventory.
6. Select your entry point and set your stops.
7. Decide where to take a profit. Know what to do when things go right and things go wrong.

STEP 1. EVALUATE THE NYSE INDEX—
WHO'S GOT THE BALL?

This is the step most investors and money managers never think about. Most investors think one way—buy stocks, always play offense. Mutual funds are the same way. They are paid to keep you fully invested in all times. The problem is you don't always have possession of the football. There are times that the market has the ball, and that's perfectly fair. When the market has the ball, its job is to score against you by taking as much money away from your portfolio as it can. The market does a great job of it as you can see from the study done at Purdue University by Professor Davis. The bearish patterns work against you much faster than the bullish patterns. Conversely, there are times when you have the ball. These are the times you must run plays and attempt to score against the market by having the strength in your conviction to buy stocks.

Another roadblock you must overcome is that you will invariably take possession of the ball when the news is the most bearish. The market will take possession of the ball when the news is the most bullish. This is the point where you must control your emotions. You will be forced to buy when things look the worst and forced to defend your portfolio when things look the best, a pattern that goes against human nature. It's like the edge the house has in Las Vegas—theirs in mathematical and yours is emotional. Someone always sells at the top and buys at the bottom. Who are these people? We call them the "Smart Money." If I had to pick a few investors I might include in this group, they would be Warren Buffett, Jimmy Rogers, George Soros, John Templeton, and Victor Sperandeo.

I do not belong to the select Smart Money group; I belong in a second group—the "Followers of Smart Money." The insiders like Warren Buffett are typically contrarian investors. They have the discipline to buy when things look the worst and sell when things look the best. When they begin operating in the market, they cast their vote by buying stock. This in turn causes the supply-demand relationship of these stocks to change, which clearly shows up on a Point and Figure chart. This is why I say the Point and Figure chart is as good as inside information.

As the chart patterns form, buy and sell signals are given. A positive change will take place in the NYSE Bullish Percent Index when enough buy signals take place to cause 6 percent of the stocks on the New York Stock Exchange to change from bearish to bullish (sell signal to buy signal). At this point, the NYSE Bullish Percent Index changes from a column of O's (market has the ball) to a column of X's (you have the ball). This is the point at which you must have the intestinal fortitude to run plays when everything you read suggests otherwise. The opposite takes place when the Bullish Percent turns negative. You are not Warren Buffett or John Templeton, but you are running a close second.

Look down to the bottom of 1987 in the NYSE Bullish Percent chart (Figure 11.1). Notice the B (November) in the chart at the 12 percent level. That was the first reversal off the bottom following the crash to signal you should begin buying stock. If you listened to the news reports and read the business periodicals, you would have been preparing for 1929. In September 1987, when the Bullish Percent reversed into a column of O's, would you have had the strength in your conviction to sell stocks or at least protect your portfolio? All the news then was bullish on stocks. The Dow had just gone to new all-time highs, and there were virtually no disconcerted investors. In November 1990, would you have believed your coach, the NYSE Bullish Percent, and begun running plays (buy stocks) when the media and prominent technicians on Wall Street were predicting doom and gloom? I know after reading this book, you will have the conviction to do the right thing.

Remember the first line of defense is knowing who has possession of the ball. When the index is declining in a column of O's, the market has the ball. When the index is rising in a column of X's, you have the ball. You must then determine your field position. Bull Confirmed at 70 percent has very little value, whereas Bull Confirmed at 30 percent has an abundance of value. The opposite is true with the bearish side of the coin. A Bear Confirmed status at 68 percent means much more risk than a Bear Confirmed status at 26 percent. Your best buying opportunities come when the NYSE Bullish Percent is on a buy signal below 30 percent. Your best selling opportunities come when the NYSE Bullish Percent Index is on a sell signal above the 70 percent level. Keep field position firmly in mind. Once you get the hang of this, you are going to love it. You will join the select few on Wall Street who understand these principles.

STEP 2. EVALUATE THE TWO SHORT-TERM INDICATORS—WHO'S GOT THE BALL SHORT TERM?

Percent of NYSE Stocks above Their Own Ten-Week Moving Average

My favorite short-term indicator is the Percent of NYSE Stocks above Their Own 10-Week Moving Average Line (Percent of 10). We discussed this index in detail in Chapter 7, but we need to touch on it again. We read this index basically the same way we do the Bullish Percent

Figure 11.1 NYSE Bullish Percent.

Indexes. We have established 70 percent and above as the upper region where the market is overbought short-term. Conversely, we consider the 30 percent level and lower to be the oversold short-term market. This index moves like a sports car and the Bullish Percent Indexes move like a bus. Therefore, we are sometimes short-term bearish and long-term bullish and vice versa. Think for a moment about the following market condition: The NYSE Bullish Percent is at 40 percent and in Bull Confirmed status rising in a column of X's, and the Percent of 10 has just given a sell signal by reversing from above to below 70 percent. What is this combination saying to you? It is saying you should postpone any further stock commitments until the short-term picture once again goes back on a buy signal. Stocks you were considering buying should go on hold as you will probably get a better price for them. Think for a moment why the Percent of 10 can move about without affecting the Bullish Percent Index. The Percent of Stocks above Their Own 10-Week Moving Average is exactly what the name implies; stocks can move above or below their 10-week moving average without ever giving a buy or sell signal on a Point and Figure chart. The Percent of 10 could run from 70 percent down to 20 percent without having much effect on the NYSE Bullish Percent Index. Here's another scenario using the NYSE Bullish Percent and the Percent of 10. If the Percent of 10 had just reversed up from below 30 percent and the NYSE Bullish Percent was in Bear Alert status having just crossed the 70 percent level on the downside, we would expect stocks to rise for the short term, but this rise should be used to sell stocks rather than buy stocks. It would also suggest that short sellers should postpone their short sales until this short-term indicator once again reverts to a sell signal and moves in concert with the main indicator, the NYSE Bullish Percent Index. Look at the combination of arrows in Figures 11.2 and 11.3 showing the respective direction of each indicator and the concept will become a little more clear.

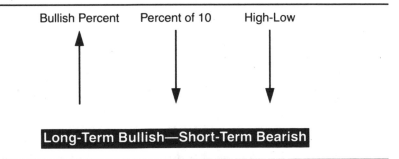

Figure 11.2   Market scenario with the three main technical indicators.

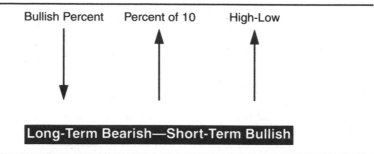

Figure 11.3   Market scenario with the three main technical indicators.

The High-Low Index

The only other short-term indicator that goes into the mix is the High-Low Index. As described in Chapter 7, this index is simply calculated by dividing the daily NYSE highs by the daily NYSE highs plus the lows. A 10-day moving average is taken to smooth out the index. We like to see this one go in the same direction as the Percent of 10. If they are not, the short-term direction of the market is suspect until they are both in concert. We use other-fine tuning indicators such as Point and Figure charts of the broad averages and some others we discussed in Chapter 7 but the Percent of 10 and the High-Low Index are our main short-term guides.

STEP 3. SELECT A SECTOR—A CRUCIAL DECISION

Once you have a good handle on the short- and intermediate-term picture of the market, you are ready to evaluate the sector. I spent a great deal of time on Chapter 8 because sector rotation plays such a key role in the success of your investing endeavor. Proper sector selection can make the difference between success or failure. I have repeated often that about 75 percent of the risk is in the market and sector. Most investors focus most of their research on the underlying stock's fundamentals and place little emphasis on the sector and the market. When evaluating a sector for investment, try to select one that is below the 50 percent level and on one of the three buy signals. It simply doesn't make sense to buy stocks in a sector that is on a sell signal because it reduces your odds of success. Once the sector rises above the 50 percent level, the field position moves to the overbought side of the ledger. The higher the sector moves, the less aggressive you should become with it. You must be prepared to take advantage of sectors that move below 30 percent and then reverse up from that level. These sectors are

	Symbol		07/29 Price	52-Wk Range	Fisc Year End	Annual EPS Estimates			ABS P/E		P/E vs S&P 500		% 5 Yr Growth		Indicated Dividend		Mkt Value (Mil.)
						F93	F94	F95	94E	95E	94E	95E	EPS	Div	Rate	Yld	
Bob Evans Farm	BOBE	H	21³/₈	24–18	04/95	1.13	1.30		16.4	NAv	114	NA	13	13	0.27	1.3	911
Chart House	CHT	H	7³/₈	16–6	12/94	0.48	0.55	0.65	13.4	11.3	93	85	18	NA	0.00	0.0	60
Checkers Drive-In	CHKR	B	5	15–5	12/94	0.31	0.18	0.26	27.8	19.2	192	144	25	NA	0.00	0.0	243
Cheesecake Factory	CAKE	SB	15³/₄	25–14	12/94	0.48	0.73	1.00	21.6	15.7	149	118	30	NA	0.00	0.0	167
DavCo	DVCO	SB	17	19–11	09/94	0.68	1.00	1.30	17.0	13.1	118	98	32	NA	0.00	0.0	111
Hamburger Hamlet	HAMB	H	6¹/₂	9–6	12/94	0.23	0.25	0.40	26.0	16.2	180	121	20	NA	0.00	0.0	26
IHOP Corp	IHOP	SB	27³/₄	34–21	12/94	1.30	1.66	2.00	16.7	13.9	116	104	22	NA	0.00	0.0	254
Lubys Cafeterias	LUB	H	22⁷/₈	26–21	08/94	1.32	1.44	1.60	15.9	14.3	110	107	10	10	0.66	2.9	590
McDonalds	MCD	SB	27¹/₈	31–26	12/94	1.46	1.68	1.89	16.1	14.4	112	107	14	15	0.24	0.9	19197
Shoneys	SHN	H	14¹/₈	26–14	10/94	1.33	1.55	1.80	9.1	7.8	63	59	18	NA	0.00	0.0	581
Sonic Corp	SONC	SB	18¹/₄	29–18	08/94	1.10	1.35	1.65	13.5	11.1	94	83	22	NA	0.00	0.0	144
Wendys Intl	WEN	SB	15⁵/₈	19–13	12/94	0.77	0.91	1.07	16.9	14.4	117	107	18	13	0.24	1.6	1555

SB=STRONG BUY   B=BUY   H=HOLD   S=SELL

Figure 11.4 Restaurants.

about as washed out as they will be for years to come. Opportunities to buy stocks in such a sold-out condition do not happen very often. When such a situation occurs, take advantage of it. Short sellers operate from above the 50 percent level because they seek to sell short stocks in groups on the overbought side of the ledger.

STEP 4. SELECT A GROUP OF FUNDAMENTALLY SOUND STOCKS FROM THE CHOSEN SECTOR

This step begins the filtering process. The idea is to find a few stocks that meet the fundamental and technical criteria to include in your inventory for that sector. The best and easiest way to find these fundamentally sound stocks is to ask your broker for his firm's recommended list. Qualified analysts are paid major bucks at their firms to do this research. Use it. If you deal at a discount broker, you will need to find some outside source for your fundamental input. Two names come to mind that could be of assistance to you: Value Line and Zachs Research. Most investors are at least familiar with Value Line.

STEP 5. EVALUATE AND INVENTORY THE CHART PATTERNS FOR YOUR GROUP OF STOCKS

It is now time to evaluate the chart patterns of the fundamentally sound stocks you selected. Not only do we want a stock that fundamentally fit, we also want to be sure there is a high probability the stock will rise. Check the relative strength chart to be sure the stock is currently outperforming the broad market. At least insure the stock is rising in a column of X's on its relative strength chart. The best way to get this information is through Chartcraft of New Rochelle, New York, which puts out a monthly book of approximately 10,000 charts covering all listed stocks and many OTC stocks. I think it's the greatest. The cost is $40 per month, but you will be able to find just about any stock you want to evaluate in that book. They also provide the weekly updates to the charts. You can't beat this value—$40 per month is about ⅛ of a point on 300 shares of stock. Chartcraft also gives you the relative strength reading of the stock and also puts a plus or minus sign in the upper right-hand corner of the chart to suggest whether the stock's relative strength chart is in a column of X's (+) or O's (−). The following are points to remember in evaluating the supply and demand picture of the stock:

1. The stock must be trading above the Bullish Support line (Figure 11.5).

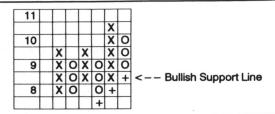

Figure 11.5   Trading above the Bullish Support Line.

2. The relative strength should be positive. Remember relative strength is calculated by dividing the price of the stock by the Dow Jones and then plotting that figure on a Point and Figure chart. The relative strength chart might look like the chart shown in Figure 11.6 after the division is done.

3. Try to buy the stock on a pullback to support (Figure 11.7); although this is not essential, it really helps with the risk reward. It's usually best to have patience and allow the stock to come to you.

4. Perform a vertical or horizontal count to determine the expected move in the stock. The price objective should exceed the average

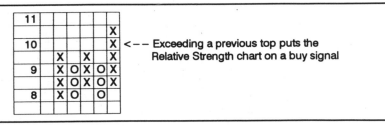

Figure 11.6   Relative strength buy signal.

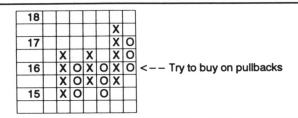

Figure 11.7   Pullback.

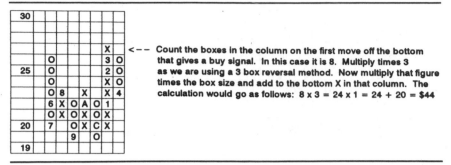

Figure 11.8 Calculating risk/reward.

expected move from the Purdue University study discussed in Chapter 3. That average move is 29.5 percent for bull markets and 24.8 percent for bear markets. The risk versus reward must be at least 2 to 1. This is a minimum expectation you should have for stocks you purchase or sell short. The chart shown in Figure 11.8 more than meets that requirement.

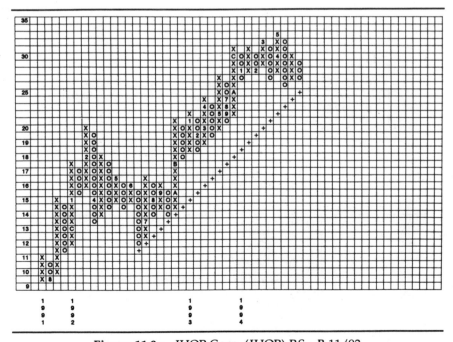

Figure 11.9a IHOP Corp. (IHOP) RS—B 11/92.

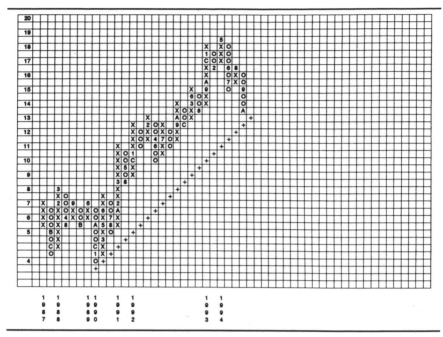

Figure 11.9b   Wendy's International (WEN) RS—S 6/84.

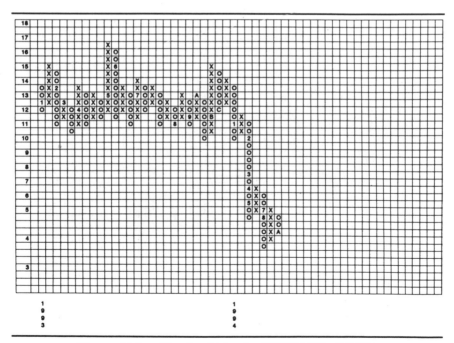

Figure 11.9c   Checker Drive-In (CHKR) RS—S 7/93.

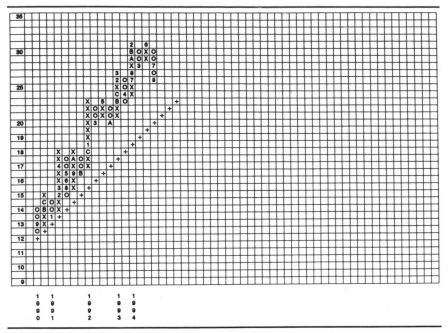

Figure 11.9d McDonalds (MCD) RS—B 9/78.

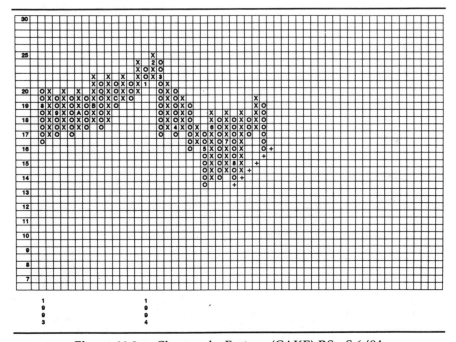

Figure 11.9e Cheesecake Factory (CAKE) RS—S 6/94.

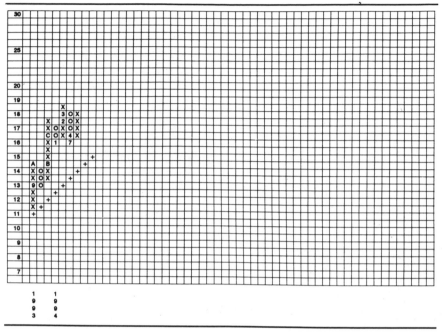

Figure 11.9f   Davco Restaurant (DVCO) RS—None.

STEP 6. SELECT YOUR ENTRY POINT AND SET YOUR STOPS

The best place to buy a stock is on a pullback because it gets you closer to your stop point and increases your risk-reward relationship of the trade. Stops should be set on the trend line for investors (see Figure 11.10). If the trend line is broken with a sell signal, stop the position out. As long as the Bullish Support line remains intact, investors should stick with the stock unless it has done nothing over 90 days. (Remember, A. W. Cohen, one of the all-time greats, suggests you stop out of a trade if it is not working after 90 days.) Keep your capital moving. Traders are a different breed and are much more short-term oriented than the investor. Traders should stop out on any sell signal and be prepared to go right back in on the next buy signal if the trend line remains intact (see Figure 11.10). This will help them cut their losses and let their profits run. If you have followed the guidelines for selecting an investment, stops won't happen often. Don't be afraid to get off a losing horse and onto a winning horse. If Pepsico (PEP) is not working for you and has stopped you out, consider going immediately with Coca-Cola (KO) if it meets your investment guidelines.

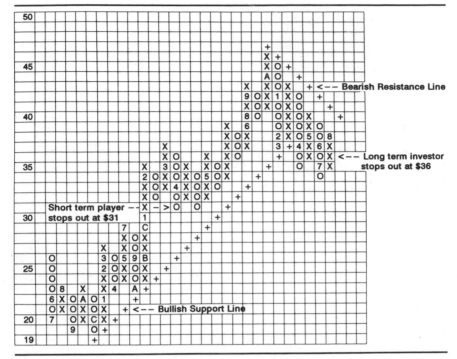

Figure 11.10   Stops for the trader and the investor.

STEP 7. KNOW WHAT TO DO
WHEN THINGS GO RIGHT

Deciding When to Take a Profit

Taking profits can be one of the hardest things investors do. As the stock moves up, hope springs eternal. Each point rise is accompanied by the hope of another point rise. We tend to fall in love with stocks. Eventually the stock tops out and supply overtakes demand. The first few points' retracement is viewed as a mere pullback in an otherwise strong uptrend. The next few are viewed with shock and disbelief as all the news is still bullish on the stock. The expected earnings are coming on stream, new products are coming to market, and the fundamental analysts are falling all over themselves raising earnings expectations. *Time* might even have had a cover story on the company. These are the things tops are made of. At this point, everyone who wants to buy has bought. The supply/demand relationship of the stock shifts decidedly to the supply side of the equation. A lack of buyers augmented by a handful of sellers causes stiff declines in the stock. Once the move is on, concern changes to fear and the decline accelerates. One analyst then reduces earnings estimates, which creates panic. The Wall Street herd follows the first analyst, not wanting to be left in the stampede, and more earning estimates are lowered. Before you know it, the investor's profit turns into a loss.

All this can be avoided by establishing some rules on when to take a profit. We covered how to establish the Bullish Resistance line in Chapter 2. The idea here is to begin taking profits when the stock reaches this line. The probability at this point is the stock will pull back to the center of the channel. You might consider taking all or part of your profits. Take action at this level. If you are adept at using options, consider hedging at the Bullish Resistance line. See Chapter 4 for other ideas on taking profits.

Alternatives to Taking Profits

1. Sell ⅓ of the position if the stock rises 30 percent.
2. Sell ⅓ of the position if the stock rises 50 percent.
3. Hold last ⅓ of the position until the stock declines to the first level where you took a profit or the relative strength chart turns negative. This will ensure you get the most out of stocks that just keep going.

One of the reasons I like this alternative method to taking profits is it forces you to take some money off the table when things are looking good. It is much easier to sell stock when things look good than it is to sell stock when everyone is scrambling for the door. Conditions change rapidly in the market and it is better to be in control.

CONCLUSION

Above all, keep it simple. The more variables you put into the equation, the more confusing it gets. Show me a person with 50 market indicators, and I'll show you a confused person. With the Bullish Percent Indexes and the Percent of 10, you will do as well as, if not better than, any other professional analyst on Wall Street. Using the guidelines outlined in this book, you will develop the confidence to have strength in your convictions and to buy when the news media are saying the worst is upon us. You will also be able to sell when the news is great and things have never looked better. We have been applying these simple principles in the market with great success for 15 years. The Bullish Percent concept is 40 years old. These indicators and guides are there for the taking.

INDEX

A

Action points, choosing, 13–14
Advance-Decline Line, 121–122
Aerospace-airlines, 147–148
Alternatives to profit taking, 231
AMEX Bullish Percent Index, 111, 131
Analysis, methods of, 2–3
At-the-money, 206
Autos and auto parts, 149–150

B

Banks, 152–153
Barron's, 59
Bear Alert market, 101–102, 145
Bear Confirmed market, 101, 145
Bear Correction market, 102, 146
Bear market results, 30–31
Bear Trap, 62
Bearish Catapult formation, 69
Bearish Resistance Line, 21–22
Bearish Sentiment Index, 120–121
Bearish signal, 36–37
Bearish Support Line, 22–23
Bell curve, 24
Biomedics/genetics, 153–156
Block Discount, 122–123

Bloomberg Financial Markets, 147
Blumenthal, Earl, 55, 95, 98, 212
Bond market indicators, 135–140
Bootleg option right, 96
Break points, 11
Bridge Data System, 118
Building, 156, 157
Bull Alert market, 99–100, 145
Bull Confirmed market, 99
Bull Correction market, 100–101, 145
Bull market results, 30
Bull Trap, 63
Bullish Catapult formation, 67–69
Bullish Percent Index, 3, 91–107
Bullish Resistance Line, 20–21
Bullish Sentiment Index, 119–120
Bullish Shakeout, 50–52
Bullish signal, 35–36
Bullish Support Line, 18–20
Burke, Mike, 8, 29, 55, 56, 62–63, 119, 142, 143

C

Call buyer, 198–199
Call definitions, 198

Call writer (seller), 199–200
Candlestick charts, 3
Catapult, 39–44
Chartcraft, 3, 45, 88, 96, 119–120, 141, 212
Charting fundamentals, 9–15
Chart patterns, 27–63
Chemicals, 156–159
Cheyenne Software example, 74–75
Chrysler example, 150–152
Cohen, A. W., 5, 29, 42, 95, 96, 98, 143, 212
Commodities, 211–216
Computers, 159, 160
Confidence, importance of, 1
Confirmation pattern, 41
Covered writing options, 32
Crash of 1987, 94–95

D

Daily Equity Market Report, 45, 94, 103–104, 144–145
Daily Range Index, 118–119
Davis, Robert Earl, 29–30, 201, 218
Degrees of risk, 99–105, 145–146
Deltas, 205, 206–210
Diagonal Triple Top, 45
Double Bottom pattern, 34–35
Double Top pattern, 33
Dow, Charles, 2
Dow Jones Bond Average, 136, 138–139
Dow Jones Industrial Average, 126–128
Dow Jones Transportation Index, 128–129

Dow Jones Utility Average, 128, 130
Drugs, 159, 161

E

Electronics, 161–162
Elliot waves, 3
Entry points, 43
Evaluation of sectors, 143
Exercise price, 205
Exit points, 43
Expiration date, 205

F

Fibonacci retracement numbers, 211
Flowchart, 10–11
Food, beverages, soap, 162–164
Football analogy, 95–98
Forest products, 164–165
Fundamental analysis, 2–3

G

Game plans, 103–107
Gann angles, 3
General Datacomm example, 76
Gray, Lee, 96, 212

H

Healthcare, 165–167
History of point and figure analysis, 2–3
Horizontal count, 25–26
Household goods, 167–168

How to Use the Three-Point Reversal Method of Point and Figure Stock Market Trading, 29–30, 42

I

In-the-money, 206
Index Trend Charts, 126–134
Institutional funds, 168, 170
Insurance, 168, 169
Intrinsic value, 206
Investors Business Daily, 122
Investors Daily, 71
Investors Intelligence, 8

J

J. P. Morgan Index, 125
Japanese candlestick charts, 3

K

Kane, Steve, 5

L

Leisure, 168, 171
Lone Star Steakhouse example, 75

M

Machinery and tools, 172–173
Market indicators, 91–107, 109–140
Media, 173, 174

Metals, nonferrous, 173, 175, 176
Mylan Labs example, 74

N

NASDAQ Composite Index, 132
New York Stock Exchange Bullish Percent Index, 3, 91–107, 133–134
Newsletters, as a source of information, 4
NYSE Bond Cumulative Advance-Decline Line, 139–140
NYSE Bond High-Low Index, 136, 137
NYSE Composite Index, 3, 91–107, 133–134
NYSE High-Low Index, 113–115

O

Oil, 175, 177
Oil service, 175, 178
Option premium, 206
Option Stock Relative Strength Book, 88
Option tools, 200–202
OTC Bullish Percent Index, 110
OTC High-Low Index, 115, 116
Out-of-the-money, 206
Overleverage, 94

P

Paper, 164–165
Point and Figure Method-Advanced Theory and Practice, 23

Precious metals, 175, 179–180
Predictability of change, 28
Price action, as a basis for charting, 8
Price change, driving force, 27
Price objectives, 23–24
Profit and Probability—Technical Analysis of the Price Fluctuations of Common Stocks by Point and Figure Method, 29–30
Profit taking, 73–74, 230–231
Profits and probabilities, 28–29
Protection-safety equipment, 180, 181
Put definitions, 200
Put versatility, 200–202
Puts, as insurance, 204–206
Puts, selling, 202–204

R

"Real Deal," The, 115
Real estate, 180, 182
Relative strength calculations, 79–89
  Chartcraft method, 79–86
  Moody and Parker's study, 86–88
  as short-term indicator, 88–89
Relative strength as short-term indicator, 88–89
Relative strength study, 86–88
Restaurants, 181, 183
Retailing, 181–182, 184
Rising bottom, 35–36
Risk levels, 99–103, 145–146

Risk reward, calculating, 70–71
Rizzello, Joseph, v–vi

S

Savings and loans, 182–183, 185
Sector analysis, 141–195
  aerospace-airlines, 147–148
  autos and auto parts, 149–150
  banks, 152–153
  biomedics/genetics, 153–156
  building, 156, 157
  chemicals, 156–159
  computers, 159, 160
  drugs, 159, 161
  electronics, 161–162
  food, beverages, soap, 162–164
  forest products, 164–165
  healthcare, 165–167
  household goods, 167–168
  institutional funds, 168, 170
  insurance, 168, 169
  leisure, 168, 171
  machinery and tools, 172–173
  media, 173, 174
  metals, nonferrous, 173, 175, 176
  oil, 175, 177
  oil service, 175, 178
  paper, 164–165
  precious metals, 175, 179–180
  protection-safety equipment, 180, 181
  real estate, 180, 182
  restaurants, 181, 183
  retailing, 181–182, 184
  savings and loans, 182–183, 185

software, 183, 186
steel and iron, 186–187
telephones, 187–189
textiles and apparel, 189, 190
utilities, electric, 189, 192
utilities, gas, 192, 193
Wall Street, 192–193, 194
waste/management, 193–194, 195
Sector Bullish Percents, 143–144
Sector rotation, 141–143
Selecting stocks, 217–231
Selection, option, 209
Sell, when to, 73
Selling short, 200–201
Series 7 exam, 4
Short sale, 69–71
Short sell substitutes, 201
Short-term indicators, relative strength as, 88–89
Signals:
    Bearish, 35–36, 59–60
    Broadening Top, 56–57
    Bullish, 35–36, 59–60
    Bullish Shakeout, 50–52
    Catapult, 39–44
    Double Bottom, 34–35
    Double Top, 33–34
    High-Pole Warning, 55
    Long-Tail Down, 53–55
    Low-Pole Warning, 56
    Reverse Shakeout, 52–53
    Spread Triple Bottom, 48–49
    Spread Triple Top, 48–49
    Traps, 62–63
    Triangle, 44–45, 60–62
    Triple Bottom, 38–39, 47–48
    Triple Top, 37–38, 45–47
Size change, 9
Software, 183, 186

Spread Triple Bottom, 48–49
Spread Triple Top, 48–49
Staby, Ernest, 143
Standard & Poors 500 Index, 132–133
Statistical analysis, 23–24
Statistical probabilities of chart patterns, 30–32
Steel and iron, 186–187
Stock selection, 217–231
Stop, managing, 69–71
Supply and demand, as a basis for charts, 3
Supply and demand, as a basis for stock movement, 7

T

Technical analysis, 2–3
Technical indicators, 109–125
Telephones, 187–189
Ten-Week Moving Average Index, 111–113
Textiles and apparel, 189, 190
Thirty-Week Moving Average Index, 115, 117–118
Three-box reversal method, 9
3-point reversal method, 8
Time premium, 206
Time Warner example, 72
Timing, 2
Trade, managing, 71–73
    guides for, 77
Trading bonds, 23–24
Trend charts of indexes, 126–134
Trend lines, 18–26
Triple Bottom, 38–39
Triple Top, 37–38

U

U.S. Dollar Index, 125
U.S. Surgical example, 14–18
Underwriter, 202–204
Utilities, electric, 189, 192
Utilities, gas, 192, 193

V

Value Line, 71, 134–135
Value Line Index, 134–135

Vertical count, 24–25
Volatility, 147

W

Wall Street, 192–193, 194
Waste/management, 193–194, 195

Y

Yates, Jim 28